SINGAPORE'S AUTHORITARIAN CAPITALISM

Christopher Lingle's account can be read on many levels — as a mystery and adventure story, as an analysis of modern Asia's economic prospects, as a portrait of one particular brand of justice at work. But above all else it is an eloquent and completely persuasive argument for the role of human liberty in Asia's increasingly-rich societies.

As Lingle makes dramatically clear in this book, he suffered persecution and financial near-ruin merely for exercising rights that most modern societies respect — and that most Asian citizens want to enjoy. Through future years, scholars and political leaders from around the world are sure to debate the right balance between individual rights and collective wellbeing, including a discussion of whether a new "Asian balance" has been found. But Lingle's case involved much cruder issues; the effort of a regime to protect itself against any criticism, and its willingness to use the legal system as a tool toward this end.

Christopher Lingle's story will be interesting to any reader — and important to all of them who care about the place of liberty in societies around the world.

James Fallows, Washington Editor of the ***Atlantic Monthly***

Many supporters of the "Singapore model" imagine a free market paradise. Lingle provides evidence that such a presumption is far from the truth. He argues convincingly that Singapore's development path, identified as "authoritarian capitalism", has various perils. Perhaps the most troubling is the prospect of a "bubble" economy emerging in Singapore, as in Japan during the 1980s. But Lingle also probes, in a way that few Singaporeans yet feel free to do, the deeper question whether a maturing Singapore will forever tolerate a nannying leadership, paying themselves huge salaries, whose main preoccupation and self-justification is that the trains run on time.

Roger Sandilands, Senior Lecturer in Economics
University of Strathclyde, Glasgow
(Senior Teaching Fellow, National University of Singapore, 1990-94)

Professor Lingle makes a significant contribution to the study of developing nations by convincingly showing that there is less to the Asian miracle economies than there at first appears. Over the long run, economic growth is not consistent with political oppression. Anyone who really wants to understand the political economy of Asian development must read this book.

Randall G. Holcombe, Professor of Economics
Florida State University

Christopher Lingle's book is an interesting documentation of the political problems of contemporary Singapore. A long remarkable period of economic growth has raised living standards to Western levels. But the political system has adjusted only slowly to the economic changes — in several important aspects, it has changed very little from what is the norm in many under-developed countries. Lingle's personal confrontation with the Singapore police and judiciary should be read as direct evidence of a Western intellectual democrat's problems in working in tightly regulated Singapore.

Kurt Wickman, Ph.D., Swedish economist

SINGAPORE'S AUTHORITARIAN CAPITALISM

Asian Values, Free Market Illusions, and Political Dependency

Christopher Lingle

Edicions Sirocco, S.L.
Barcelona
and
The Locke Institute
Fairfax, VA
1996

First published in 1996 by

Edicions Sirocco, S.L.
Apartat 30.016, 08080 Barcelona
Spain

Co-published by

The Locke Institute
4084 University Drive
Fairfax, VA 22030
USA

Printed in Malaysia

ISBN 84-85809-52-1

I dedicate this book to all my students who have taught me so much,
and to my family members who have inspired me,
especially my father

PREFACE

Many writers, especially those in academic disciplines, realize that their publications will generally command little or no response. While they are unlikely to be read, they are even less likely to be discussed by more than a few friends or colleagues. Therefore, I have mixed feelings to note that one of my publications has been widely celebrated. Since I mostly write for professional journals in the area of economics, it frustrates me somewhat that my efforts which generated extensive public interest appeared in a newspaper. Likewise, the personal consequences arising out of the reaction to the publication have been unsettling, to say the least. In an article of about 900 words, only about 20 of those prompted actions that caused my name to appear in news articles around the world.

The story begins in Singapore where I was a visiting professor at the national university. My troubles started when I wrote a response to a previously published editorial comment that appeared in the *International Herald Tribune*. Several weeks later, 2 police detectives came to my office and my home to question me. Soon after their visits, I resigned my job and left with great haste. After arriving safe at home in the USA, I received notice that I should return to Singapore and respond to the charges that I had made remarks that were contemptuous of their judicial system. However, I heeded the advice of many persons knowledgeable about Singapore's disregard for individual rights and decided not to return for the trial.

As a prolegomena to the remainder of this book, the complete text that became such a *cause celebre* is reprinted, as it appeared on the editorial page of the *International Herald Tribune*, October 7, 1994. Themes that appear in the prolegomena shall reoccur throughout the subsequent chapters. (Author's note: The passages which caught the attention of the authorities in Singapore are highlighted in italics.) Doubtless, many readers will be confused as to why the government in Singapore decided that these words should be construed as an impeachment of their institutions.

Prolegomena

THE SMOKE OVER PARTS OF ASIA OBSCURES SOME PROFOUND CONCERNS

Christopher Lingle

There are views from East Asia that are decidedly different from those of Kishore Mahbubani in his comment, "You May Not Like It, Europe, But This Asian Medicine Could Help" (*Opinion*, Oct. 1).

First, his metaphor of a "ring of fire" defined by political flashpoints along Europe's edges is figurative. Here in Southeast Asia, such a description is a literal reality, revealing much about the "Asian model" that he supports.

For the past month, much of Malaysia and parts of Indonesia have been choking under a thick cloud of smoke from Indonesian forest fires raging out of control. It is unthinkable that such a catastrophe in Europe would meet with such resounding reticence among government officials of the affected countries.

Despite registered pollution levels in Singapore and Kuala Lumpur that often surpass or hover just below the unhealthy level, the public is belatedly informed that a ministerial meeting to address this crisis will not be held until the end of October. One has to wonder what Europeans might learn from this Asian remedy.

Such inaction and refusal to comment on the internal affairs of neighbors is a defining characteristic of ASEAN, the Association of South East Asian Nations. These Asian states seem more interested in allowing fellow governments to save face than in saving lives of their citizens or preserving the environment.

The remark that "more lives are lost daily on the periphery of Europe than in the entire Asia-Pacific region" is remarkably disingenuous. This assertion is probably not true. However, there are no means for independent corroboration for what goes on in most of Asia. News that flows freely and is distributed widely in Europe results in active introspection about its consequences.

In many Asian states, the media are subject to numerous restrictions and forms of censorship, some blatant, some subtle. As a consequence, Asia's citizens can receive diluted or filtered information or remain uninformed except for announcements of self-serving government announcements. This control of information allows governments to release news on their own terms, basking in their own glory while concealing their failings.

In the particular case comparing the loss of life in Europe's conflicts, there is no solid information on how many Asians lost their lives in the political struggles in East Timor, Burma or in Tibet.

The indifference of the regimes in this region to such outrages and crises strongly supports the perception that human life is worth little in Asia. Such a response must be seen in the context of governments based upon patriarchal, collectivist ideals where society is placed above self. There is no tradition for promoting individual liberty or protecting individual rights.

Mr. Mahbubani's reference to the tragic carnage in Europe may be correct. However, he conveniently overlooks the fact that considerable numbers of peoples' lives are ruined in Asia for participating in political opposition.

Intolerant regimes in the region reveal considerable ingenuity in their methods of suppressing dissent. Some techniques lack finesse: crushing unarmed students with tanks, or imprisoning dissidents. Others are more subtle: *relying upon a compliant judiciary to bankrupt opposition politicians*, or buying out enough the opposition to take control "democratically." Trade unionists in Europe seldom face such pressures.

Mr. Mahbubani's claims are strongest when he is not comparing Europe's flawed institutions to Asia's allegedly superior ones. For example, it is hard to disagree with his advice for ending Europe's agricultural subsidies. Although consistency demands that Korean and Japanese governments muster the political will to face down their farmers on this issue, he conspicuously refrains from offering such advice to his Asian neighbors.

One is also heartened by Mr. Mahbubani's encouragement of increased global rather than regional integration. Nonetheless, his remarks do not seem to square with the initiatives for an ASEAN free-trade area or an East Asian Economic Caucus. Certainly it is wrong for Turkey to be excluded from the European Union. Meanwhile India is kept at arm's length by ASEAN.

After being called to account for regional myopia, Europeans are blamed for overlooking the three big forces on its doorstep: Russia, Africa and Islam. Mr. Mahbubani deftly side-steps the lack of mutual response among Asians to three big forces that threaten their stability: China, over-population and a rapidly decaying environment.

Meanwhile, articulate delivery masks the shrill refrain that is increasingly commonplace among apologists of authoritarian regimes in Asia.

During the Cold War, the ASEAN states used the image of a Communist menace to great effect. They developed a coherent front that provided legitimacy for their often repressive methods. It served an end that was applauded by the West. As a reward, developed economies provided these Asian regimes with national security guarantees and generally open markets while turning a blind eye to the boot kept at the throat of their political oppositions.

With the disappearance of communism as a palpable threat, some Asian regimes deflect interest from their rigid authoritarian control by pointing to the corrosive effect upon their communities from the decadent influences of the West. Yet the only certain threat associated with the introduction of liberal democracy is its weakening effect upon the choke hold of one-party political dominance.

❖❖❖❖❖❖❖❖❖❖❖❖

The writer, senior fellow in European studies at the National University of Singapore, contributed this personal comment to the International Herald Tribune.

International Herald Tribune, October 7, 1994.

ACKNOWLEDGMENTS

In reflecting upon the list of persons whom I might acknowledge for their role in the completion of this book, I feared that the list would be rather long. And so it is, although the task was more manageable than I first imagined.

Most importantly, I must thank my father and siblings who unselfishly offered the sort of support that confirms that family values are alive and well in the USA. The congenial, secure and supportive environment provided by my entire family proved to be ideal and enviable arrangements for undertaking such a daunting task.

Among all my mentors and colleagues in the academy, three stand out for their inestimable contribution toward my intellectual development. Calvin W. Sealey always provided the steady hand of friendship and his enormous intellectual abilities to support my postgraduate studies. No less debt is owed to Ethel B. Jones who so ably served as my mentor and role model while she was my doctoral thesis adviser, so many years ago. More recently, due to his generosity and deep insights, my recent collaboration with Kurt Wickman has proved to be the most productive intellectual partnership of my academic career.

In terms of institutional support, I gratefully acknowledge the support of the Institute for Humane Studies (IHS) that proved that one can learn about networking without attending Harvard. Through the IHS, the contacts I made with scholars around the world enriched my career development immeasurably. During his tenure with the IHS and now with the Atlas Economic Research Foundation, Leonard Liggio provided guidance and inspiration. Without his efforts on my behalf, I would not be faced with the pleasant task of thanking the Earhart Foundation for a generous research grant to support me in completing my manuscript. Garry Rodan of the Asia Research Centre of Murdoch University offered encouragement and research advice throughout the various stages of preparation of the manuscript. It is with great regret that I am unable to acknowledge fully the incalculable debts owed to a special friend from afar who wishes to remain anonymous.

Various readers provided most helpful review comments on the early stages of my manuscript that have doubtless improved the final version. This list includes Jim Fallows, Randall Holcombe, James Minchin, Roger Sandilands, and Bob Slaughter. Troy Beecham provided substantial assistance throughout. The efforts of all these people and many others have contributed to whatever might be good about this book. Any remaining faults or shortcomings are my own doing.

Finally, I would like to recollect my experiences at the National University of Singapore (NUS). I have warm memories of many of the students in the European Studies Programme of the NUS. My thanks go out to those who risked so much to express their support for me during my last unhappy days there during my conflict with the authorities. Since there were so many, but more importantly to protect them from reprisal, they shall remain unnamed here. Daniel and Martine Baillon were truly generous and worthy friends who offered a splendid mix of intellectual stimulation and *joie de vivre*. As a trusted confidant, Ludwig Linsmayer offered moral judgments that guided me through some stormy seas. David Martin Jones deserves special recognition for his lucid insights, trenchant criticisms, and wonderful sense of irony that guided my understanding of the political economy of Singapore and was so important in shaping the arguments in this book.

Memories of two of my supervisors at the NUS kept me focused in this endeavor. The dubious moral integrity exercized in their jobs by Ernest Chew, Dean of the Faculty of Arts and Sciences, and Jon Quah, Co-ordinator of the European Studies Programme, provide abundant evidence of the corrupting influence of mixing politics and academics. It is my hope that the observations offered in this book will undermine the capacity of such people to poison the atmosphere of learning for the sake of the future of students everywhere.

CONTENTS

GLOSSARY

ASEAN, the Association of Southeast Asian Nations, was formed in 1967 by Indonesia, Malaysia, The Philippines, Singapore, and Thailand with Brunei joining in 1984 and Vietnam joining in 1995. Membership for Burma (Myanmar), Cambodia and Laos is currently under negotiation.

Authoritarian capitalism is a system where considerable decentralization and limited government intervention in market activities is combined with extensive intrusions by government into the social and political choices of the citizens.

Authoritarian socialism is the combination of extensive government controls over the economy that is matched by substantial political repression. Most experiments in communism can be regarded as leading to authoritarian-socialist regimes.

Civil society reflects the sort of voluntary organizations that emerge spontaneously as a means for citizens to mediate the power of (democratic) governments. They also provide the interactive skills whereby individuals are socialized and serve as an inter-generational transmission mechanism for cultural values and institutions. Counted among these mediating agencies might be religious associations, educational institutions, political parties, newspapers and the media, trade unions or professional associations, and other similar groups.

Clash of Civilizations is a hypothesis associated with Samuel Huntington, who projected that future conflicts will be generated by cultural differences rather than by ideological struggles over political or economic interests.

Collectivism is an approach to social organization that can be contrasted with individualism. Institutions based upon collectivism promote the interests over the community at the expense of the individual constituents, whereby group rights are elevated over individual rights.

Command economy is the imposition of a central plan of extensive government control over an economy that might include setting production targets, the socialization or nationalization of property and resources, or the imposition of controls over market prices.

Commercialization of politics is the involvement of political parties in commerce to generate an independent source of revenue.

Communitarian democracy is a political system whose supporters who deem setting limits upon individual choices as a necessary means to promote community-oriented goals.

Comparative advantage describes a situation where some set of attributes (e.g., superior access to technology or relative abundance of resources) generates a relatively higher level of efficiency to an economic resource of one country.

Criminalization of politics is a hegemonic tactic by a ruling party to finesse the organs of government in order to create an appearance of criminality in the acts of opposition politicians or critics.

Crony capitalism describes a dependency relationship whereby a political elite offers protection and special access to markets to trusted business interests in return for political support.

Cruel Choice hypothesis offers support for an pro-authoritarian argument whereby developing economies can most readily experience economic growth if civil and political freedoms are limited. Without these authoritarian restrictions on the polity, demands for redistribution or elements of the welfare state might place a drag on the economic growth potential.

Cultural protectionism involves a set of policies that attempt to protect a particular set of cultural institutions from dilution or debasement by outside influences.

End of History hypothesis is associated with Francis Fukuyama, and foresees an increasing convergence of ideologies towards liberal democracy.

Export-oriented industrialization (EOI) policy is an outward looking development strategy that emphasizes international trade as a basis both for domestic economic growth and as a source for foreign currency.

Free rider is a person (country) that attempts to benefit from the availability of a public good without contributing to its provision.

Guanxi describes a set of informal arrangements that rely upon family ties or other inside contacts as a means to facilitate business or bureaucratic transactions. This practice is widely known among Chinese traders.

Hegemony in a political context reflects the outcome of attempts by a ruling party to insure its dominance and survival by consolidating or coopting all bases of power.

Internal Security Act (ISA) is a holdover from British colonial rule that allows arrest without warrant and detention without trial for extended periods. Although those charged are allowed to have access to legal advice, they have no legal recourse to challenge the substantive basis for their detention.

Kiasuism is a term taken from the Chinese Hokkien dialect and is loosely translated as "scared to lose."

Leninist state is one where the ruling party empowers a loyal cadre and relies upon hegemonic tactics to insure its permanence.

Liberal capitalism is an encompassing system that combines the elements of liberal democracy and market-based capitalism.

Liberal democracy is a political system that places a high priority upon the assignment of rights and freedoms to individual citizens in order to protect them from the prospective tyranny of governments.

NWEO is the "new world economic order" that has arisen from the increased global mobility of capital and the improved flow of technological knowledge.

Phobocracy is a term that describes the "rule by fear" imposed by an authoritarian regime.

Politicization of commerce occurs when access to commercial opportunities is used as a tool of political legitimization. Crony capitalism is an outcome of politicized commerce.

Politicization of crime occurs when authoritarian regimes attempt to manipulate crime statistics or public perceptions of crime to serve their own narrow political agenda.

Public goods exhibit the characteristics of non-rivalry in consumption and non-excludability. Non-rivalry implies one person's enjoyment of the good does not detract from another's enjoyment. Non-excludability means that it can be enjoyed by all members of a community, even if they do not pay for it. Examples are national defense, international peace, or a catchy tune. Because of these characteristics, public goods tend to be under produced by the market and are often provided in the public sector.

Rent seeking involves the expenditure of resources to induce a government to implement policies that bestow benefits upon an individual or upon members of a special interest group. These actions divert resources from alternative uses that could improve the well-being of the entire community.

Lobbying by businesses uses resources that might have gone into R&D or qualitative improvements in production.

Scarcity is a relative concept that involves the inevitable mismatching of means and ends. It can be seen to be the defining problem of economics that leads to predictable human behavior in reaction to limits imposed by nature and man's capacity to derive unlimited wants. These responses lead to choice and are the basis of competition.

Singapore School is represented by a variety of officials linked to the regime who allude to the existence of a unique set "Asian values" that mixes elements of neo-Confucianism with other attributes that are presumed to be uniquely Asian. In turn, these values are credited for the success of Singapore and the other "miracle economies."

Social engineering is an attempt by governments to limit the spontaneous development of individual attributes. Most often these public policies impose positive and negative incentives to encourage collectivist or communitarian goals.

Special interest groups are coalitions formed to apply political leverage in order to further the interests of some sub-set of the community. These "distributional coalitions" include consumer or labor unions as well as producer cartels. Rent seeking by these groups represent an attempt by them to financial or social advantages for their members, and that usually lead to losses in economic productivity for the remainder of the citizens.

Stagflation describes inflationary conditions that are accompanied by sluggish or negative economic growth.

Tiger Economies, also variously known as "Baby Dragons" or "Miracle Economies", are the common reference to the Southeast Asian newly industrialized countries (NIC's). Included are Hong Kong, Singapore, South Korea, and Taiwan. More recently Indonesia, Malaysia, and Thailand have been added.

Total factor productivity (TFP) is a measure of overall changes in the efficiency of inputs (e.g., labor or capital).

Voluntary export restraints (VER's) reflect bilateral agreements to restrict the quantity of certain traded goods. For example, Japan and the US negotiated VER's that placed limits on the access of Japanese cars to America.

Introduction

LIFE AND CRIMES IN SINGAPORE: AN ACADEMIC ODYSSEY TO THE REPUBLIC OF FEAR

This book is the outgrowth of an academic odyssey that began in the late 1970's. During the intervening time, I was fortunate enough to be employed as a university professor while living in various countries in Africa, Asia, Europe and North America. My exposure to life in these countries reflects a personal commitment towards a better understanding and appreciation of different economic, cultural and socio-political arrangements.

I make no claim to be an expert on Asia, so my task here has limited ambitions. First, I wish to offer a chronicle of the details of my firsthand encounter with Singapore's government during my academic appointment to the National University of Singapore (NUS). By placing the initial discussion in a human context, I hope to convey the manner in which Singapore's current leaders have been able to remain in power by operating a political system that relies upon fear and intimidation. I also hope to offer evidence that what happened to me was not exceptional and awaits others who wittingly or unwittingly run afoul of the government of Singapore. Second, I wish to develop several general themes that emerge from and are consistent with this personal account. Given my unfortunate experience with the authorities in Singapore, it is not surprising that much of my discussion will focus upon that country. Due to its small size, complaints about Singapore may seem to be much ado about nothing. Nevertheless, neither population nor geographic size are accurate indicators of importance in the modern world. A number of troubling generalizations can be drawn from an examination of the recent behavior of Singapore's rulers. It is worth noting that some of the socialist economies in the region are considering Singapore a reference model for their economic transitional and developmental strategies. Thus, the emphasis placed upon Singapore. This is justified in the understanding that the successful orchestration of the credible reputation of Singapore's ruling party has troubling implications for citizens of other parts of Asia. I will set forth an analysis that has application beyond the shores of this tiny city-state. Also to be considered is an examination of pro-authoritarian arguments that portray the unavoidable tradeoff between the emergence of democratic freedoms and economic prosperity in developing countries as beneficial. Finally, I note that many of the arguments that I set forth have not been completely worked through to a careful, logical end. Nonetheless, in light of the rapid pace of change in East Asia and other parts of the world and in response to the urging of colleagues, I felt it important to energize a debate over a variety of pressing themes in a timely manner. Thus, I made a conscious decision to move ahead with publication of this manuscript even though it involved some risk of offering imperfectly formed arguments or incomplete hypotheses.

Throughout my academic career, I have been an ardent advocate of individual rights and freedoms. Consistent with this commitment, I actively opposed apartheid during the mid-1980's while I was a university lecturer in South Africa. Following the same logic, I applauded the demise of the Soviet empire during my most recent assignment in Europe at the beginning of the 1990's. These same impulses induced me to reject the misleading impressions that tend to portray Singapore as a democratic country and a bastion of free enterprise.

As an economist, I was well aware of the enviable economic track record that is widely credited to the political leadership of Singapore.[1] However, this same training induces an instinctive tendency to examine the costs as well as the beneficial outcomes of human actions. As a political economist, I am also interested in extending this analysis in order to examine the relationship of economic policies with the emergence of democracy and a civil society. Finally, my background in international political economy has inspired an interest in global issues and the economic interdependence of different regions. In sum, my training and experience have provided me with insights into the development strategies in Singapore and other countries in the region, allowing me to pose many interesting questions regarding the same.

A specific sequence of events inspired me to write this book. In late 1993, I accepted the invitation to teach at Singapore's national university. For me it was an opportune moment to return to Asia to refresh the pool of knowledge of the region I had acquired during my appointment as Visiting Foreign Expert in Economics to the Shanghai University of Finance and Economics in 1987.

I had no intention of taking steps to undermine their government. Nor did I anticipate that I would find myself locked in a showdown with their legal apparatus. Nonetheless, it was not long after my arrival that I became aware of the suffocating, authoritarian intervention in most aspects of life there. In the course of my tenure there which covered 13 months, the available evidence and personal observations convinced me that most reports were a gross mischaracterization of the realities of the conservative, authoritarian government in Singapore. I also discovered that the government authorities took an active interest in formulating a reputation that relied upon a cunning manipulation of selective Asian traditions.

Prior to my legal confrontation with the authorities in Singapore, my research agenda over the past few years followed my interest in the nature of economic transition and development. Results of these investigations have appeared in scholarly publications as well in the popular media. While in Singapore, I continued to write editorial page comments that appeared in the *Asian Wall St. Journal*, the *Eastern Express*, the *Nikkei Weekly*, and more famously, in the *International Herald Tribune*. Doubtless, my unfortunate encounter with the government of Singapore provided me with an additional impetus to offer a more systematic treatment of issues that also relate to other countries in East Asia.[2]

The ostensible purpose of this exercise, then, is to provide a wider audience with the means to separate the myths from the realities of development in Singapore and some of the other so-called "miracle economies." In light of my own recent experience, I am particularly interested in providing some balance to the otherwise one-dimensional image of Singapore's record toward becoming one of the great economic success stories of modern times. A more complete understanding and application of economic principles may provide a means to comprehend and to appreciate fully the material progress coincidental with the uninterrupted rule by the People's Action Party (PAP). The political repression that characterizes the attempts by Singapore's leaders to continue their one-party rule has economic and political costs that are worthy of consideration. The discussion offered here is not limited to a description of the means and ends which allow PAP leaders to silence domestic opponents and to deflect outside criticism. The institutional and cultural traditions behind the governments in Singapore and in other East Asian countries will also be explored in terms of their similarities of operation as well as their long run implications. First, I offer a sketch of my unfortunate episode with the officials in Singapore as a preface to the amplification that appears in the next chapter.

If You Can't be Smarter, Send in the Cops!

In pondering my experience after invoking the wrath of Singapore's administration, citizens living in free and civilized countries may find it difficult to imagine that expressing one's opinions could lead to a police investigation leading to criminal charges. This is precisely what occurred when Singaporean officials took exception to my commentary on the use of repressive tactics by some East Asian regimes. Perhaps emboldened by their success in manipulating public opinion concerning the Michael Fay case, the government thought their actions against me would be similarly received. In an Orwellian episode, Singapore's High Court convicted me of the "crime" of expressing my opinion in a newspaper. In this article, I consciously avoided any direct confrontation and purposely did not mention any countries by name. Therefore, it is likely that outsiders who know nothing of the political affairs of the region will be puzzled by the fact that Singaporean officials drew such a clear inference that their country was the object of such general comments.

My harrowing episode began when, in the spirit of intellectual debate, I responded to the comments of a senior functionary of Singapore's Foreign Ministry. Both articles appeared in the *International Herald Tribune* (IHT). The remark that caught my eye was the stern criticism of a variety of economic and social problems in Europe. In addition to this criticism, it was suggested that a cure for Europe's ills could be found in the success stories of East Asian countries. My response was prompted by various disingenuous assertions contained in the said article which in turn raised the ire of the Singaporean government. One of the remarks made by the writer claimed that, "...more lives are lost daily on the periphery of Europe than in the entire Asia-Pacific region." This allegation may be close to the truth at the present time, but the author revealed a remarkably short memory to have forgotten the genocidal slaughter of the Khmer Rouge in Cambodia. In all events, it is troubling that independent corroboration for what happens in much of Asia is simply not available. Whereas, the free flow and wide distribution of news in Europe inspire active introspection and response, in most parts of Asia the media in all its forms faces numerous restrictions. Consequently, Asia's citizens receive diluted or manipulated information or remain uninformed except for access to self-serving government decrees.

Instead of provoking a scholarly rebuttal, as was my intention, my published commentary resulted in two separate interrogation sessions conducted by officers of Singapore's Criminal Investigation Division. In spite of the fact that I was on record stating that the police officers behaved professionally and treated me with dignity, the subtext of their visits was sufficiently ominous. In all events, these remarks were inspired by a reasonable sense of self-preservation and were intended to keep the confrontation at a low level of hostility. Persons familiar with Asia know that a smooth surface often conceals a boiling cauldron. The implied intimidation worked, and I left hastily with nothing more than my overnight bag and notebook computer. Charges were laid against me long after my departure. I did not return to Singapore on the advice of numerous people familiar with

Singapore's history who felt certain that I could expect to face imprisonment or a heavy fine or both.

Knowledgeable observers of Singapore's system of justice were probably not surprised by the outcome of my trial. I was convicted *in absentia* for contempt of court based upon my suggestion that some regimes in East Asia are able to thwart criticism by relying upon "a compliant judiciary to bankrupt opposition politicians." Also convicted were the Asian Editor and the publisher of the *International Herald Tribune* as well as the printer and distributor who were cited for their complicity in the claimed offense. Given the liberal application of Singapore's laws, the judges might have charged the street corner vendors were there not so many of them.

In turn, Mr. Lee Kuan Yew, Singapore's strongman-ruler, filed a separate libel suit against the *International Herald Tribune* and me that is still pending. In the documents submitted to the courts, he insisted that I aimed my comments at him even though neither his name nor that of Singapore was mentioned in the article. Judging from their behavior in this case, I concluded that Singapore's leaders have implemented a course of action that combines libel actions with restrictions upon circulation to lay siege to the financial base of international media owners. As will be pointed out, this approach serves them better than inspiring human rights protests arising from the arrest of editors or the banning of publications. In addition, numerical restrictions upon circulation, known (in Singaporean English) as "gazetting," are imposed upon periodicals that pass unfavorable comments about the PAP's system of rule. Non-supportive remarks about the ruling party are interpreted as "interference with domestic politics." A similar response can be expected if members of the government feel that they have been denied (unconditional) right of reply in these publications. There is no record, perhaps unsurprisingly, of the imposition of such penalties against a foreign publication that criticized opposition politicians or denied to them the right of reply.

My own misadventures provide evidence that Singapore's ruling party is willing to extend the rough handling of its critics to include invited scholars who express their opinions of government policies in the international media. Given my wide previous experience in many other parts of the world and perhaps a slightly naive acceptance of the propaganda about Singapore's commitment to democracy, I did not expect to face such strong-armed tactics.

An interesting contrast can be found in the time I spent in South Africa during the mid-to-late 1990's. During my six-year tenure there, I often engaged in direct and open denunciations of the apartheid regime in my university lectures as well as in the popular media and in professional journals. Even so, I was never subjected to any acts of repression nor was I particularly fearful that such actions were being contemplated against me. Apparently the apartheid regime was more willing to tolerate criticism. All critics of apartheid would like to believe that their actions somehow contributed to the demise of that regime. Perhaps that lesson has been learned by Singapore and other East Asian governments and explains why they have undertaken such fierce attacks upon their critics.

Organization of the Book

Like most authors, the preparation of the manuscript for this book involved the difficult task of selecting the correct balance of presentation. On one hand, I felt compelled to meet the requests from friends and colleagues around the world who wanted to be more fully apprised of the details of my disturbing encounter. I was also convinced that many others would be drawn to read this book as a result of the notoriety I gained from my misadventures with the government of Singapore. On the other hand, while satisfying this concerned curiosity was not a central concern, discussion of my own experience allows me to invite my readers to consider wider issues that relate to the institutional arrangements and implications of East Asian authoritarian regimes. In their final forms, I have aimed to present these complicated issues in a manner that is engaging and understandable to the general reader while offering some details for those who have a more specialized interest in the political economy of Asian development.

The organization of the following chapters reflects my efforts to resolve the delicate balance between relating personal encounters and offering an analytical discourse. Since most of my published work has appeared in professional journals or academic texts, I instinctively avoid the use of the first person. Therefore, the personalized account in the introduction was in many ways the most challenging to write. Therein I provide substantial details of the events that plunged my life into a state of confusion and provided me with an unwanted "fifteen minutes of fame." In this personal narrative, I have intended to convey the drama and stress arising out of the uncertainty that I faced for my personal safety.

The discussion in Chapter 2 provides an interpretation of wider issues emerging out of the intellectual debate over the implications of the "New Asian Model" as promoted by the party leadership in Singapore that was the starting point of my misadventures. My contention, then and now, is that that many regimes use the notion of the existence of a unique set of "Asian values" as a basis for the rejection of continued democratic reforms. It was my interest in these issues, and my instinctive rejection of any suggestion of a necessary set of cultural prerequisites for democracy, that led to my unexpected confrontation with the authorities in Singapore. Following my encounters with and understanding of the regimes in the region, I set out to identify a set of political arrangements referred to here as "authoritarian capitalism." I discuss Singapore's own hybrid politico-economic model and the attempts by its long-serving political party to control the impact and direction of modernizing influences.

Chapter 3 offers a critical examination of the long run economic implications of the authoritarian Asian regimes. Any examination of the progress of Singapore's economy must include a description of its transformation from a drowsy coastal city to a gleaming city of the future and a vibrant center of global capitalism. However, all is not well in the Lion City. Despite the remarkable progress, there are hints and signs of fragility that emerge out of the contradictions of the institutional arrangements that served them well in the past.

The discussion in Chapter 4 seeks to identify the means and ends of the political institutions that Singapore's authoritarian-capitalist regime applies in order to maintain its grip upon power. Through ruthless and shrewd exercise of its monopoly over political power, the PAP has been successful in deflecting the liberalizing forces of modernization (more literate work force, internet, etc.). The co-opting of the middle class has been combined with unsubtle repression and the nurturing of successors and institutions to fit the PAP's own agenda. In sum, Singapore's ruling party has perfected a special variant of authoritarian capitalism identified here as a *phobocracy*, or "rule by fear."[3] This political arrangement imposes costs and consequences upon Singapore's institutions that are often overlooked by its indigenous supporters, known collectively as the "Singapore School."

These issues are inextricably linked to my analysis of Singapore and provide a look at the wider implications of the methods of the ruling party there. In Chapter 5 there is an examination of the maturation process of regional economies of East Asia that suggests the possibility of a slowdown of economic activity. The continuing shifts of global economic activity provide some evidence of the decreased capacity of the "miracle economies" to maintain their pace of growth. A summary of the principal ideas and arguments concerning the future economic and political problems facing Singapore and other Asian countries as their stage of economic development approaches those in the West is found in Chapter 6. A glossary offers explanations and definitions of some of the technical terms that are used.

Before embarking upon the logical journey that I offer to my readers, a word of warning is in order. Some readers will doubtless find my discussion to be focused rather heavily upon criticisms of the government of Singapore. In fairness, the good people of Singapore have enjoyed material gains and social stability that are in part a function of the choices made by their political leaders. Nonetheless, I do not feel compelled to defer continuously to the record of the long serving political leaders there. It is to be hoped that my remarks will be received in the same good faith in which they are presented and shall serve to counterbalance the government's strict control over reports that emanate from the city-state and the often harsh repression of its critics. Their actions have ensured that domestic media coverage and all official documents invariably and unreservedly praise the leadership of the PAP. Therefore, I make no apologies for my mode of presentation. If indeed there is a legitimate grievance against my having expressed these views in a decidedly one-sided manner, then the reader should bear in mind that my sins in this regard are no greater than those of the regime in Singapore.

As I am convinced that what happened to me was not an isolated incident, the reason for telling my story in this manner might serve as a warning to others and that the risks of dealing with despotic governments are much higher and wider than most imagine. Anyone can expect to face the same sort of treatment when involved in a similar situation in Singapore in confrontation with other authoritarian regimes. In considering my experience, perhaps citizens of more free countries can see that allowing governments to become more repressive in exchange for promises of greater law and order or prosperity is indeed a deal with the devil.

Notes

1 Despite its tiny size, Singapore has one of the world's largest pool of foreign reserves ($46 billion). Also, the vast majority of the population is able to occupy or own high-quality public housing. More details on Singapore's economic record can be found in Chapter 4.

2 East Asia refers here to those countries to the East of Bangladesh, which includes Brunei, Burma (Myanmar), Cambodia, China, Hong Kong, Indonesia, Japan, Laos, Malaysia, the Philippines, the Republic of Korea, Singapore, Taiwan, Thailand, and Vietnam. References to the Pacific Region include Australia, East Asia, New Zealand, the Pacific Islands, and North America. North Korea and Siberian Russia might be included in either of the groupings but for their own peculiar internal problems and uncertain status.

3 Another scholar, publishing under a pseudonym, has referred to the political arrangements in Singapore as a *neurocracy*. See, J. David, "Don't Count on Me Singapore." *National Review* (May 16, 1994). For a first hand account of the political dirty tricks of the PAP regime and the climate of fear in Singapore, see Chee Soon Juan, *Singapore, My Home Too*. Singapore: Melodies Press, 1995.

Chapter 1

PUBLISH AND PERISH IN SINGAPORE: AN ASSAULT UPON ACADEMIC FREEDOM

This chapter will offer considerable details of my unfortunate episode. Some readers may interpret this as a sign of self-indulgence. That objection notwithstanding, I feel strongly that what I offer can serve as a useful vehicle in order that others might better understand the impact and personal consequences of the reactionary behavior of a hyper-sensitive regime. By dwelling on these private aspects of my ordeal, the reader may gather important insights into the general difficulties of living under intolerant governments. In all events, I use my own experiences to provide the backdrop for the likely nature of the unhappy encounters that await other critics and rivals of Singapore's ruling party.

Escape from the Republic of Fear

Few things can disrupt one's daily routine like a visit from the police to be informed that you are the subject of an investigation into criminal charges. This shock is particularly discomforting when you are an invited visitor in a foreign country whose legal system has a dubious reputation for respecting individual rights. This is precisely what happened to me when the government of Singapore took offense to my published comments that appeared in a newspaper article.[1]

Apparently the university officials recognized my expertise in the economics of European integration and valued my extensive experience in Europe as I was offered a position as Senior Fellow in their program of European Studies. Upon accepting an invitation from the National University of Singapore (NUS), I conducted myself no differently than I had in any of the other 11 countries where I had lived and taught over the past 15 years. The day began innocently enough. Even the interruption of my morning lecture to be notified that my department head, Dr. Jon Quah, wished to speak with me in my office seemed innocuous enough. However, I found that this appointment set me up for an interrogation by 2 detectives in normal street clothing. They instructed me that they were conducting an investigation into charges of criminal defamation and contempt of court. At first, I was more stunned than frightened.

My surprise was genuine in that the article referred to above contained no reference to any government or any individuals. In light of the other skirmishes of the *International Herald Tribune* (IHT) with Singapore's authoritarian regime, I assumed that the editors and lawyers were probably sensitive to what they printed about the tiny island republic. As it turns out, I had simply repeated observations and offered general impressions about the well-known methods of suppressing dissent in East Asia. Since the observations I made were readily found in more academic publications, I felt no hesitation in repeating them in the popular press. Little did I know that Singapore's regime would exhibit their willingness to go to such great lengths to prove that my criticisms of authoritarian repression described them so accurately.

Both of my interrogation sessions were quite high-tech. The officers came equipped with both a laptop computer and a portable printer. Each session lasted more than 2 hours and involved over 200 probing questions. The leading nature of their questions made it clear that they were hoping that I would make the job of the prosecutor easier by offering self-incriminating statements. After each grilling, they used their equipment to print out an affidavit for me to sign on the spot. On the first visit, they confiscated files relating to the background research for my article. After taking those materials from my office, they followed me home to collect some that I had stored there. What they took was little more than back issues of news magazines and journals that I had read over the past year or so.

It became clear from the complicated skein of questions that this was not the work of a cop who read my commentary and decided to check out things on his own. Actually, the degree of social control in Singapore is so complete that such a decision could only have emanated from the highest level. My mood became increasingly despondent given my knowledge of the habits of Mr. Lee Kuan Yew, the strongman-ruler of Singapore for over 30 years. Mr. Lee's reputation for obsessive micro-management of the lives of his countrymen is matched by his vindictive nature and the relentless hounding of his opponents.

One persistent line of questioning was to establish whether my statements might in some way construe a "threat to public order." The wording of this particular phrase was particularly ominous. There were echoes of the language of the Internal Security Act (ISA) that was a holdover from British legislation that was set up to quell dissent to colonial rule. This act allows for persons suspected of constituting such a threat to be arrested without a warrant and to be detained without trial for considerable periods. Indeed, Mr. Francis Seow, a former Solicitor General of Singapore, was detained for 72 days under this law. His "crime"? After breaking with the regime, he served as defense attorney for some prominent political prisoners and then later indicated his intention to enter into opposition politics.

My discomfort was heightened by having finished the preparation of a book review of Mr. Seow's harrowing account the day before my first visit from the police.[2] Despite his exemplary record as one of the country's highest ranking public servants, his interrogators were not reluctant to mistreat Mr. Seow while he was held without trial. With this information and a fresh memory of the regime's adamant posture to make an example of Michael Fay, I well understood the consequences of coming into conflict with authority in Singapore.[3]

After the first visit from the police, I received conflicting advice from friends and colleagues concerning the intentions of the government. On one hand, most of the Singaporeans I spoke with insisted that the police inquiry was just a "shot over the bow." They believed that the authorities expected that their intimidating tactics would deter me from future criticism. On the other hand, most expatriates suggested that I would be wise to leave as soon as possible to avoid additional heavy-handed actions that might be taken against me. Positioning myself somewhere in the middle, I decided to make contact with the news media to provide myself with some cover. Returning the fire, so to speak, I contacted the editorial staff of the Asian edition of the *Wall St. Journal* where I had published a number of articles earlier in the year to discuss the background of the problems confronting me. With the wire services also carrying the story, it was given wide international coverage in the next day's papers from New York to Hong Kong. My decision to raise the stakes by informing the newspapers was a calculated risk. I knew it might have lowered the costs to the regime of pressing their point. By speaking early to the media, I sacrificed a bargaining chip. Otherwise, I might have worked a deal whereby I would keep quiet about the investigation if the government would back away from pursuing the matter any further.

What I saw happening was a near perfect trap. To lay their ambush, even though I did not mention him or Singapore by name, Mr. Lee demanded a full retraction and an apology in specific terms dictated by him. He also insisted that I agree to pay damages for defamation and to cover all legal costs or he would initiate civil proceedings against me. Acceptance of his conditions would have amounted to an admission of perjuring myself in my signed affidavits collected by the authorities, itself a chargeable crime. There was no way out for me. Either I faced a criminal trial and the strong possibility of a prison term or I would be impoverished in defending an unwinnable civil case or both. My choices were grim: either I could remain in Singapore and face prison and financial ruin, or I could return home broke, disoriented and unemployed; but free.

It is in this context that my sense of dread overcame me. Eventually I abandoned a well-paid university position, my professional library built up over the previous 25 years, and all my other worldly possessions. After a second grilling by the same detectives and the separate notification from Mr. Lee's own law firm announcing his intention to sue me personally, I left on very short notice. I packed only my notebook computer and an overnight bag to take the next flight home. Though I stopped by my home to collect my passport, there was not even enough time to pack a change of underwear or socks. I was able to slip away before the jaws of their snare slammed shut. My hasty and nerve-wracking trip to the airport ended with a sigh of relief after the 747 lifted into the sky. In the end, total relief from my sense of agitation awaited my eventual touch down in Los Angeles. The 24 hour trip brought to end a period of anxiety that stretched over 5 days of precious little sleep and almost no food from loss of appetite. I have no doubt that many others have suffered greater ordeals for more noble causes. Nevertheless, I found that what I endured was more than enough excitement for me.

Weeks after I was safe at home in the States, charges were filed against me. Then in January 1995, I was tried in the High Court of Singapore and found guilty *in absentia*. The presiding judge ruled that I should pay a heavy fine as well as court costs amounting to tens of thousands of dollars. My "crime"? My words that appeared in a newspaper were like the tale of the "emperor who wore no clothes". A certain Asian "emperor" was obviously enraged by my challenging the carefully crafted image of Singapore's supposedly incorruptible public officials.

Flight to Freedom

Throughout the affair while I was still in Singapore, the lack of sleep and the stress of the situation made me incapable of thinking clearly about what actions were in my best interests. One colleague steadfastly insisted upon what turned out to be the proper course. At each turn, I would agree with his advice but then say that I would do it at a later time. His clear understanding of the importance of timing guided my steps over the next few days. Although he had convinced me that I must wire the funds from my local bank account back to the US, I was distracted by other things. It was only through his stubborn insistence that I actually got to the bank. After I received a fax that notified me of a family emergency, he expedited my uncertain departure plans by bundling me into a taxi to insure that I went to the airport. Because I owe a debt of gratitude to this friend, the name will not be mentioned here. Otherwise I am convinced, as he is, that the authorities would take actions against him.

In light of both push and pull factors, there seemed little other choice than for me to leave as soon as possible. I became aware that I must make cautious plans in departing from Singapore. After notifying NUS officials of my request for leave, the next move was to discuss my departure plans with officials of the US Embassy. Then at 2:00 p.m. I booked a ticket for a 5:00 p.m. flight later that same day on Singapore Airlines. In the meantime, I contacted a journalist who had covered my story in previous days to advise him of my plans. I suggested that he come to the airport along with a photographer in the event that there might be official interference with my departure. Upon seeing him at the airport, I acknowledged his presence with a furtive nod and then surreptitiously slipped him 2 different press releases. One was a statement to be published if I were able to leave; the other would be used in case I was stopped. In the event that there was a confrontation, my plans were to cause quite a ruckus. The wire services would have had access to photographs of an American citizen being manhandled by the border police of a country with a shabby human rights record. My final step was to drop a letter into the post box notifying my employer of my intention to resign as required by my contract.

During the course of my eventual escape, it was with great relief that I passed through the immigration control point without incident. Through the glass partition, I signaled thumbs up to my journalist-companions and set off for the gate to board my flight to freedom. Even then, I began to wonder if the authorities might wait until I was inside the terminal and quietly bundle me into some side room, out of the view of other passengers. My mind raced through all sorts of wild possibilities that happily were proved wrong.

But then while waiting for the boarding announcement, my nerves began to take over, inducing me to make a near fatal mistake. On the back of my business card, I scribbled the message, "If for any reason, I am unable to board this flight, please contact my family at the following telephone number in the USA." I approached a young man and asked if he were an American. In response to his nod, I handed him the note. After a brief pause, he thrust the card back into my hand and blurted, "Absolutely not! I do not want to be involved!"

Stunned by his rejection, I offered to explain, but he insisted that he wanted to know nothing more about it. I cursed my ill-fated move and resolved simply to await my fate whereupon I took a seat among the other waiting passengers.

From the first visit of the detectives, the suspense had been building. What happened next pushed me close to the breaking point. As I was trying to distract myself by reading a book, a representative of Singapore Airlines asked me if he could have a word with me. He suggested I collect my belongings and step outside the boarding area.

My heart leapt to my throat. Certainly my anxiety began to show as I felt flushed. The point of the ensuing conversation was to investigate my nervous efforts to pass my note onto the other passenger who had in turn alerted the station manager of my strange behavior. In response to the ticket agent's question, I sputtered out that since I had booked the flight just a few hours before, that I was worried about being bumped as commonly happens in the States. In order to gain some credibility, I offered him another of my business cards identifying me as a Senior Fellow at the NUS. He mused over it for a few seconds, then asked me why my name seemed familiar to him. As it turns out, my name and photo had been in the newspaper in the past few days. I explained to him that although I had been the subject of a police investigation, no charges had been filed against me.

Finally, it seemed that his only interest was for me to accompany him to the airplane to explain the matter to the passenger whom I had approached. This suggestion was a great relief to me. I carried out the mission with the greatest diplomatic aplomb and brevity I could muster under the circumstances. With all put back into order, or so it seemed, I was shown to my seat.

Boarding the aircraft was uncharacteristic for Singapore's high-tech Changi Airport. We were ferried out to the tarmac on buses and then walked up a roll-away ramp. Thus, the aircraft was situated out of sight of the main terminal. Also uncharacteristically, there was a 30 minute delay before takeoff with no substantive explanation. Given the police-state tactics of the regime and the penalties for breaking rules, I was certain that the steward who had questioned me had contacted the authorities, and they were awaiting clearance. From my seat I could see that the doors were closed, but the rampway was not pulled fully away from the aircraft. I continuously fidgeted to glance out the window awaiting complete removal of the stairs.

After an interminable wait, the ramp disappeared and the captain announced our imminent departure. As we left the ground, I released an immense sigh of relief. My neighbor, an elderly Taiwanese visitor to Singapore, remarked to me, "You must work very hard. You look so nervous." He would have never dreamed what was going through my mind, although I am certain that it was evident that I had neither slept nor eaten for the past four days.

Soon after my return home to the USA, Singapore's Ambassador in Washington, Mr. S.R. Nathan, made unsubstantiated and misleading statements about me in a letter published in the *Wall St. Journal*.[4] Referring to my IHT article, Mr. Nathan stated unequivocally that I acted to "malign the integrity of Singapore's judiciary." The unambiguous intention behind his remarks was that I had been charged, tried and found to be guilty albeit without the benefit of the trial in open court that is claimed to be available in Singapore.

Indeed, at the time of his writing, no charges had even been filed against me, and so I could not have been found guilty as he clearly asserted. Unlike Mr. Nathan's remarks, there was nothing in the arguments in my article that made specific references to any person nor any country. Relying upon his diplomatic immunity, and the open access to American publications, he felt free to act both as prosecutor and judge. While a letter I sent to him was published in the *Wall St. Journal* objecting to his statements and demanding an apology, he neither retracted his statements nor were they censured by his government. As an official representative of Singapore, it is reasonable to surmise that such remarks reflected the government's official position. Further evidence of this supposition emerged from the appearance of verbatim letters published in different newspapers in different countries by at least two of Singapore's ambassadors!

Several weeks after my departure from Singapore, I was notified that criminal charges had been filed against me. Also charged were the editor and the publisher of the newspaper as well as the printer and the distributor. The other four were charged for their complicity in allowing my words to come into public view. These rash steps are consistent with the ruling party's history of imposing its iron grip on public opinion. Obviously the specter of such actions eventually bludgeons writers and publishers into a shameful policy of self-censorship. Meanwhile opposition politicians and opponents must simply choose another place to live or keep quiet. Consequently, the political conversation becomes a hollow charade of praise and wide-eyed ignorance of abuses of power. As mentioned previously, the ruling party in Singapore uses a system of "rule by fear" and carefully constructs an illusion of democratic legitimacy. Intimidation of the domestic and international media is an important element in their phobocratic strategy.

It remains unclear whether there is a role for outside critics in bringing pressures to bear that might put a brake upon the authoritarian overreach of Singapore's regime. Citizens and rulers elsewhere truly concerned with individual rights might consider economic sanctions against Singapore in response to the same sort of barbaric behavior when practiced elsewhere. Though the historical record of the success of sanctions is mixed, there is some question as to whether Singapore's authoritarian-capitalist government merits the moral opprobrium and capital divestiture as in other countries. For example, South Africa's apartheid government exhibited the same general contempt for individual rights, and presumably both merit the same scorn, though admittedly there may be differences in the means and degree of oppression. Since the opposition to apartheid was based upon principle, it would matter little if elements of the system were reformed. Therefore, following an argument based upon principle, abuse of power by authoritarian rulers deserves to be denounced. A general contempt for individual rights is the basis of a fundamental similarity South Africa's apartheid regime and Singapore's government. Admittedly there are differences in the degree of oppression between these two examples of authoritarian government. Nonetheless, as a matter of principle, the abuse of power by any rulers deserves to be denounced even if everyone who opposes them is abused equally.

Although Singapore's authorities made much of the fact that my trial was held in open court, this did not impress anyone familiar with Singapore's questionable human rights record. Stalin often conducted open trials to allow his enemies to make public confessions before taking them out to be executed. The hypocritical remarks made by Singaporean officials come as no surprise from a regime that would send in its police to interrogate a scholar who had been invited to their country to teach at their premier university and to impound research materials . The behavior of Singapore's leaders in this affair confirms the general impressions of the repressive tactics of some Asian regimes as stated in my article. Due to the prolonged dominance of single parties or even single families in government, there is an evident convergence and consolidation of the various instruments of power. The use and abuse of the law as a weapon by a ruling party is similar to the actions taken by the communist regime in Beijing. The political imposition and institutionalization of unquestioned respect for authority serve as a convenient means for Asian autocrats to remain in power. Singapore and other East Asian countries do not exercise the Rule of Law as a means to protect individuals. Instead, rules are made by and for rulers or for the convenience of the ruling parties. What they have constructed is an illusion of law and order that camouflages a condition of "lawless order," where due process falls victim to arbitrary governance and the executive branch interferes with the autonomy of other organs of government. While there is an appearance of an orderly community, the reality is that the government's manipulation of the legal system leads to considerable insecurity for citizens.

It is apparent from the Singaporean government's own admission that opposition politicians have *never* won a case when being sued by a member of the ruling party. In regard to the appearance of a compliant judiciary, it would seem that the prosecutor's evidence put the judges in an uncomfortable position. Either Singapore's judges are capable of acting independently or they are not. If they are not, they are not likely to admit it. It is particularly striking that every opposition politician to appear before them has been found to be a scoundrel, tax cheat, slanderer or other type of distasteful character. This absolute lack of honorable opponents to a ruling party must be unprecedented in the history of politics.

As an indication of the arrogance of power evident in leaders of the ruling party, the Prime Minister Goh Chok Tong issued numerous pre-trial comments that could only be considered prejudicial. He indicated to the newspaper reporters that if found guilty, the courts would "throw the book" at me. In declaring the probable outcome of my day in court, perhaps he was merely second-guessing the "independent" judiciary. Whatever the reason, no responsible leader would speak so openly and express such a clear opinion about a pending case.

Singapore's Attorney-General insisted that I could only have been speaking about Singapore. As evidence, he detailed the outcome of the trials of the opposition politicians that had been sued for libel by members of the ruling party, all resulting in guilty verdicts. In his testimony in the High Court, the Attorney General said that Singapore was the only country where this sort of thing has happened by referring to the 11 major opposition politicians who had been sued for libel by members of the ruling party. Despite what appears to be self-incriminating evidence offered by the government's prosecutor, the High Court ruled that my remarks scandalized the judiciary of Singapore.

The prosecution made much of the fact that many of those defendants had been bankrupted by the proceedings. This struck me as a strange defense of the integrity of his country's judicial system. Their prosecutors first offered evidence that proved my statement of a compliant judiciary to be true in fact, and then they were faced with the task of contradicting their own evidence. Quirks of jurisprudential logic did not stop there. Cases involving contempt of court are normally based upon the submission of objective evidence in which the basic facts are not in dispute, but only the issue of whether contempt has been committed. Nonetheless, the Attorney General insisted upon, and was granted, the right to cross-examine Mr. Michael Richardson, the Asian editor of the IHT and one of the co-defendants. Injection of subjective testimony to interpret the content and intent of my words should have compromised the prosecution's case.

In all events, Mr. Richardson's apologetic testimony has been viewed by many as part of a pattern of capitulation to a tyrannous regime. This is particularly surprising since the paper is acclaimed to be the "world's largest news gathering network" and is owned jointly by the *New York Times* and the *Washington Post*. Prior to the trial, in order to placate the authorities in Singapore where it keeps offices and hires printing facilities, the IHT's executive published a "clarification" that acknowledged the viability of the government's case.[5] This statement appeared during December of 1994 in an edition of the IHT even though I was not consulted. The language was such that we were left without a defense. I chose not to appear nor to have an attorney represent me.

To no one's surprise, the criminal trial concluded with a guilty judgment against all 5 defendants. My conviction resulted in a fine of 10,000 Singapore dollars (about $7,000) which was the largest penalty for a contempt of court judgment in that country's history. In offering an explanation for the unusually high sum, the judge stated that my failure to show contrition for my "crime" was a deciding factor. In addition, all the co-defendants were issued an obligation to pay court costs amounting to more than 84,000 Singapore dollars (about $70,000). My personal assets remaining behind in Singapore were garnished by the court. These losses added additional burden to the forgone income resulting from my unanticipated resignation from my appointment to the NUS. By confiscating over $20,000 in my savings and pension contributions remaining in Singapore, my total personal loss from this affair amounted to over $100,000.

This sentence was less harsh than most observers expected. However, as the civil lawsuit initiated by Mr. Lee Kuan Yew is pending, the affair is not over yet. Media experts predict there shall be an inevitable settlement amounting to 6 or 7 figures. In July of 1995 the IHT was made to pay over $680,000 in a separate libel suit filed by Mr. Lee, his elder son, and Prime Minister Goh Chok Tong. That case and its broader implications will be discussed in more detail in Chapter 4.

An unsettling turn occurred in relation to Mr. Lee's lawsuit against the IHT and me. Just after the court ruling on contempt, I was issued a summons directing me to answer the lawsuit in Singapore's High Court. It was delivered to the front door of my home by a burly man who looked to be an off-duty American policeman. Obviously, the long arm of the law in Singapore can reach across continents and employ Americans to carry out their work for them here. Although I am certain that they are aware that I have no plans to respond to the summons, they were alerting me to the fact that they know where to find me.

Singaporean officials contend that the trial was not about freedom of the press. Instead, they insist that they were promoting the interests of the citizens of Singapore by protecting the reputation of the judiciary as a key institution of government. Many observers of Singapore's political machinations would declare that the only institution protected by such proceedings is the ruling People's Action Party that has held a monopoly on power for over 30 years.

To its credit, the Clinton administration issued strong protests through the State Department against Singapore's harassment and intimidating tactics against the newspaper executives and me. Then after Singapore's High Court found us guilty of the charges, the State Department issued another condemnation of the ruling. Throughout the initial and most nerve-wracking stages, officials from the Department of State in Washington were in contact with me to discuss my plight. I also received moral support and advice from friends and strangers from around the world including government officials, lawyers, university professors and private citizens. All who were familiar with the ways of Singapore's government strongly advised against returning to face trial. In the end, my decision not to return was based upon this informed advice. The consensus was that Singapore's judges were as inclined to be swayed as much by the pressures from the PAP regime as by the facts of the case.

Singapore's Courts: Scandalous or Scandalized?

As reported in the introduction, the spirit of academic debate prompted me to respond to an earlier editorial comment in the IHT written by Kishore Mahbubani, a senior bureaucrat in Singapore's government.[6]

In violation of the traditions of understatement and humility said to be intrinsic to the "Asian values" he purports to champion, Mr. Mahbubani is an aggressive and abrasive adversary of the ways of the West. On one level, I was annoyed by the prickly hubris evident in his self-righteous diatribe. On another level, I had become increasingly frustrated by the rejection of my responses to his viewpoints that I had submitted to other publications. While insisting that the curbs on press freedom in his own country were justifiable, he was exploiting his access to the free and open media of the West that I was finding closed to my ripostes. His central thesis in the newspaper article that drew my attention was an assertion that Europeans could find a cure for their economic failures and moral collapse by following the lead of the East Asian "miracle economies." Further, he insisted that a set of pan-Asian values form the basis of the unprecedented record of economic growth of Singapore and some of its successful neighbors. Obviously, he did not mention that the longevity of the PAP is based upon the institutions that support its paranoiac rule.[7]

In the process of condemning the deficiencies of Europeans in solving some conspicuous problems, Mr. Mahbubani strongly asserted that solutions to these problems could be found in the application of the authoritarian approach to government practiced by many Asian governments. My first objection to his remarks was that much is known about Europe's problems because there is a tradition for a reasonably free and open press. On the contrary, Asia's problems are kept out of sight due to legislation and other actions that stifle the press as well as the arrogant actions taken against vocal critics. My observations were certainly self-prophetic.

As indicated by the reprint of my article, the title alluded to a serious problem with massive forest and ground fires in Indonesia that were burning out of control. The smoke from the blazes was enveloping the skies and even resulted in airport closures in other parts of Southeast Asia. Meanwhile, newspapers in Singapore's neighboring states neither discussed the problem nor attempted to present expert opinion on possible solutions. Similarly, in keeping with the "hear no evil, see no evil, speak no evil" mentality that is characteristic of many East Asian governments concerning the domestic affairs of their neighbors, no pressure was placed upon the Indonesian government. Apparently the feeling was that if Indonesian authorities relied upon outside help then they would "lose face." Meanwhile, the sky over much of the Malaysian peninsula was choked with the smoke from thousands of acres of precious rain forest burning out of control. After nearly 6 weeks of clouded skies, a meeting was announced by officials of neighboring countries that would only take place several weeks later. Rather than undertake some concerted action, the newspapers quoted officials as stating that the problem would be cleared up in the rainy season.

This paranoiac control of news and information by authoritarian rulers allows them to release news on their own terms, trumpeting their successes while concealing their failings. It is truly difficult to form a reasonable comparison of lives lost in conflicts in Asia and Europe. Whereas CNN provides vivid coverage of Chechnya and Sarajevo, without similar coverage it is uncertain how many civilians perished in the political struggles in most parts of Asia. Most outsiders can know little about the loss of life associated with political repression in Burma, East Timor, North Korea or in Tibet. Also these questions are not open to public discussion since the authoritarian regimes that rule those places do not provide answers to such questions.

It may be worth examining again the passages in my article that prompted the police investigation against me. Excerpts of my statements are that, "intolerant regimes in the region reveal considerable ingenuity in their methods of suppressing dissent," and that some of these tactics are "more subtle: relying upon a compliant judiciary to bankrupt opposition politicians." Ironically, Singapore's Attorney-General insisted that the reference could only have been to Singapore. As such, he asserted that since these remarks impugned Singapore's judicial system, I had committed "contempt of court".[8] My copy of the summons provided extensive documentation of the actions taken against the numerous opposition politicians who had been tried in Singapore courts for libel, most of whom had expressed their opinions on members of the regime. As noted earlier, such evidence offered proof of my point concerning compliance of some East Asian judges.

It is puzzling that the government would single me out for such strong actions. After all, many others have made more direct suggestions about the complicity of the judiciary and other branches of government with the dictates of Singapore's ruling party. Quite a few different books that are readily available in the local bookshops were my own source of information about this problem.[9]

However, it would appear that Singapore's functionaries have a poor understanding of how civilized and responsible governments behave or how their citizens will ultimately react to repressive tactics. Interestingly, no other Asian government commenced legal proceedings against either the newspaper or me over the article. It was a miscalculation to expect anything less than widespread revulsion to their heavy-handed actions against me. Civilized governments do not send in the police and file criminal charges in retaliation to an editorial column written by a university professor that contains information that is widely accessible and previously unchallenged.

Attacks on freedom of the press by Singapore's government have earned it a fair amount of external criticism. Certainly their actions violate the spirit of Article 19 of the Universal Declaration of Human Rights that endorses the freedom of opinion and expression. During 1994, at least 2 lawsuits were filed against the IHT by Mr. Lee Kuan Yew, Singapore's strongman-ruler.[10] In one instance, he reacted to a reference by Mr. Philip Bowring on the existence of dynastic politics in parts of East Asia, including Singapore. Many observers consider that there is considerable evidence to support Mr. Bowring's observation including the elevation of Mr. Lee's elder son, Lee Hsien Loong, to the rank of brigadier general at the age of 31 after serving only 5 years in a peace time army. Then six months later he was elected to the parliament and rose quickly in the PAP party hierarchy to become Deputy Prime Minister. It is not surprising that there are many references to the fact that Lee Hsien Loong is regarded as the heir apparent for leadership in this Asian "sultanate".[11] Even his name is translated from Chinese to "the dragon apparent". Nevertheless, even after the executives of the paper published an apology in response to his demands, Mr. Lee carried out his threat and sued the paper for libel.

These libel actions combined with restrictions on the circulation of the international press are part of a shift in tactics by the regime that are discussed in greater detail in Chapter 4. The intention behind this campaign is to attack the financial base of media owners rather than to invoke human rights concerns by arresting editors or banning publications. Charges of libel and defamation are freely interpreted and argued by state prosecutors, who, like the judges, have all been appointed by the governing party during its uninterrupted rule over the past 30 years.

During the entire 30 years of independence, Singapore has been ruled by one party.[12] Indeed, something that borders upon a personality cult has evolved around the governance associated with one man, Mr. Lee Kuan Yew and his family. By avoiding some of the less subtle tactics of iron-fisted rulers, he has overseen the imposition of a sort of kid-glove authoritarianism. It may be true that opponents of the ruling party in Singapore do not disappear in the night. Instead, individuals seen as a threat to the dominance of the ruling party are likely to be subjected to a PAP smear campaign at the very least. At a higher level of escalation, they may be brought before compliant judges or other supportive civil servants whose unswerving loyalty to the party is demanded and delivered. Details in my court summons offered evidence of the ruthless efficiency of the state bureaucracy in crushing and humiliating numerous opposition figures. These brutish acts were undertaken in the open so that the disfigured victims would serve as an ominous omen to others, thus reinforcing the climate of fear.

As in Singapore, some other authoritarian regimes in the region have disguised themselves as democracies by holding elections and constructing some of the familiar political institutions. However, by rigging these institutions to serve the purposes of the ruling parties, those who rule do so by imposing a climate of fear upon the ruled. In recent elections, Singaporean citizens were put on notice that those constituencies that support opposition parties put at risk their access to publicly provided services. With control of various organs of government in the hands of a dominant party or family, individuals participating in opposition politics are vulnerable to various methods that undermine their pursuit of public office. The methods can include public vilification and character assassination by members of the ruling party. Political opposition figures face severe restrictions on access to recourse against attacks from government figures due to the regime's unmistakable influence over the courts and the parliamentary immunity of its officials. Similarly, vigorous tax audits of nettlesome critics can easily be arranged by party officials long accustomed to the trappings of power. Unfortunately, these tactics are but a few of a set of recognizable elements of a "New Asian Model" promoted by Singapore, Malaysia and some other authoritarian regimes in East Asia.

Supporters of these administrations attempt to discredit the complaints against them by the cynical suggestion that other regimes elsewhere are more oppressive, or that Western journalists make the most noise when academics or journalists are silenced. Perhaps the appropriate context for this observation is that the intelligentsia should be viewed as the "canary in the coal mine."

If the regimes are bold enough to attack them, then other less visible and more vulnerable individuals are almost certainly at considerably greater risk.

Such is the context in which journalists and contributors to the popular media operate while living in Singapore. While I was aware of the possible reaction of the regime to those voicing a contentious opinion, I imagined that as an invited scholar I would be treated with due respect. In all events, I had lived for over 6 years in South Africa during the late 1980's. In each of my lectures and in all of my publications, whether in the popular press or in scholarly journals, I directly denounced or opposed my host government's apartheid policies. At no point during that period of time did I ever face any threats from my university employer or from the government. Had there been any interference with my academic freedom, there is absolutely no doubt that all my colleagues and most students would have gone into the streets to support me or anyone else so treated.[13] It is quite telling that while the South African apartheid regime was widely considered one of the most onerous in the world, much greater space was allowed for criticism. Similarly, there was a rich and diverse intellectual atmosphere. It may come as a surprise to many that during the 1980's and early 1990's, many of the departments in South African universities were dominated by soft-left, hard-left or even Marxian academics. Obviously that serves as a partial explanation of why apartheid has been relegated to the dustbin of history. It would seem that the regime in Singapore read the writing on the wall and has decided to shut off any public debate on its policies. Many people have reproached me for my unwarranted willingness to pass judgment upon the political or cultural arrangements of other countries. Nevertheless, the logic of their argument implies that criticisms of the apartheid regime by the rest of the world were inappropriate. As for my own approach, I believe that my defense of individual freedom and the confrontational stance against the apartheid regime were consistent with my objections to the authoritarian regimes in East Asia.

The National University of Singapore and "Asian Values"?

Many commentators credit the dedication to and reverence for higher education as a source of the dynamism of East Asia. Judging from the behavior of the administrators at NUS, they have wholeheartedly adopted the position of the regime and offer an Asian approach to education. These "Asian values" involve and insist upon rigid adherence to rules and hierarchy, rote learning, and following directions from their political leaders even in academic matters.

Perhaps I had ignored a strong hint of their high level of intolerance to expressions of academic freedom earlier in my tenure at the NUS. In an article co-authored with a colleague, we raised questions about the accuracy of the reported estimates of China's economic growth.[14] We were summoned to the office of Professor Ernest Chew, Dean of the Faculty of Arts and Social Sciences, to discuss this publication. Expatriate colleagues who had lived for many years in Singapore suggested we might as well pack our bags since in their experience such summonses were never made for congratulatory reasons. Although I imagined this to be an exaggeration, we were told to expect some sort of rebuke that actually might include being fired.

Our session began with Dean Chew's blustery denial that the meeting had anything to do with the content of our article. Denouncing the impression of imposing "political correctness" in Singapore, he insisted that he called us in to advise us that attaching our academic affiliation to our published work violated university decorum. Then he presented and cited different sources of rules and regulations governing the public activities of employees. He went on to point out laboriously the intricate rules of engagement set out by the NUS concerning encounters with the press that were published in a lengthy brochure. Several paragraphs in the university handbook pointed out that professors should not discuss issues with the press that had "economic, political, social or legal" content. Dean Chew found little humor in my remark that such restraints permitted little communication with the media beyond what one might have had for breakfast. What became clear to me from this meeting was that in sharp contrast to the "publish or perish" incentive structures in American universities, the NUS apparently enforces a policy of "publish and perish."

Some additional background on this issue might be helpful in understanding the chain of events. Given the response of university officials, and in light of the revelations of others, our questioning of the accuracy of China's economic record fell in the midst of a faction fight within the government. One faction is led by Senior Minister Lee Kuan Yew and is committed to a heavy focus of investments by Singapore businesses in China. Another faction led by Prime Minister Goh Chok Tong wants the eggs spread to other baskets, including other ASEAN members and India. Apparently responding to pressure from the dominant faction of the regime, Tommy Koh, former ambassador to the US and current director of the Institute of Policy Studies, took the lead in efforts to discredit our report on China. A colleague at the NUS described an exchange between Mr. Koh and Professor John Wong, head of the Institute of East Asian Political Economy. Mr. Koh is said to have stormed into Professor Wong's office and insisted that it was his responsibility as a specialist on the region to mount an attack on our report. Under these pressures, Professor Wong later sent a letter with rather tame criticisms that was to be published later in the IHT. In the end, the intellectual broadside we expected from Professor Wong was little more than a toothless peep. Although we were left unscathed by the fury released, this episode is particularly troubling given the aspirations of Mr. Tommy Koh to seek the nomination to be Secretary-General of the United Nations.

Despite its reputation as one of the premier institutions of higher education in East Asia, it appears that there is little room for academic freedom at the NUS. It is a humorless place run by rule-bound administrators that treat professors as though they are bureaucrats rather than scholars. The administration displays an insistence upon following rules paired with zero tolerance for those who would question the rationality of those dictums. This bureaucratization of the academy became amply clear in interacting with students and colleagues. I have often been asked for my opinions on the staff and students by associates and scholars who are interested in the region. My general response was that none of my high and positive expectations for the experience at the NUS were realized. In my academic career, I have measured the quality of my students and colleagues by their ability to provide penetrating insights, to offer challenges to existing intellectual frameworks, to think laterally and the like. In turn, I always expected them to demand the same from me. Most students at the NUS suffered from the common trait of heavy emphasis on rote learning almost to the complete exclusion of using what has been learned creatively. There was a great gap between scholastic achievement and personal maturity. This was evident in the giggling, wide-eyed naiveté and parochialism that led to the most often asked question, "Please, sir, what is the right answer?"

Alas, many of my Singaporean colleagues were also intimidated into lockstep mediocrity by the power structure both in the university and in the government. These observations are less a criticism of the individuals involved than they are of the incentive system under which they operated. Most of my students and colleagues were certainly comparable in their intellectual capacities with those encountered in any other university in the world. Doubtless, many were exceptional. It was well understood, however, that those who did not cooperate would be passed over for promotions or lose their jobs. Thus, whereas the government has perfected *phobocracy* or "rule by fear," the university administration employs "management by fear." Similarly, the students tended to toe the line in anticipation of being offered one of the plum jobs in the civil service. It was a common understanding, I was surprised to discover, that like in China each class at the NUS has an informer to report on the behavior of students and lecturers to the administration. Thus, students who are too outspoken would find themselves deprived of the largesse associated with working within the well-paid technocracy. As one of my expatriate colleagues remarked, the NUS serves as little more than "an incubator for another batch of baby mandarins." Many of the full professors in the Faculty of Arts and Social Sciences are also linked directly to the People's Action Party (PAP) either as Members of Parliament or by serving the ruling party in some other capacity.

Its reputation tarnished by its behavior in response to my affair, the NUS subsequently engaged a public relations firm in mid-1995 to sell itself as an international center of learning and scholarship. Unable to change its substance but eager to change appearances, they hired Baldwin Boyle Shand, a New Zealand-based PR consultancy to counter the bad publicity arising from the unwillingness of the NUS administration to support academic freedom. The firm offered a proposal for a media campaign to release newsworthy items about the activities of researchers at NUS. Despite these plans for a high profile make-over, scholars are unlikely to be impressed. In less than six months after my departure, my immediate supervisor was faced with more than half a dozen resignations of expatriate professors.

When Singapore's government authorities took steps against me well beyond any range of my expectations, a remarkably convenient family emergency arose that allowed me to request a leave of absence from my duties. Due to the strict contractual obligations to the NUS, I could not have left Singapore without express permission from the university authorities. In absence of these arrangements with the university officials, it would have appeared that I was on the run. Happily the crisis was soon resolved upon my return. Contrary to what some Asian critics might believe about the collapse of family values in America, most Americans do cherish their families. My family was very supportive in these stressful and economically ruinous times.

Spraypaint and Newsprint

Upon my return home to the States, I was listening to a radio call-in program, wherein the DJ asked listeners to remark upon my recent run-in with the authorities in Singapore. One respondent, equating my experience with that of Michael Fay, insisted that if I had broken the laws of Singapore that I should be punished accordingly. "Cane him, too!", the caller insisted. It is important to clear the air on these matters, not so much to protect my own reputation, but to discuss a set of principles that underpin life in America.

While living in Singapore I observed the progress and the coverage of Michael Fay's much-publicized predicament. In his situation, he was accused, tried and punished for actions that would be against the law in any country. It was always my view that the debate should have focused upon whether the severity of the punishment fit the crime and whether due process was followed. Instead, many Americans expressing disappointment with an apparent decline in law and order seemed willing to impose such punishments without concern to the losses of freedoms. In noting that Singapore prides itself on being a crime-free country, lessons from my recent experience are a reminder that law and order are but one of many desirous ends in a truly democratic society.

Various striking contrasts might be drawn here. In America and in most of the West, the police and the judicial system offer protection to individuals from the actions of other individuals and especially from the abuse of power of their governments. Many critics of Singapore's regime point out that their judges and police act to protect the government or more specifically, the ruling party. In parts of Asia, government officials find it more important for them to "save face" than to promote or to protect individual freedoms.

Indeed, functionaries of Singapore's authoritarian regime speak of "Asian democracy" as though this special variant entitles them to an excessive use of power. Given the tragic precedents of various Asian communist "democracies" (China, North Korea, Laos, Vietnam) such a claim is remarkable. A common thread among many Asian governments, democratic or otherwise, is found in the suppression of individual interests in favor of the broader interests of "society." In turn, Asian authoritarian-capitalist regimes bombard their citizens with arguments that insist that limits upon various freedoms are a worthy trade-off for economic gains or security.

It is far from clear that Singapore's citizens or those of other Asian countries are happy with this state of affairs. Most decisions are made for them by a political elite that exercises social and political control through fear and intimidation. Needless to say, dread of a late night visit by the police has a chilling effect upon political dissent or open debate. Authoritarian regimes often use a form of punitive economic sanctions. For example, business licenses in Singapore are issued on a yearly basis and are subject to revocation by officials of the ruling party. Political constituencies in Singapore failing to support the ruling party find their access to publicly provided services limited or curtailed. Active political opponents have faced exceptional and thorough investigation of their tax records or character assassination by Members of Parliament who hide behind legislative immunity. Meanwhile most expatriates are convinced that their telephones are bugged and locals fear to speak openly. Even now my friends whom I left behind in Singapore have requested that I not contact them directly. Most of them are on limited term contracts and are well aware that "uncooperative" professors tend not to have their contracts renewed. In a recent instance at the NUS an expatriate professor was confronted with text copies of e-mail messages sent over the Internet. As he had made unflattering remarks about a member of the administration, his services would no longer be needed.

Clash of Cultures?

Clearly the underlying issue in my clash with Singaporean authorities is the extent to which citizens allow governments to limit their freedom. The actions taken against me by Singapore's regime are symptomatic of the dangers of arbitrary and authoritarian power unrestrained by a viable opposition party.

In reflecting upon the Michael Fay incident, many Americans expressed frustration from living in fear of criminals. These frustrations led them to express admiration for Singapore where criminals are said to live in fear of a resolute legal system. There may be some truth in this observation, but it is important to note that ordinary citizens in Singapore also live in fear of their authoritarian government.

In all events, impressions of the crime free and clean streets of Singapore are part of a well-managed propaganda campaign. Singapore's masters have carefully crafted an image as a tourist paradise and a stable place for international investors. None of the statistics concerning any aspect of Singapore are accessible for independent corroboration. While researchers are not allowed access to the raw data collected by the government, those who wish to compile their own numbers face strong actions against them for collecting the most innocuous data. One political scientist attempted to measure the extent of political awareness in Singapore by asking respondents to identify political figures by matching them with their respective posts. His computer files were confiscated and his contract was canceled on very short notice. In like fashion, journalists are discouraged from asking "sensitive" questions.

As in many countries, some Americans may be too willing to accept limits upon individual freedoms in return for promises of a greater sense of law and order. In the headlong rush to establish a more strict treatment of crime, there is a risk of losing considerable individual freedoms. Abandoning the Rule of Law is likely to result in the unsatisfactory situation of "lawless order" where rules serve the rulers. Political arrangement in those East Asian countries ruled by authoritarian-capitalist regimes reveal the Faustian nature of this bargain.

In reflecting upon the attention paid to such a tiny country as Singapore, one might be tempted to ask whether the fuss is much ado about nothing. After all, some commentators have referred to Singapore as little more than a shopping center with immigration controls at both ends. Even so, the stakes are higher than they may appear to be at first glance. China is examining whether Singapore is the appropriate model to apply to Hong Kong. Indeed, Singapore's success at combining economic prosperity with a one-party, authoritarian regime makes it an attractive model for many of the transition economies of East Asia, including Burma, Cambodia and Vietnam.

Singapore's ruling party has had a successful record in promoting its own brand of democracy by posing as a stalwart against communist threats in its neighborhood. In turn, the regime relied upon images of the destructive influence of communism upon local politics as an excuse to rule with an iron hand. Thankful western governments turned a blind eye to abuses of individual rights by Singapore's regime in exchange for a strategically important military partnership.

Ironically, while some countries in the region are ruled continuously by the same individuals or communist parties, there is an active exchange of invitations with Singapore's leaders to explore their mutual interests. Meanwhile, some of the most outspoken officials in Singapore's government have shifted their rhetoric toward a supposed external threat as an excuse to continue its autocratic ways. The excesses of some individuals and the breakdown of the family are identified as pathological components of individualist-based western institutions. By focusing upon the worst of the wicked ways of the West, Singapore's masters justify the imposition of tight restrictions upon individual rights. These tactics conveniently ignore the beneficial element of the creative force of free individuals whose actions serve as the basis for economic change and prosperity.

In an effort to provide some intellectual support to their anti-western diatribe, members of the regime in Singapore have provoked a debate over the superiority of "Asian values." Promotion of these values is an important element of the ruling party's rationale for remaining in power. Much of this relies upon a contrived notion of neo-Confucian values that are argued to be the basis for Singapore's impressive economic prosperity. On one hand, members of the regime implement a public relations campaign to portray its corruption-free rule. Acting as virtuous rulers, the government insists that it is worthy of traditional respect accorded to parents and defers to the ancient tradition of "filial piety." Expanding this tradition of respect for elders to include unquestioning acceptance of authority, they rule with an iron hand hidden behind a cloak of respectability as promoters of family values. By promoting the interests of society over the freedom of the individual, Singapore's rulers can justify punishing those with the audacity to challenge their authority. It remains puzzling to me how imprisoning the souls of individuals improves the lot of a community.

Interestingly, the regime has been able to tap into an ongoing regional debate on the emergence or the renaissance of "Asian values".[15] Given the wide diversity of this vast continent, it is unsurprising that the debate over the content or existence of shared values remains unsettled. Nonetheless, a recent survey did reveal several points of agreement. First, many respondents expressed an impatience with the behavior of the US and the tendency to impose western values upon other regions. Second, just as many Asians resented the fact that leaders of Singapore's regime and its apologists would presume to speak for them.[16]

Perhaps this whole sad episode can be dismissed as a "clash of cultures," the result of an insensitive westerner who has little understanding and no respect for a host country's traditions. Such a judgment would play into the hands of the "Singapore School" that promotes its own depiction of a particular set of pan-Asian values.[17] Their suggestion that dedication to hard work and commitment to family are uniquely Asian ignores the Protestant ethics that are argued by many to have been an integral element in the modernization of western culture. Further, it is a decidedly dubious contention that values expressed by mankind can be compartmentalized into exclusive geographic or ethnic categories. The success of this argument allows Asian regimes to inflict great human suffering by insisting that human rights are culturally specific rather than universal. If the dangers of accepting this argument were not obvious enough, the absurdity should be. This line of reasoning would allow the justification of an onerous system like apartheid by referring to a set of specific and unique cultural conditions.

As evidence that my episode did not arise solely from my lack of understanding of Asian sensitivities, there are examples of Asian academics who have displeased the government of Singapore. In separate incidents, other lecturers from the NUS have been subjected to humiliating public denunciations by government officials.

After receiving his doctorate in the US and finding a position as a lecturer in psychology at the NUS, Dr. Chee Soon Juan decided to become active in opposition politics. He sought public assurances from Prime Minister Goh Chok Tong that there would be no hard feelings if he opposed him in the 1992 general elections. Just 3 months after his unsuccessful bid as a candidate to represent the Social Democratic Party, Dr. Chee found himself involved in a scandal that caused him to lose his job and his home.[18] He had submitted a voucher for reimbursement after making payment to a courier service, which action was approved by his department head. The parcel contained his wife's dissertation that was sent back to the US for approval by her doctoral examining committee. Although his wife was no longer employed by the NUS, she had been a lecturer in the same department during the preparation of her thesis. Initially Dr. Vasoo, the head of department and a PAP member of parliament, claimed that the parcel was sent without his permission and motivated the removal of Dr. Chee from his position with the NUS. Although Dr. Vasoo offered a copy of the receipt without his signature as evidence, Dr. Chee insisted upon seeing the original document that indeed indicated that it had been approved. In explaining this discrepancy, Dr. Vasoo offered the lame excuse that his signature was removed so as not to distract attention from Dr. Chee's misdeed. After his dismissal, Dr. Chee made public statements suggesting that he considered his firing to be politically motivated. For these remarks he was sued severally for libel by Dr. Vasoo, the secretary of the department of psychology, and Dean Ernest Chew. A total of about $280,000 was awarded to the litigants.

Dr. Chee related a story to me that confirms that most of his acquaintances also viewed his firing as being political motivated. During his first year back in Singapore and before he fell from grace, Dr. Chee celebrated his marriage with over 400 friends and colleagues who attended their reception to celebrate their union. Just over a year later, when he launched his book providing a focused manifesto for the Social Democratic Party, only 1 person from that large group attended.[19]

In another incident, Dr. Bilveer Singh, a full time lecturer in the Department of Political Science, published an article in the *Jakarta Post* which suggested that despite Singapore's high rates of economic growth, "the majority of Singaporeans were living hand-to-mouth." Members of the ruling party were clearly displeased by his questioning the regime's myth that there has been an equitable sharing of the gains from economic progress. It was intolerable that he went further by suggesting that the citizenry was suffering from "PAP fatigue," an allusion to growing disaffection with the policies of the ruling party that were causing living costs to rise. Seeking to undermine Dr. Singh's credibility, the government released a deluge of its own statistics, none of which could be independently corroborated. He was then instructed by the government authorities that if he could not come up with hard evidence in support of his claims, then he must retract them. As the ruling party does not allow independent collection of what it considers sensitive data, it was known in advance that their smugly worded demands were impossible to accommodate. Knowing the rules of the game imposed by the regime, Dr. Singh tendered a statement of unconditional contrition.

In January of 1995, Ms. Catherine Lim, a part time lecturer at the university, was publicly rebuked and belittled for reminding Prime Minister Goh Chok Tong of a campaign promise of a "kinder, gentler" government. In an article reprinted in the *Straits Times*, she suggested that Mr. Goh had departed from a "consultative, consensual approach" while returning to "the authoritarian style" of his predecessors. During the 1994 National Day celebrations, Mr. Goh asserted Singapore should not follow the path of political change toward an American-style democracy such as Taiwan and South Korea have taken. Following Ms. Lim's published remarks, the prime minister's press secretary responded in a story given front-page coverage by the *Straits Times*. The article forcefully laid out the regime's intention and right to impose strict limits upon public discourse pertaining to political issues and other community matters, citing as justification, as is so often done, that the PAP's survival is necessary for the survival of Singapore. This logic suggests that faultfinding which weakens the hegemony of the ruling party also threatens the collapse of the island state. Later, Mr. Goh issued his own rebuke to Ms. Lim by establishing "the out-of-bounds' markers clearly, so that everyone knows the limits of openness and consultation." The general lesson offered to Singapore's population was that politics is only for politicians. Ordinary citizens have been put on notice that they should not offer their opinions on political issues unless they wished to actively participate in the political arena, and only then within highly prescribed channels. In effect, the regime has circumscribed the basic rights of citizens to voice their opinions through the normal channel of civil society.

Constraints upon those NUS students who wish to express their views follow them after their graduation. Not long after my departure, four of the editors of *Commentary*, a bi-annual journal published by the NUS alumni society, resigned in protest when an oversight committee cancelled an entire planned edition. These actions involved a dispute over whether or not there was a need to "balance" the views in the publication. Interestingly, the theme of the issue was "culture" and did not directly involve criticisms of the political order. Those who did resign remarked that the changing political environment was supposed to allow that views opposing the political orthodoxy enforced by PAP followers could be aired. Several articles were considered controversial since they addressed the criticisms of performance artists by members of the government's arts council. Even though the intellectual content of the articles in the planned issue was not in question, the oversight committee was loath to risk raising the ire of the government.

Besides the rough treatment meted out to Asian colleagues, there were numerous stories of expatriate colleagues whose rebuke came as non-renewal of their contracts. Instead of a clash of cultures, a more apt interpretation of the unfolding of events in Singapore is the struggle over the course of the future. Citizens in Asia and other parts of the world are going to face increasingly difficult choices. Manipulative politicians are inclined to justify the reduction of individual liberties as compensation for greater economic prosperity in what has been identified as authoritarian capitalism. It is to be hoped that this noxious political cocktail will have less allure than its predecessors, authoritarian socialism and fascism.

Honoring Repression?

No greater contrast could be found in the absence of academic freedom at the NUS than in the 1995 Convocation proceedings for Williams College. Besides its idyllic splendor in a sleepy hamlet at the heart of the Berkshire

Mountains in Massachusetts, Williams College is one of the top liberal arts institutions in the entire American university system. As happens in many universities, it was decided that bestowing an honorary doctorate upon a notable alumnus would enhance the publicity value of the opening ceremonies of a new academic year. So it was decided that an honorary doctorate would be awarded to Prime Minister Goh Chok Tong, a 1967 graduate of the Williams College Center for Developmental Economics (CDE). It was suggested that Mr. Goh should be recognized for his contributions to Singapore's economic success story. Presumably, those who supported the award felt that the ideas picked up while he was a student at the CDE influenced his policies.

Unfortunately, his selection for this high honor set off an unprecedented firestorm of protests by faculty members and students at the college. There were several reasons behind the protests, but the most salient point raised was the attacks on academic freedom during Mr. Goh's tenure as head of government. Signs and posters sprang up on the campus with the slogan, "No Honor Degree for Goh". The whole affair was brought to the wider attention of the public in a syndicated column written by Mr. William Safire of the *New York Times.*[20] Eventually a motion was passed by a vote of 63% in an open faculty meeting that stated, "*It is the sense of the [Williams College] faculty that while we recognize the significant contributions Mr. Goh Chok Tong has made to the economic development of Singapore, we nevertheless find it regrettable for Williams College, as an academic institution, to grant a duly enacted honorary degree to the Prime Minister of a government that has persistently failed to honor, protect, and promote the freedom of expression of its citizens.*"

Much to the chagrin of nearly two-thirds of the teaching staff of Williams College, the award ceremony went ahead. Nonetheless, to its credit, the college administration offered financial support to arrange for alternate forums for there to be a public discussion of dissenting views. To this end, I was invited along with Mr. Francis Seow to appear on a panel organized by Williams College professor, Dr. Sam Crane. In an independent move, the students took the initiative to raise funds and invited several other critics of the regime. They included Dr. Chee Soon Juan, a rising star in the political opposition who is Secretary-General of the Singapore Democratic Party, and Dr. Daniel Bell, a prominent political theorist who had recently left his post at the NUS. The support of the administration of Williams College for the actions taken by faculty and students was in the best tradition of academic freedom, and I feel that each and all deserve commendation. In turn, the protests were guided by intelligence and compassion, tempered by gentility, and carried out with dignity and decorum.

Unaccustomed to dealing with demands from below and revealing his inability to grasp the art of compromise and democracy, Mr. Goh stated that he was baffled by the furor. During a press conference before the awards ceremony, he mused, "I do not understand the American system, where school administrators make a decision and the faculty can object. It is confusing to me. In our country, the debate must take place before the decision is made, but once the decision is made, there must be no more debate."[21] During the same questioning period, an attempt to be humorous fell flat when he was asked if Dr. Chee might be jailed upon his return to Singapore. Mr. Goh joked, "Of course, since I am such a dictator, I will order him arrested." When he sensed that most of the journalists present took him to be serious, he quickly sought to reassure the startled assembly that any talk of arrest was nonsense.

Unsurprisingly, Mr. Goh attempted to justify the autocratic ways of his government during his visit. However, it was more surprising that an invited head of government of a sovereign state would use such a platform to impugn the integrity of an important institution of government of his host country. In a sweeping and dismissive response to a question about the judicial system in Singapore, Mr. Goh offered an improbable accusation against the US State Department. He suggested that it was following some special interests or pushing some unnamed ulterior motives in its repeated observations about the "questionable independence" of Singapore's judges from the influence of the PAP regime. In an equally reckless remark, he scandalized the British court system by suggesting that the Privy Council in London had "gone too far" and was "politically motivated" when it overturned, on appeal, the prosecution of one of the PAP's critics. In the same breath, he also derided the unflattering reports previously issued independently by AsiaWatch and the New York City Bar Association as reflecting the views of "interested parties". Mr. Goh's remarks were certainly more direct than my oblique references that led to my trial and guilty verdict for impugning one of Singapore's "key institutions of government".

Conclusion

The extensiveness of the social control imposed by Singapore's ruling party is consistent with the policies of some of the most repressive regimes of this century. It is noteworthy that South Africa initially experienced rapid gains in prosperity under apartheid. Eventually internal pressures and conditions in the world changed, exposing the irrationality of the economic, political and social relations dictated by apartheid. It can be expected that Singapore's fortunes will also shift in response to long-run adjustments. The suppression of individuality and the crushing of innovative thought is almost certain to cause the economy to falter in the long-run. Singapore's governors must shudder to realize that eventually they will be held accountable for their fallibility when the economic success story hits a brick wall. Subsequent and less autocratic leaders might also wish to hold the leaders of the current regime responsible for their remorseless and humorless authoritarianism.

Many of the apologists for authoritarian regimes in East Asia insist upon the necessity of restraining the rights of the individual to serve the interest of the greater community. However, this is a convenient device since it also serves to entrench ruling parties by eliminating vehicles for protest as the source of political and social change. Therefore, it is not surprising that governments whose officials condemn Western values seek to justify the imposed limits upon Western concepts such as individual freedoms. By placing respect for authority above reason, rules become more important than individual rights and freedoms. Like the guests in Procruste's bed, individuals in Singapore are to be fitted to the rules.

The personalized accounts given above provide considerable evidence of the machinations of the system of repression in Singapore as it was applied in my case and in others. Nothing that has transpired in Singapore's courts since I wrote that fateful passage in the IHT has convinced me that it would be wrong to suggest that their judicial system is rigged. In the following chapters, the discussion is widened to provide an analytical framework to explain the PAP regime's manipulation of its pliant judiciary system in combination with other arrangements to maintain its tenacious grip on power.

Notes

1 "The Smoke Over Parts of Asia Obscures Some Profound Concerns," *International Herald Tribune*, October 7, 1994.

2 F. Seow, *To Catch A Tartar*, New Haven: Yale University, Council on Southeast Asian Studies, 1994.

3 For differing views on the Michael Fay incident, see G. Baratham, *The Caning of Michael Fay*. Singapore: KRP Publications, 1994; and A. Latif, *The Flogging of Singapore*. Singapore: Times Editions, 1994.

4 Interestingly, I was interviewed by Ambassador Nathan as part of the hiring process for my position with the National University of Singapore. After retiring, from intelligence responsibilities in the civil service, Mr. Lee Kuan Yew arranged for his appointment to oversee the English-language daily newspaper, the *Straits Times*, before moving on to a chequered diplomatic career.

5 The full text of the "clarification" is as follows. "It has been brought to our attention [that the article] could by reason of facts later drawn to our attention be understood as suggesting that Mr. Lee Kuan Yew had sought to suppress political activity in Singapore by bankrupting opposition politicians through court actions in which Mr. Lee relied on a compliant judiciary to find in his favor without regards to the merits of the case. This was not our intention, and we do not associate ourselves with any such view which we accept would be unfounded.

We apologize unreservedly to Senior Minister Lee Kuan Yew and the Singapore judiciary." *International Herald Tribune*. December 10-11, 1994.

6 "You May Not Like It Europe, But This Asian Medicine Could Help," *International Herald Tribune*, October 1, 1994. The full text of this article appears as Appendix One.

7 A description of the paranoid responses of the PAP government is found in Ian Baruma's "The Singapore Way." *The New York Review of Books* (October 19, 1995): 66-71.

8 The charges of judicial contempt were based upon the accusation that my comments scandalized the court system.

9 Besides F. Seow's book, I also had access to S. Sesser, *The Lands of Charm and Cruelty: Travels in Southeast Asia*. London: Picador, 1993. This latter book referred to a US State Department report that cited "political control of the press, courts, and religion".

10 Another potential suit involving the IHT and the former Minister of Law, Eddie Barker, was settled out of court for undisclosed damages.

11 Despite having no experience in the telecommunications industry, a younger son, Lee Hsien Yang (also a brigadier general at 32) became a top executive of Singapore Telecom within 6 months of the commencement of his employment.

12 Although it was granted self-governing status from their British colonial masters by 1959, the time clock for statehood is registered as 1965 after Singapore's brief membership in the Malaysian Federation from 1963.

13 It is with considerable irony that I note that a colleague from the NUS accepted a substantial cut in pay to take up an academic position in South Africa. He insists that the greater degree of academic freedom and absence of an atmosphere of fear in South Africa are ample compensations for the loss in income.

14 "Don't Trust the Reports of Supercharged Growth," *International Herald Tribune*, October 25, 1993 (with Kurt Wickman). Additional work on this thesis was encouraged by a commission from the German foreign affairs journal, *Europa Archiv* ("Ist die chinesische Wirtschaft ein Papiertiger?", April 10, 1994).

15 One attempt to forge a "manifesto for an Asian Renaissance" can be found in *Towards a New Asia*, Kuala Lumpur: Commission for a New Asia, 1994.

16 See D.I. Hitchcock, *Asian Values and the United States: How Much Conflict?* Washington, DC: The Center for Strategic & International Studies, 1994.

17 The "Singapore School" shall be discussed in considerable detail in subsequent chapters.

18 Due to the fact that he had been resident overseas where he was awarded a doctoral degree, Dr. Chee was virtually unknown in Singapore. Nonetheless, he was able to attract 25% of the vote against the leader of an entrenched party.

19 *Dare to Change*, Singapore: The Singapore Democratic Party, 1994. Dr. Chee has served as acting Secretary General of the SDP from May 1993.

20 "Honoring Repression." July 10, 1995.

21 "Debate Baffles Goh." *Berkshire Eagle*. September 17, 1995.

Chapter 2

THE "SINGAPORE SCHOOL," PAN-ASIAN VALUES AND THE NEW COLD WAR

As the rulers and peoples of Asia struggle to cope with the lure of modernization, the ensuing struggle for the soul of contemporary Asia seems little different from other struggles of conservative forces against the pressures for change. The underlying stress of the modernization process is that it imposes limits upon the capacity of existing institutional arrangements to satisfy the requirements of the constituent elements of a given community. New modes of human interaction expose inconsistencies in, and raise questions about, the nature and structure of the institutions that influence or govern the behavior of individuals. Instead of a clash of civilizations, history continues to be a clash between conservative and progressive elements. On one hand, there are groups of would-be losers from a change in the *status quo*. On the other hand, there are those who seek and approve of progress not so much for the sake of change as to reap the benefits of upsetting the *status quo*. In turn, political conflicts for most of modern history have arisen out of undertakings by different groups to secure a monopoly of power in order to control the distribution of resources and wealth.

A number of commentators representing some of the East Asian authoritarian-capitalist regimes have embarked upon a risky and perhaps dangerous course. In attempting to shore up their own shaky foundations, they have provoked a debate over the viability of "Asian values" that creates impressions of unnecessary divisions between the East and the West. While serving their own selfish interests, their rhetoric has conjured up images of Cold War II.

Playing the Race Card: Beware the "White Peril"

Until the collapse of communism, the most effective subterfuge of the government of Singapore and in some of the other ASEAN countries was to brand domestic opponents as elements of the "Red Peril" of international communism. In such cases, heavy-handed actions against their political opposition were unlikely to be condemned by Western governments who were searching for strategic allies in the region. Similarly, most of the citizens governed by these regimes were either intimidated into submission or meekly accepted their authoritarian ways in exchange for economic gains and stability. Nevertheless, Singapore and several other authoritarian regimes in the East Asia have adopted a new refrain that portrays their political opponents as political lepers who would spread the filthy germs of liberal democracy and the infections of individual freedoms imported from the West. With the demise of communism, the notion of a "Red Peril" has been replaced by the suggestion of a "White Peril" emanating from the West. For example, the one-sided projections of images of Western decadence are common themes in the daily newspapers in Singapore. It is as though leaders of these countries feel that Asian cultural institutions are too fragile to withstand the onslaught of outside influences. In turn, East Asian authoritarian regimes apply this rationale as the basis of the rough treatment inflicted upon persons identified as members of a new, insidious international conspiracy of liberal democracy. Ironically, Singapore's government is now turning on its erstwhile allies and friends in the region. Mr. Lee Kuan Yew has issued numerous denunciations and warnings in reaction to the liberalizing drift that is evident in the Philippines, South Korea, Thailand, and Taiwan.

While the ruse of a "White Peril" as a rationalization for repression may be transparent, other arguments offered by the regimes seem more compelling. For example, the remarkable economic advances recorded under the direction of Singapore's leaders and those of some other Asian regimes are often seen as a tradeoff for scuttling the further progress of democratic institutions.[1] This excuse looks less credible when comparisons are made with similar economic growth rates associated with the early periods of Soviet expansion or the performance of the apartheid economy in the 1960's and 1970's. While the rigid and authoritarian methods credited for these advances would not fit well into most Western cultures, it is far from clear that Asian citizens should have their rights and dignity trampled by their governments. As they are, the political arrangements of many of the authoritarian regimes in East Asia bear an unsettling similarity to the fascism which has been resoundingly rejected by Europeans.

With the passing of the Cold War, a more essential debate about the nature of political power can now be addressed. In the past, political tradeoffs between conservative and progressive forces were often mis-cast as a choice between assigning political power to left-wing or right-wing parties, accepting communism or fascism, or supporting liberals or conservatives. Discussions of these simplistic dichotomies seldom questioned the appropriateness of the level of government intervention in the lives of citizens. In turn, individual freedoms were as likely to be crushed by communists as by fascists. Taxpayers were forced by conservatives to spend enormous sums upon defense, or liberals demanded heavy payments to expand the welfare state. Political struggles became turf wars over who should have power, rather than whether citizens should yield so much power to their leaders.

At the beginning of the 1990's, a new sense of political maturity began to emerge which has resulted in growing pressures for the marketization of economies and the democratization of polities around the globe. At the heart of this conversation are conflicting visions of the role of governments in peoples' lives. This is the core issue in the contest for the future direction for Asia and elsewhere. At one end of the spectrum is a competing vision that collective judgments provide the best method for expanding human wealth. Actions by groups of individuals who identify with this point of view tend to promote institutions, whereby a governing elite seeks to impose restrictions on the range of individual choices. Institutions designed by the governing elite reflect an impatience and intolerance for choices that are in conflict with their imposed sense of order. At the other end of the spectrum is a vision that the appropriate means of community empowerment is through an expansion of personal autonomy and greater individual control by individuals over the determination of income and wealth. Groups of individuals who identify with this vision interact to bolster the emergence of institutions that encourage expressions of individualism, especially the market. Such institutions require a tolerance for the conflicts and complications emerging out of divergent expressions of individual values and life purposes. This perspective treats individual freedom both as a means and an end for the improvement of the general community.

In an effort to justify their collectivist or communitarian vision, the banner of a pan-Asian model has been raised that masks the emergence of "authoritarian capitalism" as a successor to "authoritarian socialism."[2] Offering a new Third Way between capitalism and communism, leaders of authoritarian-capitalist regimes rely upon a variety of institutionalized interventions in the economy and the polity. In the simplest terms, authoritarian capitalism combines a large measure of economic decentralization with political centralization. By allowing for a substantial amount of economic freedom in certain market activities while simultaneously exerting a substantial element of control over political institutions, authoritarian-capitalist governments portray themselves as providing both political stability and economic growth. These arrangements should be seen in contrast to the combination of liberal democracy and competitive capitalism identified as "liberal capitalism," the hybrid of liberal democracy with a free market economy. Rulers in authoritarian-capitalist regimes maintain their grip upon power by insisting that increased political freedoms would come at the expense of lower economic growth. Social calm, political stability and economic prosperity are portrayed as compensations for the suppression of democratic pluralism, the absence of the mediating forces of a civil society, and the lack of individual freedom.[3] Due to the prevalence of one-party states and dynastic political systems, as well as a traditional acceptance of hierarchical collectivism, East Asia has proved to be a fruitful ground for the institutions associated with authoritarian capitalism. Successes in the authoritarian-capitalist regimes of Indonesia, Malaysia, Singapore, Taiwan, Thailand and South Korea have been duly noted by leaders in Burma, Cambodia, China, Laos, North Korea, and Vietnam. Former communist governments would doubtless wish to make the transition toward market economies without incorporating the institutional liberalizations and multi-party politics inherent to Western-style democracy. Although East Asian authoritarian governments receive high praise for their "miracle economies," there are reasons to doubt whether the institutional arrangements constitute a sustainable equilibrium, which will be discussed in Chapter 5.

The End of History or a Clash of Civilizations?

Two new meta-theories describing international relations have emerged in the early 1990's that point to a retreat in the likelihood of ideological conflict, albeit for different reasons. The first posits the "end of history" as described by Francis Fukuyama.[4] This thesis points to the impact of economic modernization upon demands for political modernization. Presumably, it is premised upon the dominance of the human spirit and the search for secure means to stake claims to individual dignity and recognition, which eventually translates into demands for liberal democracy. Once large numbers of persons escape subsistence levels, they are able to focus upon broader goals including demands for acceptance as autonomous adults which are achieved through meaningful political participation. In sum, industrialization elevates increasing numbers of people out of poverty and provides a momentum that promises to sweep aside autocratic governments. According to Fukuyama, there has been a steady convergence of political and economic institutions around the models of liberal democracy and capitalism. Evidence for this thesis was found in the demise of Soviet communism and the deep process of profound economic and political reform that is underway in most other parts of the world.

The second thesis portrays the future as a "clash of civilizations" according to the thoughts offered by Samuel Huntington.[5] Professor Huntington has expressed a conception of the future where three great civilizations are expected to be locked in a troubling and unstable struggle for dominance. Due to the increased economic and military power of non-Western civilizations, conflict in the future is seen as occurring along cultural faultlines rather than being based upon ideological or economic frictions. Western cultural dominance can expect to be confronted by a globalized inter-cultural struggle. These conflicts are predicted to occur at both local and macro levels. Conflict may develop as localized struggles taking place along territorial fault lines or within transnational forums where newly developed countries seek to assert greater control over international institutions.

While both of these hypotheses may be flawed for their own reasons, they also appear to be mutually exclusive. In the first instance, while Soviet communism has disappeared and Maoism is on its way out, despotic governments have undergone subtle transformation in their ways to continue the challenge to "liberal capitalism." In the second instance, a clash of civilizations is by no means a *fait accompli,* at least not in a violent sense. Perhaps a more appropriate scenario can be defined by the facilitation and widening of communication flows. What would then emerge is a competitive process whereby citizens begin to choose parts or entire aspects of cultural arrangements from a global menu. Also, in contradiction to both theories, there is no particular reason to expect that the clashes in civilizations will be played out along cultural rather than economic or political lines.

The flow of modern history then might be more accurately be interpreted as a mutual exchange of ideas and an evolution of cross-cultural institutional development. By contrast, most of the prolonged, open disharmony in history can readily be identified as civil or intra-cultural wars. Thus, these struggles were among peoples of similar cultures rather than antagonists across distinct cultural lines. Similarly, it is inappropriate to ascribe the interaction of cross-cultural institutions as arising solely out of the colonial sword or imperialist dictate.

If the past is not merely a sequence of uninterrupted, internecine clashes of civilizations, then it is probably incorrect to project the future in such a manner. An alternative interpretation of cultural interaction is that "superior" institutions traverse the globe through a competitive process of adaptation, adoption and imitation.[6] Those institutions that provide the best opportunity for individuals to attain their individual goals within a group setting and provide the most admirable results are the most prone to be copied. Cultural differences may exist, but there is no evidence that these differences are immutable or result from an absence of a set of fundamental universal values. In an open setting, citizens can choose to graft new or modernized cultural arrangements onto traditional institutions.

Opposition to change should not be mistaken for promoting those elements of ones' own culture that are valuable to the wider community *per se*. There is a constant danger that such promotion can give way to a form of "cultural protectionism" that leads to the same sort of real losses that arise out of economic protectionism. One particular instance where such a fine distinction has emerged relates to the debate over the existence and importance of uniquely "Asian values." In the hands of some of its proponents, this model of pan-Asian values identifies a number of institutional arrangements that underpins those East Asian success stories.

The Contest for "Asia": Authoritarianism, Freedom and Modernity

At the present, there appears to be a dialogue of the deaf between certain promoters of an Asian model and their antagonists. Advocates of the so-called "Singapore School" are among the most outspoken advocates of this Asian model.[7] While there is much to be praised and emulated in the value systems associated with Asian cultures, there remain numerous reasons to question the motivation behind and the content of a pan-Asian model offered by backers of authoritarian-capitalist regimes. Recent history offers a grim lesson from the cost imposed upon humanity when national socialism, fascism and communism offered a seductive alternative to liberal democracy. In all events, there is a need to discover an appropriate method of inter-cultural communication between East and West.[8]

As a first step towards understanding this communication process, it might be useful to interpret some defining elements of the political arrangements in these different regions.[9] These distinguishing characteristics differ more in time than in kind from those in other regions. The elitism of technocrats in Asian authoritarian-capitalist regimes has historical antecedents, for example, in Asia as well as in the West during earlier stages of development. There is credible evidence that the motivating factor behind the construction of this model is to provide a justification for retarding the modernization process by imposing a peculiar form of conservatism.

One unfortunate consequence of the debate over this new Asian model is that it reflects an unnecessary opening of political divisions, as if a new Cold War were to be fought on a different front. Instead of a split portraying the North against the South, this new war of words has been designed to pit the "virtues" of the East against the "decadence" of the West. Whereas political despotism under Communism relied upon the ideological justification offering its superior socio-economic system, supporters of a new Asian model defend their authoritarianism through allusions to be the debilitating impact of Western influences. Individualism and materialism are portrayed as the principal threats that might undermine "Asian values" and weaken the bases of East Asia's superior economic performance. The first salvos in this new Cold War against the West have emanated from its erstwhile strategic allies and deeply dependent trading partners in Singapore and other parts of East Asia. As if to generalize beyond their current economic performance, some East Asian commentators and politicians have asserted that there is a specific set of uniquely "Asian values" that guide their leaders and bind their citizens. However, the political dimension of this new Asian model is at once incoherent and opportunistic.

Inadvertently, the conclusion of the World Bank's analysis of the underpinnings of the high rates of economic growth exhibited by the East Asian "miracle economies" provided an additional spark in this skirmish.[10] One of the principal conclusions of the World Bank was that these admirable economic results were the result of the implementation of a prudent mix of macroeconomic and industrial policies. This guarded policy course includes control of inflation through prudent fiscal and monetary policies as well as stable and competitive exchange rates. Pursuit of this policy mix was summarized in the phrase "getting the basics right." The glowing praise offered in this report violates a cardinal rule in economic analysis. In evaluating the benefits of market actions or government policies, the long and short run costs must be taken into account. Nonetheless, some of the governments in the region, notably Singapore and Malaysia, have accepted the approving conclusion of this report as an overall confirmation of their autocratic rule.

While the geographic focus of the struggle has altered, the substance of this struggle has not changed. Although geographical divisions have been constructed to promote the political agenda of ruling parties, in reality the battle over perceptions of culture, values or of the nature of humanity involves more fundamental issues. Essentially, the clash behind the "Asian values" debate emerges out of the efforts to preserve an authoritarian political *status quo* against the forces of modernity. Consistent with the discussion in the previous section, the central element of this struggle is whether collectivism or individualism is the appropriate impetus behind political and social institutions and whether citizens or rulers should have the final say in political decisions. What is at stake in other terms is whether the political system is allowed to lead to domination by an elite or whether freedom of the individual should be explicitly guaranteed.

Advocates of the Asian model of authoritarian, centralized government as practiced in Singapore and elsewhere tend to make the claim that the pace and extent of democratization are culturally determined. As they would have it, the traditional, non-individualistic and hierarchical cultures of Asia are certain to be barren ground for the seeds of democracy. Even so, their claims for the direction of causation between culture and democracy are not convincing. There are numerous counter-examples that indicate that democratic cultures are the consequence of, rather than the cause of, democratization.[11] The logic offered by proponents of the Asian model would seem to imply that the intolerance of institutions implemented by Europe's absolute monarchs and the church should have rendered the West immune to the development of democracy. Similarly, recent developments have reversed the suggestions that a culture of dependence, irrationality, and envy predisposed Russians and other Slavic peoples to repressive governments. Regardless of any of the hiccups or setbacks, East and Central European countries have experienced considerable advances in democracy in rapid succession after the fall of the Soviet empire. It would seem that the East Asian tendency to seek consensus should be more amenable to democracy than would the atomistic individualism that is said to exist in the West. Those western thinkers who point to western institutions as the basis of democracy inadvertently support the mythology of the necessity for cultural preconditions to support the emergence of modern political arrangements. A more complete interpretation is that a democratic potential can exist in every cultural or ethnic setting.

East Asian authoritarian governments denounce western-style democracy and its focus upon individualism and freedom due to its potentially corrosive effects upon Asian institutions and the prosperity they produce. By contrast, Asian collectivism is praised for its contribution to social cohesion as a basis for continued economic growth. Collectivism and a patriarchal sense of authority fit well into the political agenda of authoritarian-capitalist regimes based upon single party democracies common to parts of East Asia. Support for collectivist political centralism is encouraged by official references to its benefits which conveniently overlook the costs imposed upon individuals. These costs are not limited to losses in individual freedom, but to the extent that they also threaten to undermine social gains. As will be argued in the next chapter, efforts to stifle individualism can be expected to lead to a decline in the innovation and creativity that are essential to progress and economic growth. Following a similar logic, government officials endeavor to condemn individualism by offering exaggerated accounts of the social costs arising from the excesses of certain individuals. Such facile reasoning identifies individualism with egoistic desires while disregarding the enrichment of communities arising out of individualist-based institutions that may promote honor and moral responsibility for one's action. Most of the important technological innovations in this century have arisen out of the creativity allowed in Western institutions. Indeed, much of it has arisen from contributions of transplanted Asians who have prospered in the freer atmosphere of the West.

Some East Asian leaders portray individualism as a dangerous development that must be nipped in the bud. As such, they would justify repression as a means to save Asians from themselves. As mentioned in the introductory chapter, with the loss of the strawman of a "Red Peril" as the excuse for the suppression of their political opponents, autocratic governments in Indonesia, Malaysia and Singapore began to point to the debilitating influence arising from the "White Peril" as embodied in Western liberal democracy. It is ironic that this posturing may reveal more about the fears for the fragility of Asian cultural institutions and values rather than judgments about Western values. Were Asian institutions so strong and superior, there would be no need to take actions to protect them.

Singapore's authoritarian-capitalist regime has manipulated "Asian values" to pursue its own limited political goals. Imposition of the notion of shared values suggests the creation of a new "opiate of the masses." As in other East Asian countries headed by one party or even a single family for decades, their survival depends upon the ruling party's ability to demand loyalty from subordinates. Thus, only the subservient prevail in the pull and tussle of political and economic life.[12] An attack on the leader is treated as an attack on the party and by implication, the state. Following this logic, draconian measures can be justified as a means to suppress political opponents who can be portrayed as traitors. The problem, in the end, is to find an optimal level of control over cadres and the citizenry without crushing their spirits. Thus, these governments rely heavily upon self-aggrandizing propaganda or, as in the case of Singapore, remarkably generous remuneration for high ranking civil servants.[13]

The elections for the Hong Kong Legislative Council (Legco) in September 1995 provide a refutation of suggestions that Asians have a different perspective on democracy and freedom. Faced with a choice between a western-style political party and a pro-Beijing party, the electorate opted for democracy over authoritarianism. The Democratic Party (DP), formed in the aftermath of the 1989 Tiananmen massacre, won 12 of the 20 directly elected seats in the 60 member chamber. Additionally, it was awarded 7 of the indirectly elected seats, and the DP was expected to form an alliance with at least 10 of the independent candidates. The pro-China party, the Democratic Alliance for the Betterment of Hong Kong (DAB), won only 7 of the directly elected seats. Neither of the leaders of the pro-Chinese parties won the seats that they contested.

Given the commitment of the DP to human and legal rights within a constitutional framework, the outcome indicates a strong preference for basic freedoms. The poor showing of the DAB occurred despite its well-financed campaign and admonitions from Beijing about supporting the DP. In the aftermath of the report of the election results, Xinhua news agency, the mouthpiece for the Communist Party in Beijing, announced its plans to scupper the Legco on July 1, 1997. This action is obvious disregard of the expressed wishes of the Hong Kong electorate. A new "provisional" assembly will be appointed, presumably with persons who view participatory democracy closer to the dictates of China's present rulers. The leadership in Beijing, like other promoters of "Asian democracy," are only interested in results that suit the agenda of a ruling clique.

There are several criticisms of these election results that merit consideration. Granted the British colonial masters have been slow off the mark to provide Hong Kong's citizens with experience in electoral democracy. However, there can be no doubt that the various elections held since 1981 have been in good faith. The limited political autonomy granted to the city-state has certainly provided citizens with an opportunity to have an active voice in politics. Even so, the tradition of a highly active, diverse, and aggressive free press has provided the basis of an active political culture. It is also the case that only 36% of the registered voters cast a ballot. This number may be artificially low since many registered voters are likely to have emigrated or be temporarily out of the country (there was no absentee ballot offered).

One of Singapore's voices in this debate and my antagonist in the IHT affair, Kishore Mahbubani, claimed that "Asian values" contribute to a greater political stability and a lower likelihood of open aggression in that region.[14] Meanwhile, he pointed to a "ring of fire," referring to the ethnic brush fires currently ablaze at the fringes of Europe. These are due, presumably, to endemic flaws in the institutions of European cultures. This contrast is misleading on several counts. In the first instance, East Asia is hardly a pacified region. There are just as many unsettled border disputes, outrages against humanity and conflicting geo-political claims in Asia as there are in Europe. Much of the difference in the conditions in these two regions is perceived rather than real. These divergent perceptions are substantially an outgrowth of the restricted press of East Asia which contrasts sharply with the open access afforded the media in most parts of Europe.

While images of the carnage in Chechnya and the tragedy of Bosnia traverse the globe, there was little coverage of the Dili massacre in Indonesia nor any on-the-site reporting from Burma. In contrast to the metaphorical "ring of fire" in Europe, in the autumn of 1994, most of the Malaysian peninsula was literally shrouded in a choking cloud of smoke. Immense forest fires were burning out of control in parts of Indonesia. Known euphemistically as "haze," it was so severe that Singapore issued health warnings for the elderly and infirm to remain indoors. Meanwhile, transportation links were interrupted by the closing of some airports and even agricultural harvests were imperiled in the most fertile region of Malaysia. Despite the availability of ASEAN as a regional forum, there was a lack of concerted action. It is likely that their inaction was associated with the importance of "saving face" as an institutionalized component of "Asian values." Neighboring governments were disinclined to offer aid or to criticize the handling of the fires so as not to embarrass the Indonesian authorities. Consequently, there was almost no public discussion about the causes or questions about the application of remedies for the choking pollution. As I suggested in my IHT article, "saving face" is apparently more important for many leaders of ASEAN countries than is saving the lives of their citizens or protecting the regional environment.

Perhaps living by double-standards should be included in the list of "Asian values" offered by the Singapore School. While Mr. Lee and Mr. Mahbubani denounce any critique of their internal politics, they are ever ready to offer criticisms and denunciations of arrangements in any other country. While Mr. Mahbubani plies his views in academic journals, Mr. Lee plays the role of the omniscient elder statesman to the hilt. Touring the world, he has scolded Australians for not being "Asian enough" while condemning the West's obsession with individualism. In turn, they deflect complaints against violation of human rights in Singapore by treating them as the utterances of "cultural imperialists." Mr. Lee's pronouncements on the failing of others seem to be offered as though they reflected universal values. The Singapore School apparently has also discovered its own sense of "Asian" logic.

There is ample evidence that allusions by authoritarian-capitalist regimes to a set of exclusive pan-Asian values as an explanation of their country's economic success follows a kind of cynical logic. Assertions that individual freedom and pluralistic democracy are alien concepts to Asia are little more than a part of politically convenient arguments. The conceptualization of unique "Asian values" serves to deflect the encroachment of modernization and the liberalizing institutions that would weaken the grip of Asian rulers upon political power. In particular, rulers of one-party states have found it to their benefit to praise respect for authority as a component of Confucianism or some other supposed pan-Asian values.

Exploring "Asian Values"

No one doubts that Asian cultures have generated values that are worthy of praise and emulation. Nonetheless, numerous questions surround the content and intent of assertions that proclaim that recent economic success in the "miracle economies" of Asia is associated with a renaissance of certain "Asian values."

One source of early support from Western democracies for many of the East Asian regimes was their shared opposition to the anti-democratic forces of communism. However, many of these same East Asian governments clearly do not support liberal democracy nor liberal capitalism. As in the contrivance of "Asian values," defenders of these authoritarian governments have conjured up the notion of "Asian democracy." It might seem that there would have been a reluctance to claim special Asian qualities for democracy given the auxiliary misapplications of the term by other Asian regimes (e.g., Kampuchea, North Korea). Similarly, any attempt to lump together Asian values would require a consideration of many traditions that are peculiar to a subset of Asians. For example, female circumcision is almost certainly limited to those Asians who are Muslims. Many of the East Asian authoritarian-capitalist regimes seem inclined to apply the vocabulary of democracy to divert criticism for their repression by referring to regionally-specific values. Individual rights and freedoms are belittled as being irrelevant to Asians especially since these are asserted to be the source of the moral collapse of the West. In short, "democracy" as practiced in much of East Asia involves extensive control of political and economic relations as well as social engineering. Therefore, East Asian authoritarian capitalism relies upon many of the problematic institutional arrangements that may generate the same sort of contradictions that characterized authoritarian socialism.

The presumption of the existence of an "Asian" democracy arising out of some unique and monolithic constellation of identifiably pan-Asian values seems to be dubious. For example, while some leaders in East Asia account for their restrictions upon the development of democratic institutions along Western lines, other Asian leaders insist on an alternative point of view. India's Prime Minister Rao and President Fidel Ramos of the Philippines insist that democracy is the way forward for developing countries. Secondly, many of the laudable "Asian values" are recognizable in the value systems outside the region, as alluded to in Chapter 1. Clearly the decidedly strong work ethic, dedication to education, and thriftiness often associated with Asians are descriptive of values observed in the other parts of the world. Certainly, these same values are recognizable in the Protestant work ethic.

The ensuing debate over the notion of "Asian values" raises several issues. First, there may be an erroneous impression that these articulate observations emerge from a community embroiled in its own active public discourse. This impression is far from the truth since the repressive nature of many of these East Asian governments ensures that there are strict limits upon access to Forums to air opinions unless they have a seal of approval from the ruling party. For example, in Malaysia as in Singapore, the domestic media tends to be subservient, while the foreign media often confronts open censorship or is subject to numerous restrictions. While satellite dishes and transmitters are manufactured in Singapore and the Singapore Broadcasting Network beams its programs to the outside world, these same devices and transmissions are almost totally banished from its own shores. There can be no true political dialogue or debate when alternative viewpoints are shut out or silenced from within. However, this does not mean that there are no internal dissenters. It was my experience, which was confirmed by other expatriate colleagues, that Singaporeans would intimate in nervous whispers what they really thought. Some even asked foreigners to speak out for them knowing that the consequences for themselves are so grave.

On top of these politically imposed restrictions upon internal debate, there are various cases where scholars in one ASEAN member country are banned from visiting another. In late 1994, the government of Indonesia pressured the authorities in the Philippines to limit a conference organized by foreign and Filipino scholars to discuss the independence movement in East Timor. Outsiders who would wish to voice critical opinions of Asian culture or to report on repression in parts of Asia are most often dismissed as inappropriate intruders into domestic affairs, or excoriated as neo-colonialists by paternalistic rulers. While there may be a disturbingly high probability of becoming a victim of gratuitous violence in America or other parts of the "decadent" West, there is the equally troubling frequency of East Asian authoritarian regimes taking steps to silence those citizens or outsiders who would challenge their authority.

The idea of a single Asian model of democracy or "Asian values" based upon a dominant Asian culture appears to be based upon spurious logic. Even supporters of pan-Asian values are of mixed minds on this issue, at times speaking of the values of East Asia or Southeast Asia, perhaps even widening the focus to all of Asia. Singapore's regime has shifted from a selective sampling of genuine neo-Confucian values to a contrived set of pan-Asian values dressed up in order to provide appeal beyond the Chinese citizenry. In all events, family values have been invoked as a simplistic depiction of a uniformly-present glue preventing Asians from succumbing to the moral decay and social chaos that their leaders have said pervades Western culture.

There are obvious flaws in this assertion. Were family values the essential element in Asia's value system that underpins economic success, then Burma, Pakistan and India would not be so underdeveloped. If family values must be mixed with repressive authoritarianism, then Vietnam and Laos should have performed better economically. Perhaps family values, repression and dominance of Chinese part of the required mix, but in that case China would have enjoyed economic growth much sooner. In light of the willingness of so many Asians to sell their children into prostitution or to engage in infanticide based upon gender, it is difficult to validate the primacy of the family among Asians.

Even so, if one accepts family values in Asia as a building block, the edifice itself is on shaky ground. Specifically, family orientation may be a greater threat than is Western individualism. Widespread corruption is likely to arise where family ties or connections are considered to be more important than the objective application of rules. More generally, an appearance of stability is unsustainable if the social order does not emerge from the consent of the governed. Basing the aversion to open discourse on a fear of ensuing instability betrays a weak foundation. If these values provide such a formidable anchor, then they should be able to withstand equally formidable challenges. In the end, insistence upon family values in order to rationalize filial piety and respect for authority as important "Asian values" reveals a cynical political opportunism of leaders who seek to limit challenges to their authoritarian control.

Despite the incoherence in the claims for a unique set of "Asian values," champions of authoritarian-capitalist regimes continually manipulate such values to rationalize their authoritarian rule. A common and conspicuous assertion is the officially enforced requirement of the veneration of authority. Although filial piety is a cornerstone of Confucian ethics, similar institutional arrangements are promoted by countries in East Asia whose values were not directly shaped by these traditions. Moreover, the underlying purpose of this ruse is to encourage unquestioned acceptance of the dictates of incumbent parties to promote the survival of despotic rule among all ethnic groups in the population. Following a neo-Confucianist version of logic, virtuous rulers deserve the full respect and automatic loyalty of their citizens by carrying out duties forthrightly (e.g., keeping the peace, providing conditions for economic prosperity, and not over-burdening the population with taxes). In Singapore, the concept of a "loyal opposition" is treated as an oxymoron according to the wishes of the paramount leader, Mr. Lee Kuan Yew. In turn, advancement of their own sets of "Asian values" allows repressive governments to dismiss outside criticism either as inappropriate external meddling or impertinent cultural intrusions. If these more subtle parries do not suffice, complaints of neo-colonialism or protectionism can be used to great effect to rebut human rights complaints.

It is also problematic in that the purveyors of pan-Asian values tend to point almost exclusively to the beneficial consequences associated with "Asian values" while ignoring negative consequences. In reversing this mode of assessment, only the costs of western institutions are considered while benefits are overlooked. This single-dimensional approach satisfies self-serving political backers of governing regimes. The same set of values that are said to promote prosperity is also invoked as an excuse to stifle the critical introspection of citizens. Whereas it is seen as an unacceptable sign of weakness for leaders to wonder aloud about the state of cultural and political order, it is too often treated as an insupportable heresy for others to do so.

Those offering criticism, or commentary that does not unconditionally praise the political *status quo*, are likely to invite strong rebukes from rulers of authoritarian-capitalist regimes. A variety of reactionary steps are readily taken by some East Asian governments against ordinary citizens, academics, journalists, opposition politicians or even outside observers. Their responses range from a mild caution to citations for criminal defamation or libel, detention without trial, and, in the limit, armed military or police action. By placing severe restrictions upon freedom of speech, the regime limits the few opportunities or forums where citizens can communicate changing preferences directly to other members of the community. Similarly, critics find it difficult to air their views before the general public. Evaluations concerning civic discourse and discussions about the "Asian values" are left to the domain of outside critics and the proponents of the autocratic political systems. The conversation between the rulers and the ruled is most often a self-righteous, paternalistic monologue where citizens are more likely to be on the receiving end of a sermon rather than being able to air their grievances or concerns. In the end, the stability of Asian societies may not be due to a regionally-specific set of culturally-determined values. Appearances of social cohesion are just as likely to be the result of the iron grip of petty despots who exploit an illusion of a pan-Asian set of values to remain entrenched in power. More ominously, these regimes may also rely upon an effective campaign of fear and intimidation of their critics as well as ordinary citizens.

What is happening in parts of East Asia is an experiment to spark economic progress through minimal, selective market interventions while keeping a tight rein upon social and political change. As suggested above, authoritarian capitalism is similar in substance and form to communist experiments and the various forms of authoritarian socialism. In both instances, individuals are treated as servants of the enforced socio-political order and objects of social engineering. Rights and freedoms become remote abstractions that are swept aside if they threaten the plans of the ruling party. Repression in Singapore has been candy-coated with allusions to communitarian values and references to its participatory democracy.

The success of these propaganda ploys is aided by the contrast of East Asia's economic dynamism and an imposed sense of political stability with what appears to be systemic decline in the West of economic and social institutions. This contrast is overstated in various ways. First, many of the difficulties faced by Western countries are the result of adjustments imposed by the forces of modernity that all evolving societies can expect to encounter. Second, another aspect of modernity is a more mature electorate and self confident population that is actively involved in relatively open civic discussion and self-directed criticism. When combined with a free and open media, the image of social collapse might become greatly exaggerated in a frenzy of introspective critical analysis. Thus, the shortcomings and problems in the West are well-chronicled and often discussed *ad nauseum* in a remarkably free atmosphere. Controls over the media and other restraints upon communication enable East Asian rulers to trumpet their successes and conceal their failings while pointing to the seemingly intractable problems encountered elsewhere. By joining the chorus of Western self-criticism, proponents of these authoritarian political systems promote the impression that the institutional arrangements of the West involve only costly consequences, and are engaged in a self-destructive cycle. However, these impressions ignore that civic communication in the West involves a free-for-all of individual opinions expressed as a matter of constitutional right or cultural conviction.

Arguments that pair the benefits emerging out of "Asian values" with the costs of Western culture are decidedly limited as well as misleading. Similarly, such arguments reveal a materialist bias that establishes a dubious logical link between the economic success of these economies and authoritarian repression. An important element of this argument is an insistence that restraints upon individual freedoms were and are a necessary element for economic progress, at least in East Asia. Meanwhile, the Western fixation on individual rights is portrayed as the source of a destructive moral drift and lagging economic performance. While these unimaginative assertions imply that material gratification is the only, or most worthy goal, of mankind, they also ignore the fact that current weak growth in the Western economies is partly explained by the economic life-cycle. It is no surprise that growth rates for the developed economies of the US and Europe compare unfavorably with the vibrancy of the budding economies of East Asia. Upon catching up with the developed world, the "miracle economies" can be expected to exhibit less miraculous growth rates.

Modernization offers the likelihood of the evolution and fusion of cultural values marked by a mutual exchange of ideas and an evolution of cross-cultural institutional development. Those institutions that provide the best opportunities for individuals to attain their goals within a group setting and provide the most admirable results will survive and be copied. Governors of East Asian authoritarian regimes would do well to ponder these facts. Interference with this historic, inexorable progress by authoritarian-capitalist regimes or conservative religious leaders will only inflict economic costs upon and retard cultural progress in their countries.

East Meets West but Whither the Twain?

Any investigation of the debate over "Asian values" should include an investigation into the observed differences in Oriental and Occidental institutions. This approach would be helpful in determining whether these differences reflect mismatched stages of socio-economic development or are the result of endogenous differences in fundamental values. Among the observably different characteristics of Eastern and Western institutional arrangements, perhaps the most conspicuous is between Western individualism and Asian collectivism. A particularly distinctive contrast can be found within Confucian-influenced settings where filial piety, a tendency to seek consensus, and the dictum "society above self" are ingrained features. Collectivist Asian regimes tend towards an imposed social order where rules set by those wielding political power are meant to be unquestionably accepted by the polity. Individualist-oriented Western governments exhibit the tendency where reason is applied toward conflict resolution between private and social interests. Consequently, cultures based upon individualism tend towards an outspoken citizenry whereas collectivist cultures rely upon reserved understatement. Nonetheless, similar differences were observable during earlier stages of development in the West.

Paternalism has a history of giving way to authoritarianism. Many Asian regimes simply do not tolerate direct criticism and strongly resent indirect criticism. Though Asian cultures generally rely upon an indirect method of dealing with problems, even this approach is not acceptable to officials in less secure political settings. Strict limits upon dialogue with Asian authoritarian regimes are not limited to outside critics. Criticism by citizens is no more welcome in Burma or China than it is in Indonesia, Malaysia or Singapore. Even though there are remarkable advances recorded under the direction of some Asian governments, the rigid authoritarian methods credited for these advances would not fit well into most Western cultures. In all events, Asian authoritarian capitalism bears closer resemblance to fascism and other authoritarian systems than to most institutional arrangements presently observed in the West. In particular, many East Asian regimes denounce what they consider to be the destructive openness of the free press in the West. It is worth repeating the irony of their spokespersons having ready access to the Western media to denounce press freedom.

An interesting outgrowth of the disparate traditions in the East and West is the differing contributions to the historical development of political institutions. While the implementation of effective electoral democracy is the great contribution to political arrangements emerging from Western culture, bureaucracy is the most significant contribution of China in the East. While liberalism and individual freedoms found fertile ground in the West, Asian institutions tended to develop along distinctly conservative and collectivistic lines. In turn, capitalism evolved in the West toward liberal capitalism. Now, some leaders of high performing East Asian economies appear to have instituted the model of authoritarian capitalism described above. As such, they follow neo-mercantilist, export-oriented industrialization (EOI) policies while imposing strict controls on political activities. Not all of the countries remain stuck on the authoritarian path. There are mixed reviews of the impact of rising incomes and modernization upon East Asian governments. Some of the authoritarian-capitalist regimes are loosening up on the degree of political centralism, even if they maintain the same level of market intervention. For example, the Philippines, South Korea, Thailand and Taiwan began their moves towards multi-party politics in the early 1990's. In all events, the ruling parties in Indonesia, Malaysia and Singapore have tended to strengthen the government institutions to entrench their political control. These institutional arrangements appear to be converging with those observed in Burma, China, Vietnam, and perhaps North Korea.

A contrast in the orientation of business activity in the East and West is also affected by the observed tendencies associated with individualism and collectivism. Individualist-oriented cultures encourage and reward innovation of free-spirited entrepreneurs who are as inclined to challenge the political *status quo* as they are to upset market arrangements. In the past, most Asian rulers have either imposed autarchy or have evolved by relying upon imitation that depended heavily upon access to the open markets of more advanced economies.

It is far from clear that the political control imposed by East Asian authoritarian-capitalist regimes is in an equilibrium state. The good news is that, in the end, archaic and obstructive institutions can be expected to be swept aside through the choices of individuals whether these institutions originate in Asian or European values. On one hand, despots and autocrats are mortal as are their dynastic heirs. On the other hand, the effects of modernizing influences arising out of economic prosperity are the highly probable source of an eventual weakening of their grip upon power.

Defending the Political *Status Quo*: the "Cruel Choice" Thesis

Those countries undergoing radical transition, whether erstwhile communist regimes in Asia or former communist regimes in Europe, each must resolve the political and economic issues that influence their patterns of development. The search for a workable model has led some to the conclusion that authoritarian rule may be a "necessary evil" as a means for speedy economic development. In this sense, the trade-off between political freedom and economic prosperity is portrayed as a cruel choice.[15] Authoritarian capitalism reflects a current incarnation of this trade-off.

The logic of this trade-off suggests that the sacrifice of political freedom and civil rights for economic growth places those countries with democratic institutions at a disadvantage relative to authoritarian, even totalitarian regimes, during the transition process. Similarly, it implies that while economic freedom might be required for development of political freedom, the reverse may not be true. In fact, not only might political freedom not be necessary for economic development; indeed, it could be an obstruction. A variety of reasons are cited for this "growth first" strategy, including the problems arising from the formation of powerful interest groups. If they demand redistributive policies, there may be a reduction in long-term economic growth if the redistributive policies lead to economic inefficiencies. Similarly, there are the threats and realities of tax revolts as well as open political debate and change of rulers that may place substantial fetters upon political decisions.

Thus, it is widely believed that authoritarian governments can more readily ensure rapid economic progress. This might be achieved through the extraction and disposition of savings from a relatively docile population. Dissent, where allowed, would tend to be muted, and political debate subject to the whims of the ruling party. Governments that rely upon democratic approval tend to encounter political constraints in extracting a target level of savings or generating revenues through raising or imposing taxes. They also confront demands to provide funds for an expansion in current consumption or are pressured to redistribute the present stock of income and wealth.

In spite of these claims, competitive capitalism joined by liberal democracy (liberal capitalism) can be seen to provide a good platform for economic growth through its system of incentives and the relatively wide disbursement of a direct personal stake in economic development. Access to personal rewards from involvement in the making of the economic pie is the source of a strong motivation for individual effort. Increased productivity and creativity arising from the incentive structures of liberal capitalism would offset the presumed advantages of coerced accumulation under authoritarian capitalism.

Of particular interest is the impact of the differing institutional arrangements of these two competing systems upon the role and the development of "true" entrepreneurs. Since "true" entrepreneurs are individualists, they are more likely to emerge in an environment that allows them to challenge the *status quo*, whether it is the competitive structure of a market or authority structures. This would include opposing government policies that obstruct opportunities for the expansion of their individual economic fortunes. When authoritarian regimes endeavor to control economic activities, they often do so by attempting to construct entrepreneurs through the awarding of special privileges to political sycophants. Nevertheless, an economy that does not generate "true" entrepreneurs will suffer from the lack of an internal source for sustained economic growth. Their malaphoristic cousins tend to be most interested in restricting competition and in maintaining various aspects of the economic or political *status quo*.

Liberal capitalism also provides for freedom of social and economic mobility as a means for individual empowerment. Clearly, the middle class is not the only social segment to have a vested interest in promoting democracy. Alternatively, authoritarian capitalism relies upon a sycophantic arrangement between the ruling party and obedient bureaucrats, party cadres, select business interests and other cronies.

While it may be obvious, it is worth noting that there are numerous examples of authoritarian regimes that exhibit little or no economic success, e.g. Cuba, Zimbabwe, Burma, Bangladesh, Pakistan, Afghanistan, Iraq and Iran. Thus, the imposition of authoritarian rule or repression are neither necessary, nor sufficient, conditions for economic growth. In sum, the visible hand of the interventionist state does not guarantee successful economic development. Policy makers are as fallible as the private decision makers they seek to replace. This fallibility is to be expected regardless of whether the guiding principles are based upon ideology, like communism, or a paternalism guided by Confucianism.

Even Japan's much-heralded MITI has been shown to have chosen as many losers as winners in the decades of interventionist promotion.[16] Such evidence exposes the long-run failure of neo-mercantilism that has been stealthily disguised as export-oriented, industrial development strategies. For example, China's economic malaise is symptomatic not only of the long-run effects of the gradualist approach to its economic transition policy, but also the problems of neo-mercantilism. In China, as in most authoritarian regimes, the primary purpose of extensive controls over the economy is to maintain and to protect the existing structure of political and economic interests. The wrong-headedness of such attempts to exercise extensive controls arises from and is shared by the abject failures of central planning.

On balance, whatever economic success might be associated with authoritarian guidance is a thing of the past. Comparative quantitative studies indicate that democratic governments have performed better than authoritarian ones from 1987 onward.[17]

Modernization and Authoritarian Capitalism

Social engineering, supported by "cultural protectionism," constitutes one of the striking similarities between authoritarian capitalism and authoritarian socialism. However, while authoritarian-socialist regimes tried to exterminate the middle class, authoritarian-capitalist regimes have sought to clone a middle class to serve their own ends. Both systems have also been relatively effective in eliminating or de-constructing the non-governmental organizations that characterize a civil society.[18] Western political theory assigns a special role to the emergence of a civil society, which serves as a system of checks and balances by recognizing divisions and providing some protection for diversity. Free association allows for the development of a web of mutually restraining institutions formed by the choices of individuals to pursue their own life purposes by providing the interactive skills and the means for the socialization of individuals into their culture. Such associations also serve as a inter-generational transmission mechanism for cultural values and knowledge.

By eliminating or controlling sources of countervailing powers to the state, authoritarian-capitalist regimes reduce the autonomy of their citizens and impose upon them a greater sense of insecurity. Political stability defined as continuation of rule by a single party involves a fable wherein security for members of the ruling party results in deep anxiety among the rest of the population. In the absence of alternative or mediating institutions, supporters of these governments argue that they are able to uphold their end of the social contract as justification for their continuance. One important difference between these two competing systems is that while communism anticipated the withering of the state, authoritarian-capitalist regimes envision their survival as a necessary element of the future of the state.

Modernization theory is the final refuge of hope for those who would oppose the continued political hegemony of authoritarian-capitalist regimes. Despite long experience with a relatively large and growing middle class, authoritarian-capitalist regimes in Asia have been surprisingly slow to show signs of liberalization.[19] This tardiness in demanding greater political freedom has occurred by resolving some of the paradoxes of authoritarian socialism in allowing private property and by encouraging involvement in market activities. The intrusiveness of the policies of authoritarian-capitalist governments also holds citizens' interests captive through their high degree of dependency upon the ruling party. The resulting lack of confidence induces voters to associate their own survival and prosperity, as well as that of the interests of the entire country, with the continued political success of the ruling party.

Although these governments are unlikely to find a permanent inoculation against modernizing pressures from the competitive influences of alternative institutional arrangements, they have certainly been effective in holding back these forces of change. Nonetheless, just like the competitive pressures of free trade, market-like forces will eventually undermine attempts to intervene with the true preferences of their citizens. Perhaps they have been successful in pushing the long run further out into the future, but they cannot do so forever.

Conclusion

Numerous questions arise from the debate over "Asian values." Even if there are observable differences in individual and human values, these may be the result of different stages of economic, social and political maturity rather than the consequence of regional peculiarities. Authoritarian-capitalist regimes have aspired to deflect the influence of modernization upon their rigid political frameworks by imposing a set of values that serves the cynical political agendas of ruling parties. A constructed set of kinship structures replaces the spontaneous formation of a free civil society to serve the needs of citizens. The aims of political stability in this context can be measured as little more than the survival of incumbent rulers.

Ultimately, the imposed institutional framework combined with a variety of traditional arrangements can be expected to reduce the long term economic growth potential to the region. Survival and success in the open and highly competitive international economic environment that is emerging will require flexible institutions and innovative, risk-taking entrepreneurs. Authoritarian capitalism is unlikely to provide the conditions to meet these requirements. In reality, the cruelty of the choice to trade-off political freedom for rapid economic growth is that short-run gains are likely to be masking unforeseen long-run losses.

In the end, the "Asian model" will have to stand the test of time. In the post-industrial international economic order, those communities with the most flexible institutions and those that are most able to innovate are the ones that are best positioned to prosper. Cultural collusion offers a better chance of long term prosperity than does an antagonistic clash of civilizations or the imposition of cultural protectionism. It is arguable that those conditions can best be met in a setting that guarantees individual freedom and eschews collectivist repression. Steps should be taken to avoid imprisoning society, such as through increasing the autonomy of individuals. It is impossible to liberate society by imprisoning the human spirit. Few would argue that the rights of the individual should not be treated as anything less than absolute. Neither then should the rights of the community be treated as such, especially when it is the rights of the rulers being protected over those within the community.

It remains unclear what internally generated actions are ultimately capable of leading to a check on the overreach of authoritarian-capitalist governments like that in Singapore. Again in terms of outside pressures, those countries truly concerned with individual rights might consider imposing economic sanctions, even if this blunt tool of international disapproval has a poor record of success as seen in the case of the universal condemnation directed at the apartheid regime. How long can Singapore's authoritarian government deflect moral condemnation and capital divestiture that has been the response elsewhere for similar misbehavior.

The economic costs of a stunted growth potential are certain to trigger accompanying social and political costs. At some point, civilized governments shed their materialist bias and acknowledge that a measure of the national standard of living must also include abstractions such as individual freedoms and rights. Contrary to the assertions of the government of Singapore, there is little evidence that the trade-off can be sustained. According to revisionist interpretations of Singapore's economic record, there is little that can be labeled new or miraculous about its recent growth path. Chapter 3 shall provide an overview and analysis of the economic institutions of Singapore's authoritarian-capitalist system in support of the assertion.

Notes

1 While other parts of the world were experiencing sluggish or negative growth in the late 1980's and early 1990's, some East Asian economies have had sustained growth. The average growth rate for Southeast Asian economies was 7.4% for 1971-80, and 6.1% for 1981-90. In spite of recessions in most Western economies, East Asian exports to them expanded at an annual rate of 15 to 20 percent.

2 While this peculiar form of capitalism may follow certain communitarian arguments, the accompanying political system remains remarkably bereft of the essential elements of a civil society. This model is neither new nor is it observed only in Asia. Chile and the South African apartheid regime rightly fall into this category.

3 Some organizations that might serve as a mediating influence between the power of the state and the rights of the individual are political parties, newspapers, religious groups, trade unions and other voluntary associations that might wield political influence. Many of these associations also fall under the term non-governmental organizations or NGO's.

4 An elaboration of the argument is presented in *The End of History and the Last Man*, New York: The Free Press, 1992.

5 This much discussed thesis appeared in "The Clash of Civilizations?" *Foreign Affairs* (72, no. 3, Summer 1993).

6 Survival and imitation appear to be "objective" indicators of the superiority of institutions.

7 The so-called "Singapore School" has been particularly aggressive in promoting "Asian values" as a mobilizing myth as an element of its own nation-building process. Much of the commentary is offered by officials of the ruling party or organizations that are connected to the regime. For example, see K. Mahbubani, "The Dangers of Decadence—What the Rest Can Teach the West," *Foreign Affairs* (vol. 72, no. 4, September-October 1992); "The West and the Rest," *The National Interest* (Summer 1992); "The United States: Go East, Young Man," *Washington Quarterly* (vol. 17, no. 2, Spring 1994) and "Live and Let Live — Allow Asians Choose Their Own Course," *Far Eastern Economic Review* (June 17, 1994). Also see B. Kausikan, "Asia's Different Standard," *Foreign Policy* (no. 92, Fall 1993), and F. Zakaria, "Culture is Destiny: A Conversation with Lee Kuan Yew," *Foreign Affairs* (vol. 73, no. 2, March/April 1994).

8 A response to some of Singapore's spokespersons can be found in E. Jones, "Asia's Fate: A Response to the Singapore School," *The National Interest* (Spring 1994) 18-28.

9 An attempt by a distinguished group of Asians to engage this debate while avoiding political influences can be found in *Towards a New Asia*, Kuala Lumpur: Commission for a New Asia, 1994.

10 *The East Asian Miracle: Economic Growth and Public Policy*, Washington, DC: Oxford University Press, 1993. This report will be discussed in more detail in a later chapter.

11 For a discussion of the democratization process in Asia, see E. Friedman (ed.), *The Process of Democratization: Generalizing East Asian Experiences*, Boulder: Westview Press, 1994.

12 By politicizing most aspects of life, those so-called "soft authoritarian" regimes readily evolve into "soft totalitarian" regimes. Whatever the coherence of the former, certainly the latter involves a contradiction in terms.

13 The Prime Minister of Singapore earns about $720,000 each year plus perquisites. This exceeds the combined salaries of any 3 European heads of state.

14 K. Mahbubani, "The West and the Rest," *The National Interest*, Summer 1994.

15 See J. Bhagwati, "Democracy and Development," *Journal of Democracy* (July 1992, vol. 3, no. 2) 37-44 and J. M. Marvell, "The Myth of Authoritarian Advantage," *Journal of Democracy* (October 1994, vol. 5, no. 4) 17-31.

16 R. Beason and D. Weinstein, "Growth, Economies of Scale, and Targeting in Japan (1955-90)." Harvard Institute of Economic Research, Discussion Paper 1644, 1993.

17 See A. Przeworski and F. Limongi, "Political Regimes and Economic Growth," *Journal of Economic Perspectives* (1993, vol. 7, pp. 3-21).

18 For a discussion of the importance of civil society in the evolving democracies, see E. Gellner, *Conditions of Liberty: Civil Society and its Rivals*. New York: Allen Lane, Penguin Press, 1994 and F. Fukuyama. *Trust: The Social Virtues and the Creation of Prosperity*. New York: Free Press, 1995.

19 For discussion of this problem see D. M. Jones, "Asia's Rising Middle Class: Not a Force for Change," *The National Interest* (Winter 1994/95, no. 38) 46-50.

Chapter 3

AUTHORITARIAN CAPITALISM IN EAST ASIA: FROM MIRACLE GROWTH TO A MIDDLING FUTURE?

Moving from the Bottom of the Heap toward the Top?

Imagine a tiny country with a small number of inhabitants clustered on a few islands only a few degrees north of the equator. As if being bathed in the sweltering tropical torpor were not enough of a handicap, add to this image a dearth of natural resources and a geographical positioning at the base of a deeply impoverished sub-continent. Now picture a richly diverse population dominated by a non-indigenous racial group that represents a substantial majority. This is an apt, if incomplete, picture of Singapore. Upon throwing off the yoke of their colonial master, the residents of this small city-state were set adrift to find their own fortunes. With these images in mind, the survival of such a country, much less any trace of success, is worthy of acclaim.

There is no question nor any doubt that Singapore's post-Independence leaders have contributed to a remarkable transformation of an under-developed economy. Since being granted self-rule by the British, Singaporeans have experienced enormous improvements in many aspects of their material life. For example, figures released by the government indicate that per capita income has risen from about $1,000 in the early 1960's to more than $15,000 in 1995. Over the past 30 years, Singapore's domestic production is reported to have increased at an average annual rate of over 7 percent. In the same span of time, the average annual rate for Germany's economy was $2\frac{1}{2}$ percent, while the US economy grew at $1\frac{3}{4}$ percent. There has also been a remarkably low rate of inflation and an even more remarkably high rate of savings. Impressive social advances were also experienced during the same period, with substantial improvements in the quality and availability of schooling leading to dramatic decreases in illiteracy. Singapore now boasts a highly-skilled and technologically-sophisticated labor force. Since labor demand and real wages have grown rapidly, there is little unemployment, and poverty has been largely eliminated. Infant mortality also fell sharply to a level that is now about one-half the rate in the US.

Given that the World Bank included Singapore among an elite group of East Asian countries identified as "miracle economies," it may seem inappropriate or implausible to raise questions about the means or the ends of Singapore's rapid rise towards modernity. Even so, beyond the accolades there are a number of interesting questions to be asked. For example, the cost of living in Singapore places it among the six most expensive cities in the world, while wages for its workers rank only twenty-ninth in the world. Certainly it would be appropriate to ask if there were associated costs along with these impressive gains and to undertake the identification of them. It would also be of considerable interest to know if Singapore's approach to development can serve as a suitable road map for other countries. Answers to the first question will be part of the answer to the second question. It is this set of tasks that we take up here.

Singapore's Free Market Illusions

There is considerable irony in the championing by its supporters of the "capital friendly" nature of Singapore's economic policies and legal system. In light of the wider evidence, it is surprising that the Heritage Foundation ranked Singapore as number two in the world in terms of economic freedoms.[1] Singapore enjoys a reputation as one of the world's great entrepots, allowing the free flow of goods and resources through its port. However, there are many government obstructions to, interferences with and involvements in domestic commercial activities. Regardless of its international free trade policies, there is substantial interference with commercial matters that covers many of Singapore's different home-based markets. One striking exception to the image of free-wheeling capitalism in Singapore is found in the politically inspired restrictions on the communication and information industries. Government restrictions upon information flows and their opposition to freedom of the press are likely to retard the most important bases of the modern, information-based economy.

In terms of its domestic policies, Singapore's policies share as many notable similarities with state socialism than with free market capitalism. The most striking similarity is the extent of government control over savings and investment. Nobel Laureate Franco Modigliani upset the PAP rulers by criticizing the enormous build-up of foreign reserves, and what he considered to be an excessive rate of savings. In addition, besides the more common monopolies in the telecommunications industries, the government is extensively involved in real estate markets, including a massive public housing program. The ruling party, its affiliates and the government are also partial owners in various industries. Some of these are extensions of colonial-era statutory authorities. Others include newspaper publishing, shipping and ship building, transportation and others.

Macroeconomic policy interventions are reflected in extensive controls over the labor and currency markets. Trade union activities are co-opted through government control, and a National Wages Council was established in 1972 as a tripartite advisory board to establish guidelines for wage increases. The Monetary Authority of Singapore (MAS) pursues active foreign exchange interventions to guide exchange rates, as much to sustain an export-oriented industrialization (EOI) policy as to hold inflation in check. Foreign banks must be licensed by the MAS, which only grants them "offshore" licenses. Thus, foreign banks are allowed to incorporate in Singapore, but they may only operate in the international markets. No foreign banks have been licensed to compete in domestic banking operations since the early 1970's. Those that are allowed to compete in the domestic retail banking market face severe restrictions on the opening or moving of branches and the installation of ATM's. Several key industries are totally blocked to foreigners. The authorities have recently announced that the domestic insurance market is "saturated" and no longer allow new entry. Also, no foreign firms are allowed to invest in the manufacturing of armaments in Singapore.

Such actions are far from consistent with free markets. Interestingly, some detractors of Singapore's regime oppose what they wrongly interpret to be its ideological commitment to free markets. Similarly, some supporters offer praise for the same, though erroneous, reasoning. Careful investigation of the laws, economic policy, and regulations provides strong evidence that Singapore's economy is not a free market haven. This conclusion is evident in the blatant disregard for individual rights and the substantial market interventions. Clearly, the regime is driven more by political opportunism than by a commitment to free markets or any free-market ideology.

Preconditions To and Political Control Of Singapore's Development

Various conditions beyond the prudent judgments and strong-armed tactics of its leaders underpin Singapore's well-chronicled prosperity. Despite self-serving statements to suggest that the regime started from scratch, there is ample evidence that Singapore was well-endowed at independence.[2] The oft-repeated observation that Singapore had no natural resources has given way to a realization that the latent abilities of its labor force have contributed significantly to its strong economic performance. In fact, Singapore's positioning on the main sea route between India and China has always been crucial to its economic vitality. When Great Britain allowed for self-rule in 1959, Singapore's location then accounted for it being the pre-eminent economic center in the region. Its colonial heritage dealt Singapore various other valuable cards. These include a forced exposure to English as the principal trading language, the privileged access to trade links with the developed world and the British Commonwealth, as well as the establishment of a highly regarded legal and commercial code. These factors converged in a post-war setting where ample slack in the world market allowed for expansions and shifts in manufacturing and trade.

Besides these institutional arrangements, a number of other factors further contributed to Singapore's successful pattern of economic development. In the mid-1960's, Britain transferred to the government of Singapore its substantial housing stock previously provided for its military personnel under the Far East Command. This in turn lowered development costs for the new island republic and allowed taxation to remain relatively low. Also left behind by the British was the Central Provident Fund (CPF) that had been established in 1955. This provided the regime with access to low interest funds for their pet projects. In the absence of the obligatory contributions of workers and employers, the government would have had to borrow on the open market at considerably higher rates and with considerably more accountability than the present system allows. This lack of accountability seems important. As shall be discussed in greater detail at the end of this chapter, rates of return on public investment in Singapore have been substantially less than in Hong Kong.[3]

Another factor in Singapore's growth is that its status as a city-state meant that it never had to confront the sort of adjustment problems normally faced by nation-states. For example, many other developing countries had to resolve a rural-urban migration problem arising out of the Green Revolution, as displaced peasants crowded into cities. Therefore, Singapore gained a distinct comparative advantage in being able to pick and choose immigrants from work-permit workers to non-tenured academics in the university system who could then be kept in line by threat of dismissal.

A final, and perhaps decisive, factor was the fortuitous timing and strategic positioning of the take-off period. The timing of Singapore's rapid growth in exports was such that there was no great threat to the domestic economic *status quo* of the industrialized economies. Equally important was promoting the prosperity of the various countries in the region to serve strategic interests in checking the influence of China and other communist regimes. This aspect of geo-political strategy meshed neatly with Singapore's own requirements for foreign investments, which could be supplied by multinationals from the US and other Western allies.

Electoral support for the PAP regime is heavily dependent upon delivery of economic progress. Therefore, it seeks a balance between controlling actors in domestic markets while appearing open to outside investors. In addition to the attributes of "authoritarian capitalism," PAP rule has led to a peculiar form of crony capitalism that promotes the notion that the fortunes of the country are not an admirable end in itself. Instead, economic progress serves as a means for the ruling party to maintain its political dominance. Besides the substantial government interventions in the market, the Singapore regime (and its counterpart in Malaysia) also resorts to actions that can be described as the "politicization of commerce" and the "commercialization of politics" that are discussed later in this chapter.[4]

A substantial degree of government control and ownership of commercial activities in Singapore is affected through a state enterprise system. This involves a complex skein of statutory boards and government-linked companies (GLC's). In many of these cases, the GLC's operate as monopolies and are held through 4 conglomerates (Temasek, MND, Singapore Technology Holdings, and Singapore Health Corporation). In turn, the GLC's employed over 83,000 workers. In 1990, the GLC's, along with the 15 statutory boards, controlled 74.7 percent of all local profits. Of the 7 domestic companies involved in knowledge-intensive, high value-added industries, all except one are GLC's.

It is of some consequence that the technocratic directors and managers of these government commercial ventures have acquired increasing autonomy. Despite the importance of the state enterprises, there is virtually no parliamentary or judicial oversight. The government holding companies are exempt from filing reports or accounts with the Registrar of Companies and recent statutes mandated restricted access to data from and information on these enterprises. Also, these state enterprises are characterized by a high concentration of power in the hands of a group of "trusted" directors, and that concentration appears to be increasing over time. The extent of these "interlocking directorates" is evident in that by 1991 over 27 percent of the directors were interlocked with nearly 61 percent of the GLC's.[5] Consequently, an increasing proportion of the economy is being managed by a relatively small group of people. Obviously, there are natural limits to the ability of the regime to ensure that state enterprises are run by technocrats who share the PAP's ideology. As the diversity and number of the state enterprises continue to expand, either sycophantic directors must assume additional directorships or new members of the team will have to be brought on board. Without institutional restraints, it will become harder to manage the behavior of new directors. Eventually, the way will be left open for abuse of power, and there will be a growing potential for greater inefficiency, or possibly corruption.

Besides involvement as owners of commercial activities, the PAP also exercises political dominion over the trade union movement. A critical element of this control stems from legislation, like the Employment Act and the Industrial Relations (Amendment) Act of 1968, that transferred bargaining power from workers to employers. To consolidate this control, the pro-PAP National Trade Union Congress (NTUC) was recognized as the sole legal trade union federation.[6] In turn, the regime was able to divert trade union attention away from interest in workers' rights towards serving as cheerleaders for the PAP. It has even threatened to expel those members who would support the opposition. By making the position of Secretary-General of the NTUC a cabinet level post, Singapore joined the ranks of socialist states where top leaders of the ruling party also served as officials in the trade union movement. A lack of independence of the labor movement may be evident in that, despite a labor market defined by shortages of skilled labor, there have been negligibly few labor stoppages since 1967.

Costs of the Conservative Struggle Against Change

Economists tend to be most concerned with efficiency and long run adjustments. While their critics suggest that concern for the former implies that economists have little concern for humane values, focus upon the latter is seen as a cop-out on their part. A particular objection is that there is no exact time frame for the long run adjustment processes in economic analysis. Economists generally treat the long run as the period of time before their predicted adjustments are observed. This construct is often seen by non-economists to be an intellectual dodge whenever theories do not bear fruit in the immediate term.

These complaints notwithstanding, the following discussion places an emphasis upon the issues of efficiency and the implications of the long-run adjustments of the current institutional structures in Singapore. This discussion will also serve as a guide to economic activity in other parts of East Asia. At the outset, a basic premise is that these observed institutions should not be understood to constitute a state of equilibrium. There are good reasons to see the current record of high economic growth as a transitory phenomenon. Suppositions of the superiority of a particular cultural or economic system tend to be fatally flawed if they overlook their transitory nature. In the end, the most critical element in any social arrangement is its compatibility with the forces of the discovery process that drives the market and non-market choices that people make. It should be obvious that this characteristic is not dependent upon a culturally-specific milieu.

By treating life in the present as a reflection of ongoing long-run adjustments, most economists insist upon the importance of the processes of dynamics and change in social analysis. Apparently, it is a human weakness to become entrapped by what might appear to be the verities of today and to extrapolate them into the future. Perhaps the true failing of hubris is to become a slave to a particular set of beliefs and structures based upon immediate experience or that of the recent past. Obviously this logic applies to economic development in the West as well as in the high performing East Asian economies.

The presumption here is that competition and change ought to be perceived as the central elements behind economic analysis. Competition emerges out of the ubiquitous human dilemma in resolving the problems arising from scarcity, which is treated as a defining aspect of human existence.[7] In other words, competition is the manifest outcome of making choices arising from the sacrifices required to acquire the things we desire. This might be most easily conceptualized by considering the issue of mortality in that humans face competing pressures in the use of their unavoidably limited life span. Costs emerge then out of these decisions and are measured in terms of what else might have been accomplished with the expended time and other resources when one course of action is chosen over another. Changing costs become an important input in the decisions made by individuals based upon their life purposes and the means at their disposal. Competition then is the outcome of a natural and often unconscious thought process of choice making. In turn, competition acts as a motivating force that drives social, political, cultural or economic change.

Choices made by individuals acting either alone or as members of groups both reflect and generate the competitive forces that generate these changes. Following this logic, the notion of a static social or economic equilibrium makes little sense. As stated previously, the passage of time can be viewed as the process of transition between momentary equilibria, all of them made fleeting by a new round of choices sparked by the presence of new and unexpected information. Although some market adjustments may be nearly instantaneous, developments in social and cultural institutions tend to reflect a relatively slower, evolutionary pace.[8] Similarly, unless supported by the force of law, the community can readily abandon experimental arrangements that do not serve them well. In a modern setting a continuation of lawful but consistently socially harmful acts can most often be traced to some government policy that invokes a perverse set of sanctions. In other words, anti-social or economically irrational acts are not likely to be repeated by large numbers of persons for a long period of time unless there is some institutionalized payoff from doing so.[9]

Choice-making behavior then serves as a discovery process whereby humans search for the best means to serve their collective purposes. Even if the process is not consciously undertaken or articulated by the human actors, these choices are continuously subjected to conditions that test their consistency with the pursuit of individual life purposes and collective goals. Introduction of new information through invention or imagination guarantees the dynamics of the process by allowing for the imagining of new life purposes. The progress and change of communities are relentless, and while it may be delayed or observed over a given period of time, this process can never be halted completely.

Although scarcity requires that choices be made which in turn inspire competition, the qualitative element of choice is influenced by the incentive structures arising out of social, cultural, political and economic institutions. Culturally-specific values may set limits to choices by establishing a payoff matrix for behavior. However, the incentive structures can normally hold in the short run. Those arrangements that turn out to be counter-productive for the purposes of the bulk of the community will be altered or abandoned in the long run simply as the course of daily choices is made. In the end, superior institutional arrangements are discovered or emulated though the simultaneous choices of individuals as they search for the means to accomplish their constantly changing ends and means.

Conservative forces may try to halt the inexorable forces of change. Indeed, they may register temporary success. For example, the survival of authoritarian-socialist regimes for nearly 70 years in East and Central Europe involved a concerted effort to stifle the market by interfering with the forces of change and competition. Now in Singapore, and some other parts of East Asia, authoritarian-capitalist regimes constitute the new conservative, anti-modernist force. Therefore it appears that there is no clash of civilizations. It is just another round in the continued struggle between modernizing forces that arise out of choices expressed by individual citizens that clash with the conservatism of rulers who wish to hold back progress as they hold on to power. In light of their nominal commitment to democracy, these conservative rulers seek moral and cultural justifications for their conservatism. However, the core of this conservatism is anti-democratic in its refusal to acknowledge or to allow the joint expression of their citizens' political preferences. The obstruction of market transactions is an equally anti-democratic act in that it limits the expression of preferences by individuals.[10]

Anti-democratic actions under authoritarian capitalism reflect another, more basic, conflict of views. Attempts to restrain changes in this setting involve an explicit and forceful subjugation of the individual to the collective. An assertion of the superiority of the values and visions of the political leaders removes the opportunity for citizens to act as individuals. This form of conservatism invokes a self-fulfilling prophecy that insures a level of dependency, immaturity and insecurity among the populace to exercise their own choices. Following these methods, these rulers impose a self-realizing prediction based upon their conspicuous contempt for the ability of the citizenry to choose for themselves as individuals.

Claims for culturally-specific characteristics, that rulers share with the ruled, as the basis for restricting individual actions seems to be a bizarre form of racism. In legitimating their autocratic rule, certain Asian leaders reveal a lapse in logic. While these leaders recognize in themselves the virtues of wisdom stemming from their cultural heritage, they attribute inferior qualities to their citizens who are a product of the same background. For example, Mr. Lee Kuan Yew of Singapore is on record to have referred to his fellow citizens as "digits." Such a disdainful remark reveals that Mr. Lee interprets the value of Singaporeans as based upon how they fit into his master plan. During the convocation ceremonies at Williams College, Mr. Goh made the stunning revelation that there was a need to maintain the ISA in Singapore due to the political immaturity of his fellow citizens. To such rulers, ordinary people are treated as means for government-directed projects instead of treating them as capable persons, and who thus cannot be trusted to make their own open political choices. This attitude of Asian leaders has shaped the hierarchical traditions of political rule for centuries. The following section will examine some of the economic consequences of the Asian political arrangements.

Economic Effects of Asian Political Institutions

Economists are interested in the impact of organizational forms and institutional arrangements upon incentive structures that influence economic choices. Recently, there have been efforts to trace the evolution of institutions relative to their impact upon efficiency and costs. This "transaction costs" approach to understanding institutions provides economists with additional tools to evaluate the interaction between political and economic institutions. The provision of a framework to measure the economic impact of public policies has been one of the most valuable contributions of modern economics. This approach to institutional analysis is well suited to the task of generating some additional insights into Asian authoritarian capitalism.

One of the most striking public policy myths is the depiction of the openness of East Asian economies. This impression is supported by the substantial reductions in trade barriers. Nonetheless, there continues to be a significant amount of protectionism and intervention in these economies, especially in domestic markets.[11] Import-substitution policies continue to provide protection for domestic industries, such as automobiles in Thailand and Malaysia. As suggested above in the case of Singapore, monetary policy of other countries in the region tends to be heavily interventionist, often with the aim of maintaining a stable exchange rate as part of neo-mercantilist export-oriented trade policies.

The "politicization of commerce" is observable where market intervention is manifested through special interest group pressures or preferential arrangements offered by the regime to trusted individuals. This can also be seen as a subtle form of corruption which provides privileged opportunities for those commercial activities that serve political ends. Crony capitalism allows governments to take an active hand in the economy as a means to solicit political support. There are also instances where Asian authoritarian-capitalist regimes rely upon the "commercialization of politics" (political business) whereby political parties or government institutions use insider information and political influence to engage in lucrative commercial activities.[12] Characteristic examples of the commercialization of politics are found in the People's Liberation Army (PLA) of China, as well as in the commercial activities of the ruling parties in Malaysia and Indonesia. These strategies reflect various methods to reinforce the political hegemony of a (quasi-Leninist) one-party state. In the case of China, the Communist Party has reduced intra-governmental tensions by allowing the military to develop their own revenue sources to carry out their modernization schemes. In Malaysia and Indonesia, the ruling parties have greater autonomy from the citizens by generating revenues through business ventures. A similar approach involves the co-opting of the emerging middle class, either through offers of positions in bureaucracy or access to lucrative private sector arrangements for individuals who are trusted by the regime. Corruption and money politics flow readily out of these institutional arrangements, as is readily evident in many East Asian economies. It is perhaps most problematic that these arrangements provide the temporary illusion that decisions made by technocrats, bureaucrats or politicians can always be trusted to improve upon, or to replace, the decentralized decisions of entrepreneurs. A similar error of reasoning was evident in the belief that central planning and socialized property could improve upon the price system of a market economy.

One of the more problematic elements of the institutionalization of autocratic rule is that restraints upon freedom of the press and free speech not only shut out political conversation but also restrain economic activity. A free and open news media are important means towards other ends, such as those which allow individuals to identify and to accomplish their life purposes. In turn, the absence of a free and protected media reinforces the dominance of one-party rule by stifling the emergence of political opposition. Control over information flows and communication channels allows despotic regimes to create and sustain myths about their successes, while concealing their failures. Among the numerous ends and means associated with these illusions is the misleading perception surrounding economic performance. Certain East Asian economies have certainly exhibited high rates of economic growth. However, as in the control of information in other areas of life, internally generated economic data are also jealously guarded. If data is not readily available for outside scrutiny by independent sources, these figures should be interpreted cautiously if not treated with outright skepticism. If things were really so good, then they should be openly and readily available. Just as public access to government data inspires greater confidence, the suppression of such data ought to breed suspicion. What is being questioned in this instance is not the big picture, but it focuses the attention upon the shading and the relative magnitudes. The fact that access to these statistics is so tightly controlled supports the contentions that the data are considered to be important enough, and sensitive enough, to hide. Recently, Singapore joined China in taking harsh steps against journalists who reported economic figures in a manner that displeased their official policies.

Some traditional institutions peculiar to parts of East Asia are inclined to stunt long term growth and development. It is widely believed that without the use of networks of family and political connections (*guanxi*), little can be accomplished in China or in those parts of Asia where overseas Chinese family businesses dominate. These informal connections are not limited to person-to-person or family-to-family arrangements. Access to special favors from bureaucrats or regulators is a particularly important aspect of *guanxi* in the transition process in China and in many of the emerging market economies. Indeed, the extensiveness of bureaucratic control and the politicization of life creates an extreme dependency of the average citizen upon figures of authority. Negative welfare impacts upon economic growth potential can be expected from this particular institutional arrangement when it relies upon special contacts with government officials. *Guanxi* is a zero-sum redistributive game that results in the familiar socially wasteful consequences associated with conventional rent-seeking behavior. In a deregulated economy, it is more important whether resources are most efficiently used rather than who has the best access to the bureaucrats.

Asian institutions based upon collectivism are widely seen as the source of strength, and an important contributing factor, to the emergence of the "miracle economics." As stated previously, many regimes (Indonesia, Malaysia and Singapore) depend upon political repression and interference in the economy to insure their political survival. As such, these economies have nominally free enterprise economies that are largely guided by an authoritarian hand, and where competition is encouraged, but only on terms set by the governments. That large scale economic success in the private sector often depends upon the complicity of these regimes reflects a form of crony capitalism. As mentioned above, institutionalized collectivism and the suppression of institutions that promote individualism inhibit the emergence of entrepreneurs. As discussed in detail in Chapter 5, these countries are likely to find themselves stuck in a parasitic phase of development. Without homegrown entrepreneurs, such countries lack domestic, or even regional sources of innovation and progress. Many Asian economies also continue to direct the bulk of their exports outside of the region. They cannot expect to continue to be dependent upon North America and Europe for innovations as well as for markets for their externally traded goods and services. More recently, Singapore has become dependent upon other countries to make up for their labor market shortages at all skill levels.

Ironically, the supporting institutions of the "miracle economies" may imperil continuation of their own performance record as well as the promise of future developments of the Pacific Basin. Recent spurts of economic growth coincidental with East Asian authoritarian-capitalist regimes may dissipate under the weight of their own internal contradictions. By continuing to stifle the development of individual-oriented institutions, their economies can be expected to falter, subjecting the tenuous political base of these regimes to erosion. As individuals seek institutional arrangements that allow them to pursue their individual life purposes within a collective setting, authoritarian capitalism provides little room for the soaring spirit of individuals. A community of spiritually-deprived individuals is almost certainly unable to represent a sustainable condition of social equilibrium.

As suggested above, it might be more accurate to explain the differences in Eastern and Western political institutions on the basis of different stages of development. More mature Western institutions have developed enough confidence to allow greater play to individualism. Meanwhile, Asian political elites opportunistically continue to promote a conservative form of collectivism. This gulf is most distinct in Confucian-influenced settings where there is an insistence upon filial piety that is combined with a politically-inspired demand that citizens place "society above self." Asian authoritarian-capitalist regimes demand respect for a social order where rules set by those in power are to be unquestionably accepted by the polity. Collectivist societies tend to rely upon reserved understatement as is evident in the importance of "saving face."

Like all other arrangements, actions taken to "save face" involve costs as well as benefits and like *guanxi*, it is a zero-sum game. The importance of face-saving behavior stems in part from the desire to create an appearance of consensus and to avoid open conflict. It may appear that social arrangements that are based upon the avoidance of conflict or placing someone in an embarrassing situation should be beneficial. However, the action of saving face may have more to do with appearances than with substance. Rigorous adherence to such a convention allows many problems to be masked from outsiders who do not understand how to look behind a veneer of placidity. The fable of the child who insisted that the "emperor has no clothes" apparently has no counterpart in modern Asian culture.

The zero-sum nature of the convention of saving face can be observed at several levels. At the personal level, if one person is allowed to save face, another is often forced to lose face. Saving face is based upon a pecking-order in that the position of a superior is more important. At the national level, the tradition is obviously well suited to the maintenance of hierarchical or even authoritarian rule since it closes down opportunities for individuals to object openly to unreasonable rules or conditions. In transnational dealings, compromise tends to be more elusive when negotiations over conflicts are more complex.

Perhaps the most important cost of this imposed approach to "consensus building" is that it lends support to, and reproduces, hierarchical structures by limiting challenges to authority. Without proper checks on political leaders or business managers, the short run gains of consensus building may lead to substantial long run costs from corruption, injustice, or inefficiency. With increasing pace of change in technology and management practices, authoritarian or hierarchical rule may increasingly aim to develop institutions that focus upon face saving and an imposed sense of consensus. When group interests are decided by a hierarchical structure in a rapidly changing world, there is an increased likelihood that the decisions will impose costs upon larger numbers of individuals. Institutions that force individuals to subjugate themselves and muzzle those who would be challengers to the *status quo* are becoming obsolete due to increasingly globalized capitalism and the rapid pace of change. At some threshold, there must be an outlet for grievances or restitution to those who are disadvantaged by the interests of the larger community. As income and wealth increase among Asians, silencing the voices of individuals will involve increasing costs to the integrity of their respective communities.

It may be less clear to some observers that the repression of freedom of speech as a means to maintain the political *status quo* is itself an identifiable form of protectionism. As a form of "cultural protectionism," it retards the flow of numerous commercial ventures including newspapers and magazines, films, books or any other forms of intellectual property. In a global economy that is becoming so heavily dependent upon information technology, cultural protectionism will invoke very high costs. By imposing restrictions on information flows, cultural protectionism imposes a double blow to emerging economies. Attempts to protect cultures are almost certain to inhibit cultural developments in Asia in much the same manner as their trade counterparts inhibit economic growth. Nonetheless, by eroding the development of an information based economy, cultural protectionism can also retard the economic growth potential of these countries. Those regimes in Asia, or elsewhere, that ignore this process can be expected to lose out on the promised prosperity of the Pacific Century, and may contribute to its untimely demise.

Continued global economic progress requires the free trade of goods and services. It also depends upon the unimpeded development and flow of knowledge-based commodities that are more consistent with the individualist institutions associated with liberal capitalism. Similarly, cultural progress requires an open competition between political and cultural institutions regardless of their cultural or geographic origin. Authoritarian-capitalist regimes in Asia are seeking to impose a form of "cultural protectionism" designed to isolate their communities from the infectious influences of the West that encourage the liberalization of controls over the individual.

Cultural Protectionism and "Asian Values"

Governments around the world seek legitimization for their policies of "cultural protectionism." It is interesting to note that France, and some partners in the European Union, share similar protectionist inclinations with regimes in other parts of the world well known for censorship. National governments intervene in cultural affairs for their own reasons. More openly authoritarian regimes use cultural policy as a means to exercise political hegemony. On one hand, the communist bureaucracy in Beijing pursues a similar policy in vigorously "protecting" the Chinese people from democratic, and some economic, freedoms. Singapore's government, and to a lesser extent the Mahathir regime in Malaysia, has embarked upon a vigorous campaign to "protect" its respective citizenry from what is claimed to be the destabilizing influences of western individualist-based institutions. On the other hand, France's cultural protectionism, though a bit more benign, is a thinly veiled mirror image of cultural imperialism.[13] Critics of cultural policy seeking principled arguments to oppose cultural protectionism need look no further than South Africa's disastrous experiment with apartheid.

Arguments for protectionism, as a general policy, quite clearly exhibit great resilience. While this logic has been applied to various aspects of public sector action, its most irrepressible example can be found in trade restrictions. In most instances, inhibitions on trade are promulgated by opportunistic politicians. While these populist policies provide benefits for a supportive interest group, the motives are disguised behind an announced intent to serve the common good. It is readily apparent that advocacy for trade protectionism is not limited to socialist ideologues who reject either the projected merits of the market or the benefits of free trade.

The purpose of the ensuing arguments is to identify common elements in various protectionist arguments in search of consistent and principled reasons for accepting or for rejecting them. An important source of the explanation for the survival of protectionist arguments can be found in the allure of these arguments to special interest groups, in this case a European cultural elite.[14] This argument is important here since the political motivation behind the "Asian values" debate clearly involves a form of cultural protectionism.

Under representative democracy, the need to capture the maximal number of votes to maintain, or to gain, public office results in the great sensitivity of politicians to the demands of well-organized special interest groups (SIG's). Nearly all protectionist policies impose costs upon the general public, while yielding benefits to a narrowly defined interest group. Nonetheless, arguments in support of such policies are often phrased to reinforce a widely nationalist rhetoric. It is only by stripping away the rhetorical cover that the substance of protectionism can be seen for what it is: a zero-sum game, whereby gains for one group are offset by losses to another. In this framework, it becomes transparent that protectionism is motivated by SIG's that seek to divert public policy to serve their narrow advantage. Politicians are induced through lobbying and other pressures to promote policies that transfer resources from the general community in return for the political and financial support of the SIG.

Trade barriers are the most commonly discussed form of *economic* protectionism. The familiar examples of economic protectionism involve trade restrictions including quotas, tariffs, and "voluntary export restraints." However, there is a wide variety of protectionist policies. All of these arise from the demands made by political coalitions that seek to serve a special interest. *Moral* protectionism results from a treatment of a certain set of morals as though they had universal and objective content. This may be observed as a form of paternalism that uses the force of law to prohibit certain vices. Moral protectionism might involve highly selective choice in the criminalization of certain acts. These actions have often been referred to as "victimless crimes" and may include prostitution, sale of pornography, life styles such as homosexuality and the use of certain prohibited drugs. What might be merely vices become defined as illegal acts. *Political* protectionism may lead to restrictions on immigration, banning of political parties or outlooks, or attacks upon freedom of association.

More broadly, *cultural* protectionism may appear as a positive force that involves ethnic nationalism or social nepotism, or provides approval of some particular cultural expression. In its negative form, cultural protectionism involves censorship and the promotion and protection of ethnic or group rights at the expense of individual rights. Examples of the latter can be found in apartheid, certain demands by "Green" parties or neo-fascist political parties to protect national heritage, and the Jim Crow laws in the USA. All of these actions or policies rely upon the same sort of means, i.e., government tools of intervention. Similarly, all tend to be rationalized by the assertion that they serve collectivist or "communitarian" goals.[15] However, most forms of interventionist protections are susceptible to the same objections that were correctly raised in opposition to apartheid.

The tools for all these variants of protectionism involve (often extensive) governmental intervention and are based, presumably, upon the expectation of net "social" benefits. While not all protectionism is based upon good intentions, the political apologies offered by supporters suggest this to be so. Yet, regardless of intentions, the essential results are strikingly similar in that individual rights are made subservient to group rights. Contrary to the expectations from majoritarian democracy, the preferences of minorities are, in effect, allowed to overshadow majority interests. Minority rule displaces majority rule regardless of whether the minority is a political, economic or ethnic elite. While the effects may appear elsewhere to be benign, authoritarian regimes apply similar collectivist, utilitarian claims (e.g., establishment and protection of certain group's rights under apartheid) in order to justify their repressive methods. In all events, basing policy upon good intentions is not enough to bring desired results. It is not enough to suggest that one is promoting a particular (good?) cause. Despite the rhetoric to the contrary, and whatever the intentions, protectionism seldom, if ever, serves the interests of the general public.

It might be instructive to reflect for a moment upon the broader, more generalized issue of the nature of public sector action. In the first instance, government interventions depend upon, and are funded by, compulsion rather than choice. Thus, the further one moves away from unanimity, the greater will be the presence of external costs. These "negative externalities" are costs borne by the growing number of those opposed to, or adversely affected, by a given policy. It must also be recognized that the aim of protectionist interventions is to generate or support the establishment of "monopoly rights." Decisions to protect one group from competitive market forces are very likely to be determined by SIG pressures. In this sense, promotion of one group's preferences, whether as a cultural policy or due to racial segregation, necessarily implies either coercion or the shifting of costs to other, perhaps larger, groups. This occurs whenever politics serves as the dominant means for determining the distribution of goods or income and wealth. In the case of apartheid, white dominance of the South African power structure, and their historical isolation from other racial groups, was an important factor in the emergence of legal obligations to enforce racial segregation as a form of cultural protectionism.

In order to determine whether a principled counter-argument can be applied to cultural protectionism in all its forms, it is useful to investigate the interest group dynamics, as well as the collectivist means and ends, that characterized apartheid. In the end, by viewing apartheid as a form of cultural protectionism, protectionist policies ought to be subjected to the same scrutiny. If they are vulnerable to the same criticisms, then these policies deserve to be abandoned on the same general grounds.

The limits on economic and social activity imposed by cultural protectionism (including apartheid and other forms) work against the most critical elements of capitalism: free choice in trade by individuals and unobstructed, competitive markets. The massive extent of state interference with market exchange provides solid evidence of the links between apartheid and other forms of oppressive interventions. The efficient operation of capitalism requires free exchange within a system of private property rights. To the contrary, apartheid represented an effective "nationalization" of holdings of property due to legal restrictions on their uses. Apartheid laws restricted not only the sale and ownership of property, but they also placed restraints upon labor and capital markets. In a very real sense, the apartheid state overshadowed all economic transactions, in the same manner as authoritarian socialist regimes. In all events, the crucial conclusion drawn from the above reasoning is that the nature and consequences of apartheid lie within interferences with free exchange induced by demands from special interest groups. If such policies should be discredited, then it should be on the basis of principle, not simply on special (racial) pleading.

Other forms of cultural protectionism may seem innocuous in terms of their outcome, but these are subject to the failures of state action to meet their prescribed ends. This divergence between intentions and results of public policy arises out of the unintended consequences of social action. In other words, collective solutions may fail to improve upon the private sector decisions that are seen to yield inefficient results. In the current discussion, the state serves as a substitute for an enthusiastic cultural elite in directing an adequate level of funds into the Fine Arts. Indeed, it must be recognized that there is a high probability that the politicization of public intervention can result in misdirection or misappropriation of resources. Imposition of an artificial set of relative prices for goods and resources may worsen matters in those activities where state action is supposed to remedy market failures.

Policies aimed at protecting cultural products can be expected to lead inevitably to a situation of non-competitive monopoly power. This tends to lead to diversion of large amounts of taxpayers' money into various "cultural enterprises." As predicted by conventional economic analysis, one would expect to find underproduction and higher prices. For example, greater funds may go to a single arts company driving up the hiring costs of performers as well as other production costs for all others. Further, it could then be argued that the diversity, and thus the richness, of cultural expression is actually constrained by the interventions of the government into the arts industry. The concentration of public funds or assets into a single expression of the arts deflects funds from less conventional, but equally rich, art forms. Without government intervention in this sector, there might well be a richer diversity in cultural expressions offered by the domestic market at lower, and almost certainly at more affordable, prices.

It is often argued that the broad community risks the loss of certain cultural expressions, especially in the arts, based upon a presumption that private source monies are inadequate to support them. Yet such a conclusion begs empirical verification. The skeptic's query along this line ignores that present high levels of payment are carried out in an environment distorted by the presence of state interventions. Subsequently, various native cultural expressions and private sector involvement are "crowded out" in the manner described above. Interventionist claims for cultural protectionism overlook or ignore *a priori* arguments that explain inefficiencies and inequities arising from government regulation and bureaucratic actions. They also conveniently ignore the responsiveness of both the supply and demand of the arts to real economic impulses. Elitist judgments are invariably granted greater weight than are the expressed choices of individual citizens. In the end, attempts by cultural elites to implement a public policy often results in an *exploitation* of those citizen-taxpayers who have no direct interests in a given cultural expression.

Grants of special protection for cultural products are based upon the familiar claims presented by, e.g., industrial monopolists or producer groups, racial groups, trade unions or dynastic political parties. Each and all seek to prosper at the expense of the rest of society. Government regulations and restrictions involve the almost unavoidable result of protecting some element of the *status quo* at the expense of both present and future competitors, as well as inflicting injury upon consumers. Protection of vested economic or cultural interests to serve political ends is a well established, cynical political game. It would appear that the goal of minimizing the inefficiencies resulting from politically inspired interventions, including monopoly privilege, would require expanding the extent of private sector decisions.

Apartheid has been described here as a particularly offensive form of cultural protectionism that relied upon extensive state intervention to promote the interests of a particular nationalist group. Obviously there is no suggestion that any other governments wish to set up separatist racial policies. However, the close correlation of the cultural policies of Singapore's government with those of the apartheid regime provides a serious indictment of the same cultural protectionist instincts that motivated the French to nearly derail the conclusion of the Uruguay Round of the GATT talks. Cultural protectionism, under the guise of the promotion of pan-Asian values, may unintentionally weaken the links between developed countries in the West and some of the countries in East Asia.

The mechanisms of cultural protectionism can be expected to interfere with the continuation of economic growth and development. Stifling the economic and political atmosphere serves to stunt the emergence of homegrown entrepreneurs. In a surprisingly candid interview in a local newspaper, one of Singapore's most successful bankers admitted to the shortage of entrepreneurial skills in his country.[16] Mr. Wee Cho Yaw, Chairman of the United Overseas Bank and an active participant in many business-related organizations in Singapore, observed that Singapore is producing few "true" entrepreneurs. Further, he added that the "Government's strong link of companies" makes it difficult to do business. Mr. Wee stated that if he were young, he would look outside of Singapore to go into business.

Singapore's lack of true entrepreneurs is compounded by the fact that many of the older generation of business leaders had little technical training or interest in technical matters.[17] Since many of the large fortunes in Singapore developed from trading, these larger commercial organizations were driven by quick profits. Those that entered manufacturing often did so when the government's import-substitution policies closed the economy to the importation of tradable goods. Now, Singapore's homegrown industrial capitalists face the formidable task of moving from inward-looking production for their domestic market to competition with low cost producers in the regional market.

As suggested in the previous chapter, true entrepreneurs are contrarian, free thinkers who thrive in a free environment. They are also notorious for seeking the refreshing oxygen of an environment of freedom. Starved of this talent and dependent upon outside technological innovations, authoritarian-capitalist regimes of East Asia are unlikely to be able to carry forward their economic successes into the future.

Economic Growth Limits and Long-run Market Adjustments

Considerable attention has been focused upon East and Southeast Asia due to the remarkable record of high economic growth in those regions. Although numerous studies chronicle the upward path of the "miracle" economies, with some notable exceptions, fewer works have applied dispassionate economic analysis to examine this phenomenon.[18] For example, the recent country reports of the prodigious growth of Southeast Asian economies commissioned by the World Bank were prepared by economists residing in those respective countries. Doubtless they were under some pressures to reflect the often self-serving account dictated by the political conventional wisdom. Thus, it was not surprising that the principal summary comment applauded the regimes for getting the "basics right." Presumably, the remark reflected upon economic fundamentals rather than an evaluation of human rights policies or the nature of civic discourse in most of those countries. Once again there was no effort to examine the cost side of the equation arising from the development strategies of the East Asian economies.

While there has been a great deal of praise and interest in the Southeast Asian "miracle" economies, a consensus is lacking on the nature of cause and effect linkages that underpin their economic performance.[19] In looking at the impressive record of the high performing East Asian economies, some observers simply rely upon casual empiricism to confirm their own ideological biases. For example, promoters of the free market might praise the relatively open international trade policies of these economies as the source of high economic growth. The problem with taking this simplistic assessment is that it overlooks the extensive interference with other aspects of domestic market activity common to governments in the region. Others may praise the judicious guidance to the economy by technocrats as a model for other countries to follow.

Since judgments over the "success" of the market interventions of Singapore's regime are colored by the observer's ideological positioning, an objective measure should be applied. One such objective measure of the performance of government intervention is the rate of return on capital investment. In spite of similar beginnings, a recent study found an unfavorable comparison in the growth in output per worker as well as in the growth in output per unit of capital between Hong Kong and Singapore.[20] These differences are likely to have consequences for the long run growth potential of their respective economies. Judging from the reported findings, the forecast is not so rosy for Singapore's future.

In 1960, both Hong Kong and Singapore were island-state dependencies of Great Britain that were at about the same level of economic development.

Since then, they have experienced similar annual increases in real per capita income (6 percent). Certain differences are noteworthy, however. Hong Kong generally followed a path of market-driven, *laissez-faire* economic development. Singapore's government was heavily interventionist in deciding upon the industrial direction as well as the timing of investments, in its domestic economy. This active involvement in the market was supported through the program of mandatory worker and employer contributions to the CPF pension scheme. Hong Kong had a similar pension scheme and began this time period with a stock of well-educated refugees from communist China. Singapore began its post-independence era with a poorly educated work force.

For a variety of reasons, including the use of public expenditures for what many would interpret to be purely political ends, over-investment has led to Singapore displaying one of the lowest returns on capital investment in the world. The subsequent losses of utility to the general population from the misallocation of resources emerge from the same sort of elitist planning, arrogance and forced savings exhibited by authoritarian-socialist regimes. Admittedly the regime in Singapore has been able to deliver some of the fruits of their focus upon long-run economic growth. In all events, the test will come in the long-run when the costs of the misallocations come home to roost. Authoritarian-capitalist regimes in Singapore and elsewhere should remember that long-run adjustments to economic and social contradictions were the cause of the instability and eventual collapse of authoritarian-socialist regimes in Europe and other parts of the world.

Asian "Miracle" Economy: Facts and Fables

Some recent studies have found that the reported growth rates for the "miracle" economies are less than miraculous when comparing them with the similarly impressive results of Soviet-style economies in their early periods.[21] Although in the case of the Soviet Union and in some of the "miracle" economies, the absence of independent corroboration allowed for tightly-guarded economic statistics to be exaggerated for political purposes, this point was not raised. The most important point of comparison was the high degree of forced saving and sacrifice of current consumption shared by Soviet-style and Asian "miracle" economies. Growth in tangible output in both these instances can be explained by growth in the quantity of inputs of capital and labor applied to production, a process that has logical and physical limits. High rates of investment in physical capital, increased labor participation rates, employment expansion, and rapid increases in investments in education and health are blunt and unsustainable means to generate economic growth. Only by accepting a simplistic extrapolation of previous trends can the exceptionally high rates of real economic growth be expected to continue. Nonetheless, the continuation of high growth rates would require that qualitative improvements match the quantitative increase in inputs. In other words, without a boost in productivity gains for the added inputs, economic growth will slow down due to diminishing returns. Sustained long-run growth requires that there be increases in the total productivity of the factors of production. Although Singapore's reported average annual real growth of domestic income for the period 1960-91 was $8\frac{1}{2}$ percent, only $1\frac{3}{4}$ percent of that total can be attributed to increases in the productivity of factors of production. As in the case of the Soviet Union, the remaining $8\frac{1}{4}$ percentage points are attributable to mere quantitative increases in the inputs used for production.[22]

An interesting implication can be derived from the comparison of the relative performance of the Asian "miracle" economies. In terms of raw data on improvements in output per capita, each of the "miracle" economies ranks in the top 5 of a total sample of 118 countries. The thesis that these results derive from massive increases in the quantity of labor and capital is confirmed by the data on the growth in output per worker. Although the gains in output per worker compare favorably with the rest of the sample, they are considerably less impressive than gains in output per capita. Other developing economies, such as Egypt, Greece, Syria and Cameroon, performed equally well in this category. While the gains in economic output of the "miracle" economies more than offset population increases, the dramatic increase in the number of workers in those countries resulted in substantially lower gains in output per unit of labor.

In looking at gains in "total factor productivity," the "miracle" economies fall from grace in being outpaced by Bangladesh, Uganda, Iceland and Norway. However, it appears that Hong Kong, with the least amount of government intervention and thus the least source of policy distortions, performs best in terms of improvements in "total factor productivity." Apparently, industrial policy targeting by the governments in the other 3 "miracle" economies made them less responsive to market impulses. By providing government-directed incentives for production, industrial policies tend to interfere with resource allocation due to greater lags in the decision process.[23] In this light, there is no more reason to believe that the "Asian model" of government-directed development is any more "miraculous" than the Soviet model. Neither is it clear that those rates are sustainable.

Singapore's economy deserves specific scrutiny due to a presumption that its policies are an appropriate model for developing countries in the region, and perhaps elsewhere. As suggested above, Hong Kong's development record is based upon gains in "total factor productivity" in response to the market. The crude explanation for Singapore's record is that government-directed investments were derived from taxes and forced savings. It may be possible, in the short run, to "buy" growth through the payment of subsidies and other transfers to multinationals, but this is an unsustainable development scheme. Much like the record of the early days of the USSR, Singapore's leaders oversaw massive injections of expenditures for physical capital (factories and machinery) as well as human capital (health and education). Clearly, there are notable differences in the development paths. Resources in the Soviet Union were mobilized for inward development under autarky while the "miracle" economies pursued export-oriented industrial strategies. Another critical difference was the near total absence of private property rights under authoritarian-socialist regimes. Even with the considerable limits upon private property under authoritarian capitalism, prices and markets do function, even if imperfectly. Nonetheless, there are various signs that returns to investments in Southeast Asia are diminishing. Changing patterns of global capital flows are one of the most important of these indicators. Should the inflow of foreign capital be interrupted, Singapore's present high rates of saving will make it very difficult to raise sufficient capital in domestic markets to sustain such high levels of economic growth.

Another potential problem for long term growth in Singapore is the real estate boom that has most of the characteristics of a speculative bubble that could burst at any time. Land prices have been soaring in Singapore for many different reasons. Most obviously, the small amount of land area has been stretched by domestic uses in competition with the demands by the multinational corporations that operate there. In the early 1990's, many firms, fearing the uncertainty from the takeover of Hong Kong by the communist Chinese regime, have either shifted their operations or opened representative offices in Singapore. Although locals are shielded from some impacts of these cost increases due to the substantial holdings of public housing, the economy as a whole cannot be immune. As in the case of Japan's bubble economy, many investments and purchases are leveraged against inflated real estate and stock holdings offered as collateral.[24] In such a tight market, small increases in interest rates could trigger dramatic adjustments requiring compensation in other areas of the economy. Those who have purchased stocks on margin accounts could be forced to dump their shares on the market, or those with big ticket purchases to repay may simply default. A sharp plunge in the stock market would reverberate back into the real estate market. The situation is worsened by the fact that one of the largest players in the real estate market is Temasek Holdings, a GLC. Faced with a collapse of Temasek, the government would be forced to honor its obligations by tapping the publicly held pension funds in the CPF accounts. In a stroke, the savings and gains of the past 3 decades could disappear. It is particularly problematic that there is little access to information about the financial status of, or the exposure of, Temasek or any of the other GLC's. As in other cases of financial bubbles, there is a tendency for market participants to suspend reality.[25] Therefore, it is not surprising that many intelligent and aware investors are willing to be caught up in the soaring real estate and land prices in Singapore. Apparently the political leaders and technocrats in Singapore believe that past successes in guiding their economy will allow them to contain the effects of a bursting bubble. If so, this belief ignores centuries of evidence that it is simply impossible.

Many readers might feel that the weight of evidence in favor of continued growth in East Asia is indisputable. Even so, these objections might be put to rest by examining another similarity between the East Asian "miracle economies" and the early impressive record of Soviet economic performance. Numerous people accepted on face value the existence of a real foundation for their respective growth patterns which could be extrapolated into the future. No less of an economist than Nobel Laureate Paul Samuelson predicted in the 1973 edition of his classic textbook that the Soviet economy would catch up and then surpass the US standard of living by the early 1990's. Nothing then or now could be further from the truth. Even the CIA warned that the Soviet economy would become larger than America's by the early 1970's. After all, the economy of the USSR had been growing from a low base in the 1950's and then at 8-9% a year during the early 1960's. The Soviet approach followed the same path of input-led growth as have the East Asian "miracle economies." On the basis of this sort of evidence there should be good reason to encourage a closer look at the underpinnings, and to question the future prospects, of East Asian economies. This task will be undertaken in Chapter 5.

Conclusion

There is no question that the performance of Singapore's economy benefited by escaping or avoiding the contradictory development policies that plagued economies in Africa, South Asia, and Latin America. Recognizing the detrimental economic consequences of import barriers, policy makers in Singapore began to implement an enabling environment for private sector growth. This environment can be defined as providing macroeconomic stability, judicial protection of contracts and property rights, an adequate provision of infrastructure, and a reasonably transparent or predictable policy mix.

Nonetheless, the irrepressible force of economic change in the new global economy will impose continuing pressures for government policy makers. Besides the difficulties arising from the limiting factors associated with the contradictions arising out of authoritarian capitalism, Singapore's regime also faces constraints arising from various institutional arrangements that endanger the ability to maintain its exceptional rate of economic growth. Due to its size and positioning in the global economy, Singapore is highly dependent on the outside world. Besides the dependency upon foreign capital and technological advancements to facilitate its economic development, its economy requires access to foreign markets for their manufactured goods as well as a continuing dependency upon guest workers to fill gaps in the labor market. Such comprehensive exposure to international economic integration will almost certainly challenge its autonomy in domestic social policy in the changing world of global capitalism.

A considerable portion of Singapore's enviable economic performance can be traced to the initial availability of relatively cheap labor combined with access to mature technology in the production and assembly of relatively simple products. However, more recently a combination of resource bottlenecks (soaring land prices, shortages of skilled labor and middle management talent), along with an appreciating currency, has led to higher costs of operation in Singapore. These rising costs, along with increased global and regional competition for foreign investment funds, may mean that the combined real estate and foreign investment booms may soon be over for Singapore. Even if the absolute level remains high, the rate of inflow is almost certain to decline. As new emerging markets bid to contest the same markets, actors in Singapore's economy must work increasingly harder to identify and to develop a new set of competitive advantages.

In addition to the pressures of the changing global market place, Singapore's regime must also seek to resolve the paradoxes of authoritarian capitalism where its strategy of internal political isolation comes into conflict with the necessity to be responsive to outside economic pressures. Chapter 4 provides a close look at the peculiar elements of Singapore's governmental system and offers some additional background to understand the methods behind the political dominance of the PAP regime.

Notes

1 B. Johnson and T. Sheehy, "Index of Economic Freedom," 1994. Although a distinct correlation was found to exist between standard of living and the "economic freedom index," there was no effort to examine the relation with political freedoms or civil liberties.

2 W.G. Huff, *The Economic Growth of Singapore: Trade and Development in the Twentieth Century*. Cambridge: Cambridge University Press, 1994.

3 G. Becker and I. Ehrlich, "Social Security: Foreign Lessons," *Asian Wall St. Journal* (March 31, 1994). Young, A., "A Tale of Two Cities: Factor Accumulation and Technical Change in Hong Kong and Singapore," *NBER, Macroeconomics Annual 1992*. Cambridge, MA: MIT Press, pp. 15-62.

4 For the origins of these terms, see E. T. Gomez, *Political Business: Corporate Involvement of Malaysian Political Parties*. Townsville, Aus.: Centre for East and Southeast Asian Studies, James Cook University, 1994.

5 W. Vennewald, "Technocrats in the State Enterprise System of Singapore." Asia Research Centre, Murdoch University, Working Paper No. 32. November 1994.

6 Through its ownership of businesses, the NTUC is financially independent of the PAP, though both share the same ideology. The current president of Singapore, Ong Teng Cheong, served as NTUC Secretary General while simultaneously serving as Deputy Prime Minister in the PAP Government.

7 Scarcity must be distinguished from the notions of rarity and shortages. Rarity is a phenomenon that is linked to the absolute amount of some items, but not necessarily others. Shortages stem from market imbalances and can be resolved by price adjustments. Scarcity is more elementary and basic than rarity, and is a defining and limiting characteristic of life as well as those things that humans seek to have or to consume.

8 Reversals of cultural institutions might require shorter time periods than will the replacement by alternatives.

9 Similar acts that impose harm to the community might be continued if there is no, or a relatively small, penalty attached to them.

10 Interestingly, restricting choices that involve commercial interests often provoke less public resistance than do other government mandates.

11 World Bank, *East Asia's Trade and Investment: Regional and Global Gains from Liberalization*. Washington, DC: World Bank, 1994.

12 E.T. Gomez, *Political Business: Corporate Involvement of Malaysian Political Parties*. Townsville, Aus.: Centre for East and Southeast Asian Studies, James Cook University, 1994.

13 Promotion of the French culture through the Alliance Francaise is an example, *par excellence*, of the latter. In the 1960's, the administrators over French dominions in Polynesia forced native and Chinese inhabitants to take on French surnames so they would be "easier to pronounce."

14 Benefits that accrue to few citizens other than the cultural elite involve policies which range from financial support for film production or artificially low admission prices to cultural events, like the opera.

15 In addition to those listed above, the policy consequences of moral protectionism might include professional licensing, Blue laws, and drug "wars."

16 "I'm No True Entrepreneur, Says UOB Chief," *The Sunday Times* (23 July 1995) p. 6.

17 Yoshihara, K. *The Rise of Ersatz Capitalism in Southeast Asia*. Singapore: Oxford University Press, 1988.

18 Hong Kong, Singapore, South Korea and Taiwan comprise the Asian "miracle" economies, also known variously as the dragon or tiger economies.

19 One conventional argument for economic growth in Asian economies points to export-oriented development policies. In this sense, industrial take-off is prompted by relatively higher profit opportunities leading to large-scale exports. A variety of arguments challenge this conventional wisdom with much of the debate focusing

upon the effectiveness of government intervention. A recent summary of these viewpoints is found in D. Rodrik, "Getting Interventions Right: How South Korea and Taiwan Grew Rich," *Economic Policy* (April 1995, no 20) pp. 55-107.

20 A. Young, "A Tale of Two Cities: Factor Accumulation and Technical Change in Hong Kong and Singapore," *NBER Macroeconomics Annual, 1992*, Cambridge: MIT Press, 1992.

21 A. Young, "Lessons from the East Asian NIE's: A Contrarian View," NBER Working Paper No. 4482, October 1993. For supporting argumentation, see also P. Krugman, "The Myth of Asia's Miracle," *Foreign Affairs*, vol. 73, no. 6 (1994): 62-78.

22 R. van Elkan. "Accounting for Growth in Singapore," in K. Bercuson (ed.) *Singapore: A Case Study in Rapid Development.* Washington, DC: International Monetary Fund, 1995.

23 Decision lags can be expected to be longer since technocrats that direct industrial policy cannot gain directly from changing market conditions. Without personal incentives, the response time is likely to be slower since individual technocrats are unable to capture a share of profits gained from new market openings. Conversely, private sector producers can be expected to be more alert to changing market conditions since they can capture some of the potential gains in profits.

24 Interesting background to the instability of Japanese financial institutions can be found in Christopher Wood's, *The Bubble Economy: The Japanese Economic Collapse.* London: Sidgwick & Johnson, 1992.

25 A fascinating and entertaining account of bubbles and speculative frenzies is found in, J. Bulgatz. *Ponzi Schemes, Invaders from Mars and More Extraordinary Popular Delusions and the Madness of Crowds.* New York: Harmony Books, 1992.

Chapter 4

SINGAPORE'S DYSFUNCTIONAL DEMOCRACY: A CYCLE OF PROPAGANDA, FEAR AND DECEPTION

Glossy advertisements promote images of a vibrant, open economy known variously as "Singapore, Unlimited" or "Singapore, Inc." Equally well chronicled is Singapore's reputation as a clean, crime-free city. Yet few outsiders realize that the pristine images of blissful security and prosperity conceal a dark, forbidding side. While other countries in the region have moved towards greater democracy, Singapore has been lurching in the opposite direction.[1] As suggested in an earlier chapter, *phobocracy* as "rule by fear" is an apt description of the system of government that has been put in place by the PAP in Singapore. One of the illusory results of this method of governing is a false appearance of law and order. In turn, the reality is a "lawless order" where the Rule of Law is replaced by the rule of man. The implementation of legislation and the pursuit of justice is made to serve whatever purposes the regime may see fit, including the stifling of their political rivals and critics.

Given that the regime in Singapore spends millions of its taxpayers' dollars devising propaganda and providing images for the outside world, there is no need to add to their self-congratulatory chorus here. Indeed, it is more important that the imagery offered by Singapore's government promotes the reputation of the ruling party rather than reveal what the balance of benefits and costs are to Singapore's citizens. Meanwhile, Singapore's PAP regime continues in its campaign to hold critics at bay through a combination of guile and force. Despite remarkable success with promoting domestic prosperity, the loss of the unifying impact of an external threat of communism has unmasked the insecurity of Singapore's regime. Reflecting its own doubts about its ability to maintain power, the leaders of the ruling party have fabricated a set of "Asian values" and declared itself a champion of these ideas.[2] In particular, these "Asian values" betray the regime's hostility towards individual freedoms by portraying them as inducing a corrosive influence upon a stable sense of community. This campaign applies a veneer of neo-Confucian values to justify their autocratic grip on domestic politics. By declaring these values to be those of the nation, the PAP regime has tried to equate moral restraint with political constraint in the eyes of citizens in order to limit their participation in political debate.

Notwithstanding its confused content, the notion of "Asian values" serves the agenda of the ruling party well. One argument is that the cultural essence of Asian societies favors the interests of the collective in place of the individual. In order to exploit the legitimacy derived from the global affinity with democracy, a new model of "communitarian democracy" has been constructed. This softens the otherwise sharp contrast with western forms of democracy with a focus upon individual rights and freedoms. Yet it is chimerical to imagine that abuse of individual rights is consistent with protection of legal rights over property or the enforcement of contracts. Those delivering special favors to particular interest groups possess the same arbitrary ability to remove privileges. In the limit, protection of contracts and property depends upon a deep commitment to individual rights, *per se*. Given the extensive direct and indirect commercial holdings by the government, Singapore's compliant judiciary can be expected to protect the economic interests of the government as reliably as it protects the political *status quo*. Likewise, the lopsided majority in Parliament enables the regime to force through legislation to their own benefit and with a minimal amount of public consultation. For example, in mid-1995 there was a removal of the right for citizens to withdraw their pension funds in their CPF accounts at the age of 55. Little heed was paid to the minimal amount of publicized objections. As in covering most other controversial issues, the *Straits Times* published letters and articles that were mostly supportive of the regime.

Telling the Big Lies: Crime and Justice in Singapore?

Joseph Goebbels stated that the best way to mislead people is to tell a big lie and to repeat it over and over again. It seems that the regime in Singapore has followed this advice well in promoting its squeaky clean image. After nearly 3 decades of rigid single-party rule, Singapore's rulers have successfully sold the world on a variety of really big lies. These lies, so often repeated by unsuspecting journalists or visitors to the Lion City, can be summarized in one sentence, such as follows: "Singapore's independent judiciary provides crucial support for democratic institutions operated by incorruptible public officials who oversee a crime-free community."

It is true that Singapore's performance in some of these categories looks good relative to its neighbors in East Asia. Yet, a close inspection reveals that such assertions are merely self-serving propaganda as a means to rationalize the regime's "soft authoritarianism" to the rest of the world. In all events, Singapore provides a poignant counter-example to the global trend towards increased democracy. There is substantial evidence that the increasingly hard line position of the government will serve the ruling party's interests at the expense of the rest of Singapore's citizens.

Disorder in the Courts

There are several pre-conditions for the success of a state-sponsored lie, whether it be big or small. Perhaps the most important single element is to ensure that the judicial system does not interfere with the plans, programs and policies of the executive branch of the ruling party. In the case of Singapore, this occurs by an interesting sleight of hand. Reflecting a Jekyll and Hyde split, the courts enjoy a reputation for enforcing contracts and protecting property rights, especially when the commercial interests of multinational corporations or other foreign investors are involved. Unfortunately, strict adherence to due process and the Rule of Law is less often applied to domestic political opponents or critics of the regime. The authorities insist that trials are held in open court and that defendants are allowed their choice of legal representatives. However, this is an illusion if one accepts the earlier suggestions that their judges are widely believed to be predisposed to the government's case. Another element of the illusion of blind justice is the practice of allowing Queen's Counsels (QC's), the elite English barristers, to appear in Singapore's courts. According to some QC's, their appearance as highly respected jurists has provided unwarranted credibility to Singapore's legal system.[3]

The Rights of the Accused in Singapore: Bound by Justice?

A particularly disturbing aspect of Singapore's trial system is that "confessions" extracted while in detention tend to be treated by judges as unconditional evidence of guilt.[4] Confessions provide a simple substitute for the lengthy arguments required to establish technical proof of guilt. Now the regime has shifted to a less costly approach for the state while placing enormous burdens upon defendants. A recent ruling by the Court of Criminal Appeals, the highest court in Singapore, radically widened this advantage given to criminal prosecutors. In cases where 2 or more people are jointly accused of a crime, a person can be convicted solely on the confession of the co-defendant.[5] Such a ruling goes even beyond the point where the accused are guilty until proven innocent. In other words, a person can be literally hanged if the co-accused confesses to a crime although there may be no other independent evidence of the guilt of either parties. Apparently, this tendency was implemented after government prosecutors became frustrated by the cumbersome and costly requirements to establish the guilt of an accused. When neither the means of extracting "confessions" nor their accuracy is challenged in the courts, the police are encouraged to elicit them by whatever means are necessary. These problems are exacerbated by the absence of a system of effective checks and balances among the various branches of government.

Another area where due process in Singapore doubtless suffers is from the abolition of the jury system by the regime upon finding its citizenry to be too unpredictable in returning verdicts. Similarly, until an embarrassing and unfavorable ruling against the regime involving one of the very few active opposition politicians, Singaporeans had access to the Privy Council in London that serves as the court of highest appeal for British Commonwealth countries. From 1989, this avenue for appeal arising from disciplinary matters and for cases falling under the Internal Security Act was abolished through amendments to the constitution and Parliamentary actions. Meanwhile, back at home, at least one judge who was foolish enough to issue a decision that went against the government was "penalized" for his judgment. As an additional check against the risks of judicial discretion, the sentences associated with many crimes have already been decided through legislative mandate. With guilt of an accused often pre-determined by the ever zealous constabulary's ability to extract confessions, judges have little input in the process that passes for justice in Singapore.

A change in the schedule of fees associated with court costs has also served to place justice outside the reach of the common citizen. Following the tradition of British courts, Singapore's judges consult with the prosecution and require that the costs of a trial be paid by the loser of a given case. The level of these fees for filing documents and the daily charges for appearing in court is set by judicial decree. These fees were substantially increased in amount by the current Chief Justice, Yong Pung How. At the present high rates, ordinary citizens find it extremely costly to undertake litigation or to defend an accusation in court.

The Emasculation of Singapore's Judiciary

Numerous references to the dubious integrity of Singapore's judiciary are available in print. As mentioned before, Francis Seow has provided extensive commentary on the pliancy of Singapore's judges. His remarks are particularly insightful in that they are drawn from his prior service there as Solicitor General and president of Singapore's Law Society, a group rather like the bar association in the US. His statements have been corroborated in reports by the US State Department on human rights issues which point to the fact that the regime has a near perfect record in winning court cases against its opponents.[6] Asia Watch, part of an international network of human rights organizations, has also published a particularly damning expose of Singapore's different tactics, including references to the complicity of the courts with the PAP's exertion of political control.[7] It might be surprising to many to find that even the New York City Bar Association found the decline of the Rule of Law in Singapore to be serious enough to warrant a lengthy report detailing abuses of executive power.[8] Their report summarizes three main areas of human rights abuses that include the use of the Internal Security Act (ISA) to detain non-violent offenders; institutionalized restrictions on the independence of the judges and lawyers, and restrictions on freedom of speech, association, religion, and the press.

Loyalty to Singapore's ruling party is widespread in other branches of the bureaucracy. This faithfulness of civil servants is prompted by a carrot and stick approach. The "carrot" takes the form of generous sinecures and high salaries for sycophants of the regime. Confusing payoffs for loyalty as rewards for merit allows Singapore's Prime Minister, for example, to be paid more than the combined annual earnings of the heads of government of the USA, Germany, Canada and Great Britain. The "stick" is the fear of reprisal against those who might dare to defy the regime's imposed and enforced consensus. As there is but one level of government, there are no alternatives to joining the PAP if one wishes to be active in public service.

Illusions and Social Control

Another important pre-condition for governments to succeed in telling the really big lies is to exercise control over the media. Success of the regime in this area is especially remarkable since the media at large have been tamed without provoking widespread condemnation of its tactics. The attack on the media then has two prongs. Control over the domestic media arises out of the government monopoly on TV and radio as well as the prohibition of satellite dishes. Although government ownership of the broadcast media is fairly common elsewhere, this practice is reinforced by the regime's tight control over newspapers, publishing, and receipt of external television transmissions.

Apologists for the ruling party often insist that the PAP regime has been returned to power continuously over the past 30 years in "open and free" elections. The element of truth behind this prevarication is swamped by other realities. Singapore's sham democracy is evident in that the exercise of extensive controls over so many important public institutions enables the regime to neutralize political opponents. In turn, there is one element of Singapore's political history that is almost certainly unique. On the basis of court rulings, almost every major political dissident in post-Independence Singapore has been found to be a tax cheat, a reprobate, a liar, a member of some international conspiracy and/or a (bankrupt) libeler. Apparently the only virtuous or capable political figures are members of the ruling party.

The trend of the PAP's declining electoral fortunes speaks volumes about its waning popularity and the level of discontent among Singapore's populace. In 1972, 1976, and 1980, the PAP won every single parliamentary seat. Thereafter, it lost 2 seats in 1982, 1 in 1988, and 4 in 1991, and its share of the total vote has been in steady decline (77.7% in 1980, 64.8% in 1984, 63.1% in 1988, and 61% in 1991).[9] During the presidential poll in August 1993, Ong Teng Cheong won a narrow victory after what can only be termed token opposition.[10] Strict prerequisites for candidacy were imposed that included having held one of several senior public offices, all of which were appointments of the ruling party including cabinet minister, speaker of parliament, and attorney general. It would have been almost impossible for a non-PAP candidate to satisfy this particular requirement. Otherwise, a prospective candidate must have been the chief executive of a private company worth in excess of sixty million dollars. Another layer of the pre-selection of aspiring candidates involved a vetting by a 3 person committee that was made up of 2 government appointees. Only about 400 citizens met the first set of criteria and the applications of 2 opposition politicians were rejected by the screening committee. At the last moment, Mr. Chua Kim Yeow, a non-partisan, retired accountant-general, was coaxed into standing as the opposition candidate against the PAP. During an interview, Mr. Chua proclaimed his opponent to be a "far superior candidate." Notwithstanding his self-effacing remarks and his extremely limited campaign activities, Mr. Chua won over 41% of the votes cast. Uncharacteristically, and in spite of Singapore's faultless high-tech image, the reporting of the results was delayed for nearly 8 hours due to unspecified technical faults.

Attracting only 58% of the vote in the first substantive presidential poll under such loaded conditions can only be seen to be an important indicator of electoral alienation, especially since the PAP leadership made it clear that it expected to win no less than 65% of the votes. The general election of August 1991 resulted in the worst ever showing of voter support for the PAP when it won "only" 67 of the 71 parliamentary seats. Despite winning 40 percent of the vote, the opposition was awarded only 4 seats. The PAP's sustained electoral decline has occurred in spite of conspicuous patronage and cultivation of a carefully groomed elite to insure the permanency of its dominance.

Singapore is often praised for being clean, green and crime-free. However, as economists remind us, benefits always have associated costs. For example, it may be objectively true that Singapore is clean and green, yet the latter claim is more a manipulated perception than a reality. This perception is itself the result of complex control of the flow of information. It may be true that drive-by shootings are unheard of in Singapore. Nonetheless, according to a report of the United Nations, Singapore's account of murders, violent crimes and robberies (59.4 per 100,000) places it above its neighbor, Malaysia (42.2) and even Australia (57.5).[11]

Some casual confirmation of this fact is found in the frequent announcements of canings and hangings in the local newspaper. These reports are meant to reinforce the image of a government commitment to a rigorous maintenance of law and order, and they also provide some cursory statistical confirmation that many more violent crimes are actually committed than is the general impression. This misleading impression stems from the apparently safe streets, especially in the more prosperous areas or in the central business district. In spite of the regime's intractable position on inflicting harsh punishments, there is little evidence that people are dissuaded from their errant ways.

Besides manipulating their criminal statistics, the regime also treats social, economic and political data as state secrets. Those who have tried to construct an independent data set, or to gain access to those data collected by the technocrats hired by the regime, have met either stiff resistance or court actions. In 1993, the government initiated a case against the editor of the *Business Times* and four others who were involved in a report that cited unreleased economic growth figures. The editor, a government official, a journalist, and 2 employees of a securities firm were all found guilty and fined for failing to protect the secrecy of official information. It is a mystery that although it is obvious that data provided by the government are tightly guarded and not subject to independent confirmation, their figures are accepted with remarkably little skepticism by outsiders.

Even the widespread impression of a low income tax rate is illusory since the country's tax system is quite progressive. The top income bracket attracts a 55% tax rate while corporate taxes are a flat 40%, as compared to 17% in Hong Kong. The corporate tax bite in Singapore is relieved somewhat by a liberal deduction policy for corporate expenses that allows cars to be charged off to companies. Since high-level corporate executives have most of their expenses paid in this manner, there is a very large number of luxury vehicles cluttering the streets of Singapore. Similarly, companies often provide their executives with houses and country club membership. Therefore, it is not surprising that expatriate executives expend so little energy finding fault with the political arrangements in Singapore. It would be against their own personal interest to do so if their criticisms led to dismissal or transfer.

Another illusion relates to an impression of the lack of corruption in Singapore that is made more believable on the basis of the dismal experience of many of its neighbors. Nonetheless, overt financial corruption is more than offset by the moral corruption wherein the civil service serves the ruling party rather than the citizenry. Surely, the complicity of the judiciary with the wishes of the regime is a form of corruption. In reality, corruption in Singapore is merely internalized and professionalized through the regime's reliance upon crony capitalism. Nonetheless, those members of the ruling party or officials in the government who have been caught tend to face punishments only slightly more severe than that meted out to teenage vandals. It is difficult to imagine that in spite of the extensiveness of dubious commercial activities in the region and Singapore's wide open financial market, there has never been an accusation or a conviction for money laundering. Following the policy of détente with Burma's tyrannical government, a few companies with suspected ties to the drug lords of the "Golden Triangle" have opened in Singapore.

Having a muzzled media, a mute political opposition, a compliant judiciary and a fiercely loyal group of civil servants makes it easy for the regime to get away with such big lies. Critics of its political system are waved off by the insistence of apologists for the regime that it practices "Asian democracy" driven by "Asian values" that have little concern for individual rights or freedoms.[12] Those who point to the compliance of the judiciary would unavoidably be forced to appear in those same courts.

Thus, paranoiac control over information, rule by fear, the imposition of paternalistic dependency, intimidation of opposition politicians and an effective propaganda campaign allows Singapore's authoritarian-capitalist regime to hide behind an unwarranted pristine image. Informed observers of the reality of life in Singapore would advise others to limit their unreserved praise for its clean streets and little else. Of course, rule by fear is itself an outcome of social construction. The regime uses the specter of impending disaster and crisis should the reins of power be assumed by a party other than the PAP. Officials of the regime constantly point to the potential instability of the region or the possibility of mis-handling of the economy should other leaders be selected. Deputy Prime Minister Lee Hsien Loong has suggested that democratic progress in other Asian countries will lead to sure disaster. "If we follow the examples of South Korea, Taiwan or the Philippines, in the name of democracy and universal values, we shall come to grief."[13] As if reinforcing a sense of conservatism based upon dread of the unknown were not enough, implicit and explicit threats of retaliations against political opponents and critics or disloyal voters also guide the choices of the population.

Singapore's "Total Defense" and Rule by Fear

The imposition of "rule by fear" involves a variety of subtle arrangements. Least visible to outsiders is the striking sense of dependency between ruled and ruler. The formation of this dependency relationship is the outcome of a careful weaving of reality along side fable. This begins with the fact that Singapore's existence as a nation-state is an unnatural outgrowth of a colonial legacy and its peculiar geographic positioning. An immigrant Chinese majority (76%) cohabits a small island with a broadly multicultural populace in the midst of a region otherwise dominated by Malay-speakers who are mostly Muslims.[14] The endemic insecurity arising out of this situation is exploited by Singapore's ruling party, which insists that stability must be maintained at any cost. Delivering this stability has become a preoccupation and a source of credibility for the regime, which it articulates under the concept of "Total Defence." This concept combines the conventional notion of national defense against military invasion with defense against a variety of outside influences that might dissipate the moral, physical or economic strength of the population.

Pursuit of "Total Defence" provides the regime with a justification to impose severe limits upon the choices of citizens. It also reveals a thinly veiled fundamental distrust in the ability of the populace to engage in responsible self-government. Rather than encourage development of mature democratic institutions, the ruling party clings to its monopoly on power through imposition of a hierarchical and paternalistic system of governing. Democracy, Singapore-style, was summarized by National Development Minister Lim Hng Kiang, "you need to trust your leaders to represent your interests and your tastes."[15]

A side-effect of this regime's paternalism is that it has been able to reinforce other layers and sources of fear upon the electorate. Singaporeans are barraged by newspaper stories that discuss the consequences and causes of the deep-seated sense of insecurity known there as *kiasuism*. This term is derived from the widely used Chinese Hokkien dialect, and, translated freely as the "fear of failure," has emerged as a defining element of Singapore's peculiar political culture.[16] Excessive paternalism and its imposition of the demands for conformity have created a political sentiment of detachment and irresponsibility among voters. With the citizenry mired in a deep sense of reliance upon the paternalistic supervision of the regime, there is little room for individual initiative, especially since such behavior is apparently met by greater threats of punishment than promises of reward. For a country with few natural resources other than the talents of its population, there is considerable risk that a cost of the imposition of political stability is an entrenched tendency toward mediocrity. On the one hand, control over the media and information flows allows the ruling party to promote its own successes and to conceal its failures. On the other hand, opponents of the PAP are portrayed as threats to continued stability and security that exacerbate the fragility of the city-state in an uncertain world. Constant reminders of the unquestionable superiority of the current leadership serve to convince the population that their participation in public dialogue is not only unnecessary, but also that citizens do so at their own risk. Strident and aggressive action against opponents to the PAP regime provides ample warning to the voters.

Those citizens who are brave enough to challenge the ruling party in a political contest find themselves the object of a concerted campaign to discredit them. Tactics of intimidation are not reserved solely for opposition politicians. The regime inverts the notion of a democratic election. Plebiscites in Singapore are not a test of the worthiness of politicians to serve the citizens. Instead, they provide an opportunity for the government to discover whether a given constituency is worthy of their virtuous rule. An unworthy electorate that might cast its votes for the opponents of the ruling party is subject to a variety of subtle punishments. Government ownership of the vast bulk of housing along with the extensive intrusion of the ruling party into businesses, infrastructure and the universities provides it with the capacity to inflict considerable pain on those citizens who raise their voice in opposition.

Ironies and Contradictions of Singapore's Nation Building

Encouraged by their success in manipulating and directing economic life since gaining independence from colonial administration, Singapore's ruling mandarins have directed their talents towards "nation-building." Not content with stripping the entrepreneurs of autonomy, the People's Action Party has effectively sought to co-opt, to divert and to dilute political culture. Those unaware of the wily political antics in this single-party state would benefit from a deconstruction of the myths and operative elements revealed in the 1994 National Day celebration. It was a piece of pure (political) theater.

Beyond its pure indulgence as an expression of national pride, the Happening displayed the same sort of organized spontaneity and dubious patriotism witnessed in the aftermath of Kim Il Sung's death. Actually, it was nothing more than the outcome of a synthesis of psychological manipulations that are part of Singapore's "total defence" strategy. Construction of a Singaporean national identity is a crucial element of this strategy.

Dispassionate observers would be forgiven for interpreting the notion of Singapore's nation-building to have arisen from the decisions of a cabal of self-selected rulers. The construction of national images under the guise of an "Asian model" or the promotion of "Asian values," reflects the regime's intention to smuggle its own values into an ethnically diverse community. On one hand, this course of action might be driven by an objective need to cope with a potentially fractious community composed of a rainbow mix of ethnic groups. On the other hand, the regime's assertion of the primacy of a regional set of values reflects its aim to thwart the importation of a set of values that might lead to a demand for greater protection of individual rights and the formation of a truly accountable democratic system. As such, national celebrations and "nation building" become entangled with promoting the consolidation of political power in the hands of the PAP.

On the 29th anniversary of its nationhood and its brief, ill-fated flirtation with the Malaysian Federation, the many years of sustained economic growth provided good reason for celebration. As in the past, the event offered a surreal combination of Busby Berkeley kitsch combined with the orchestrated frenzy of a rally at Nuremberg. However, the character of Singapore's National Day and the identity it celebrates raises some interesting questions.

In the political understanding of the PAP government, Singapore's newly affluent citizens cannot be trusted to form their own identity, neither individually nor collectively. Instead, the government constructs it for them. Just as one-party domination by the PAP was, as the World Bank Report put it, "integral to Singapore's rapid industrialization and growth," so now the state technocracy manages every aspect of Singapore's identity. The aim is to forge, as one National Day song proclaims, "One Nation, One People, One Singapore."

Whatever the intent behind it, the act of engineering a unified Singaporean nationalism involves numerous problems and contradictions. As a multi-ethnic city state dominated by immigrant Chinese amidst an Islamic-Malay world, there is no common mother tongue, no unifying religious beliefs, and, regardless of the regime's insistence to the contrary, nor are there commonly held "Asian values." Undaunted by such heavy constraints, state technocrats single-mindedly pursue nation building and "people bonding." Central to this social engineering is the continuing fiction of an impending external threat to inspire dread among the populace. Whereas threats of a "Red Peril" were an effective means or mobilizing theme for loyal Singaporeans in the 1970's and 1980's, by the 1990s the external threat has become increasingly diffuse. The chosen substitution of images of liberal, Western institutions as the source of potential instability and impending economic decline involves an inherent contradiction in that Singapore's economy is highly dependent upon the investments of Western MNC's.

Alternatively, the PAP might have alluded to the real or imagined threat posed by resurgent Islam in Southeast Asia. Yet, Singapore's geographical location renders this gambit to be much riskier. Faced with the anxieties caused by an otherwise unidentifiable enemy, Singapore's MinDef (Ministry of Defence) has identified what it terms "Five Pillars of Total Defence."

Psychological defense, one of the Five Pillars, was much in evidence in the course of the 1994 National Day rally held before an audience of 70,000 in the National Stadium. A cast of 3,000 performers moved through an elaborate geometric ballet that included flashcards, fireworks and laser technology. The flashlight section of the show involved a carefully choreographed dance routine symbolizing the "cohesive community" that is Singapore. The dancers were dressed as different Asian flowers reflecting the different ethnic communities that were announced to live harmoniously in the tense little island state. Such harmony presumably depends upon "Total Defence" as suggested in the subsequent routine where several hundred "Spiritual Warriors" appeared. Having established the conspicuously xenophobic notion of "Total Defence," a subsequent laser display incoherently depicted a Global City rising like a seagull, reaching out to embrace the same world from which it must be defended. The finale was even more incongruous in its display of an overly made-up 8 year old girl presented seductively on a silver platter singing out "A Better Tomorrow." The song led into a mass tap dance routine as a schizophrenic symbol of the meeting of East and West that culminated in a giant pink birthday cake and fireworks. Then, after a sudden pause, the assembled masses were moved to swear a solemn pledge of group loyalty to the city state.

Apart from its economic success and its *kiasu* (scared to lose) pragmatism, there is little else that unites Singapore's fragmented citizenry. As pragmatism is the only real "value" upheld by all Singaporeans, its National Day celebrations can be seen as a self-serving charade for the praise of the ruling party. In turn, it is this same essential pragmatism that will ultimately undermine the technocratic dream of Singapore's tenuous unity. There can be no doubt that, even with ample evidence of vocal and public support for the ruling party, citizen loyalty to a regime that governs on the basis of fear cannot run very deep.

The dysfunctionality of Singapore's democracy arises out of the contradictions imposed by its authoritarian-capitalist regime. Acts of considerable discouragement for political participation by professional and non-governmental organizations have limited the availability of expertise to opposition parties. While co-opting or destroying the institutions of a civil society may have made it easier to govern in the short run, it has bred a community of uncivil citizens. The insecurity of a *kiasu* culture lies behind the loutish manners that Singaporeans often display at home and abroad as revealed in constant reports in the *Straits Times*. Their boorish behavior is obviously a source of irritation and embarrassment to the political leaders as communicated through frequent public denunciations by officials, or through frequent newspaper commentary. Not surprisingly, there is little voluntarism among Singaporeans in spite of aggressive publicity campaigns to promote charitable works. In short, the PAP regime's imposition of an extreme dependency of citizens upon the state has crippled individual incentives in the same manner as the welfare state distorts economic incentives.

While Singaporean social behavior is a cause of concern for their rulers, the peculiarities of their behavior as economic actors are also notable. During my career as an academic economist, I have relied upon the model of an "economic man" as a classroom tool to explain market behavior. This conceptual construct depicts decision makers as calculating persons who weigh costs and benefits at every margin for every choice. Prior to my assignment to Singapore, even though I found that this was a useful tool for evaluating market behavior, I never encountered a real life counterpart. However, I was amazed to find that Singaporeans behave very much like an "economic man" in that consumption patterns are altered on differentials of a few cents, or jobs changed for a few extra dollars. In Singapore, an inordinate number of decisions seem to be motivated by material considerations to the exclusion of other concerns. The phenomenon of job-hopping has reached epidemic proportion and is the source of worry to business interests as well as the government. Consumers are extremely demanding and brusque, if not rude. Apparently, the creature that economists only conceptualized has been brought to life by the incentive structures and policies implemented by Singapore's regime. Economic man is alive and well in Singapore, and he (she) is not a very nice person to encounter.

Besides a fixation on their economic status, rule by fear and its accompanying dirty tricks have desensitized Singaporeans by hollowing out their spiritual and moral concerns for other members of the community as evident in the transcendent *kiasu* culture. Maybe the best example of this problem is that most Singaporeans appear to be unmoved by the plight of Mr. Chia Thye Poh, Singapore's long suffering political prisoner. There is a conspicuous lack of protest over the fact that he has been detained for over 20 years without having been charged with a crime. Neither has he ever appeared in court even though he continues to have his liberties tightly circumscribed.

No number of assertions about the superiority of an Asian model can resolve these contradictions. The regime's chosen tactics are either to close down debate in public forums or simply be blind to these problems. Either approach is likely to make these problems even more intractable.

Social Engineering and the Crippling of Civil Society

Singapore's social engineers differ from their counterparts in centrally planned economies only in the subtlety of their methods. In both instances, government policies have been aimed at expunging the sense of individuality from members of the larger community. This approach depends upon the forging of myths that promote group or communal consciousness, and replaces the notion of the individual as a bearer of rights. Consequently, rights or freedoms for individuals are allowed only when they advance a grand viewpoint that is constructed and manipulated by the political power structure. Just as in medieval times, man becomes a servant to a higher master, instead of being allowed to confront life as a relatively free agent. Following the lead of the Soviet Union, there are frequent public campaigns to encourage citizens to forgo their individual interests for the collective good.

Social engineering in Singapore involves a complicated set of policies that all serve, by design or chance, to ensure the continued political hegemony of the ruling party. A few of them shall be discussed here. As mentioned above, the ruling party has announced the selection by its own technocrats of a non-sectarian set of "shared values" to "secure social cohesion and collective orientation." Identification of a unique set of "Asian values" followed by Singaporeans is meant to serve as an inoculation against the possibility of outside influences, especially the lure of Western pluralist political systems. This scheme also allowed the government to deflect challenges to its own position by portraying them as challenges to the very core of the values of all Singaporeans. The injection of a set of requisite values into the public consciousness allowed the ruling party to be indistinguishable from the organs of government. In this way it could portray attacks on the PAP as attacks upon Singapore itself. The construction of shared values by the government has allowed it to alter its image of blatant authoritarianism and to replace it by an imposed notion of consensus. This has also combined with a cultivated impression of a move towards a more consultative approach to governing associated with the second generation of leaders.

Another more conspicuous element of social engineering by the PAP is reflected by the dabbling of Lee Kuan Yew in what might be called "pop eugenics." Encouraged by a notion of educational elitism, tax and other incentives, marriage and child-bearing by women with university degrees are encouraged and child-bearing by those with lesser credentials is discouraged. Policies guided by Mr. Lee's simplistic notions also led to the formation of the Social Development Unit (SDU) that served as a match-maker for the more reluctant diploma holders, the Social Development Section that catered to less-educated people, and the Family Services Unit that served members of Singapore's armed forces.

In light of the fact that the government is the principal provider of housing, the most powerful element of social engineering can be found in the ethnic allocation of public living quarters. Although ethnic quotas in the allocation of new housing stock by the Housing Development Board (HDB) had a longer history, they became public knowledge in 1987. The official position on this element of government housing policy is to encourage integration of the culturally diverse population. The political reality is that the government is able to ensure that potential pockets of political dissent do not form along ethnic lines.

In order to help the citizens so that they do not lose sight of the "correct" set of values, the regime also pre-empted the formation of voluntary organizations by setting up state-sponsored associations. In so doing, these actions have stunted the emergence of the elements of a civil society. Included among the para-political institutions are PAP kindergartens, the Community Centres that are coordinated by the PAP as well as Citizens' Consultative Committees and the Residents' Committees.[17] These officially designated "grassroots organizations" were established, and are backed, by the government. The shared philosophy and incestuous association between the PAP with the only legal trade union organization, the National Trade Union Council, have insured political support for the ruling party as well as labor peace. It is a bit far-fetched to imagine that spontaneous initiatives or critical judgments are likely to emerge out of politically constructed organizations that are funded by a government that governs on the basis of intimidation and fear.

An explicit limit upon the truly spontaneous associations has been imposed by a variety of laws or enactments. The so-called Societies Act requires any organization with more than 10 members to register with the government. Meanwhile, speakers at public rallies must first have approval by the police, as must any public assembly that includes more than 5 people. Members of opposition parties have been denied permits to speak at public functions while there is no report of a rejection of applications filed by PAP members.

The discussion in Chapter 1 revealed the general approach and tactics that the PAP imposes to cut off dissent from the university community. This approach has been extended to professional associations as well, as is evident in the government's handling of the Law Society that served as a legal entity to oversee the self-regulation of the legal profession. In 1986, the Law Society dissented to proposed government legislation — the Newspaper and Printing Presses (Amendment) Act — that would impose restrictions on the circulation of foreign publications carrying criticisms of Singapore politics. In retaliation for a dalliance in legislative matters, the Legal Profession (Amendment) Bill forced a change in the leadership and the disciplinary procedures of the Law Society. Henceforth, the Law Society could only comment upon legislative matters when requested by the government to do so. Once again the regime sent a message that only those directly committed to political careers should pass comments upon political matters. Given the rough treatment of those who pass ill judgment upon the regime, their comments had best praise government actions.

No Island Is a Man

It might be useful to digress for a moment to describe Senior Minister Lee Kuan Yew, the founding father of a self-styled Asian authoritarian-capitalist regime in Singapore. His governance of and influence on the island state that he oversees reveals two sides of his ruthlessly efficient abilities.[18] On one hand, Mr. Lee has gained the respect of admirers around the world for overseeing the emergence of one of the world's "miracle economies." During his tenure of office, he oversaw the implementation of capital-friendly policies and shrewd public sector investment in people, as well as in infrastructure, that are credited for raising the per capita income of Singapore to developed country status in the space of less than 30 years. As an English-trained lawyer of considerable mental acumen, he has drawn accolades from friends and has won the respect of his foes. Upon graduating with top honors from Cambridge University in the late-1940's, Mr. Lee returned to his home to become a key figure in the struggle for self determination. A masterly handling of his friends and foes in the independence movement eventually placed him securely at the top of a superbly coordinated and highly disciplined party structure. His strident anti-Communist stance during the Cold War also made him an important figure among grateful Western allies. A considerable part of the successful development of Singapore resulted from Mr. Lee being able to surround himself with a band of skilled technocrats. In exchange for their bureaucratic and technical skills and, more importantly, for their unswerving loyalty, they are paid lavish salaries. This unquestioning sense of allegiance to their strongman-ruler pervades all the organs of government that, while serving the country well, has served to place Mr. Lee in a virtually unassailable position.

On the other hand, as the somewhat benevolent despot of the tiny island-state, Mr. Lee's dominating presence has been marred by a skillfully repressive grip that has effectively stifled the emergence of an effective political opposition. Mr. Lee and the PAP have been remarkably successful in beating back political challengers. As discussed earlier, at least 11 opposition politicians have faced libel proceedings initiated by either Mr. Lee or members of the PAP, many of whom were bankrupted as a result. It would be fair to say that opposition figures have had an unusual lack of success in Singapore's courts. Mr. Lee has been particularly harsh upon those who disappoint him or reject the secure embrace of being part of his inner circle.

Muzzling the Media

By providing a forum for diverse and trenchant views, an open media constitute important components of a civil society. Singapore's ruling party has apparently recognized that unless the media are subject to strict controls, it might undo its political manipulation of the other mediating structures of its political environment. A most unlikely scenario has developed as an outgrowth of the PAP's interactions with the media. The non-titular leader of one of the world's smallest countries has been able to intimidate some of the most influential news media organizations in the world. In so doing, a definite and successful pattern lies behind Mr. Lee's autocratic behavior. He and his associates combine a tight rein on those imprudent enough to oppose him while taming the domestic press and intimidating the international press. Various pieces of legislation empower the government in their battle with the media. Control over the domestic media is legislated through the Newspaper and Printing Presses Act. This law requires that, unlike other publicly traded companies, newspapers must issue both ordinary and management shares.[19] Selection of editors, acquisition of management shares and appointment of the board of directors all require the approval of the Minister of Information, Technology and the Arts (MITA).

A similar set of tactics is in force with respect to the international media. For example, amendments to the Newspaper and Printing Presses Act (1986) allow for the restriction of the circulation of publications that "engage in the domestic politics of Singapore." Perhaps the most effective tactic used to silence their critics in the press is the regime's reliance upon their pliant judges. Given Mr. Lee's distinguished career as a lawyer, it is not surprising that the judicial system plays such an important role in the tactics of his government. Following the fate of opposition politicians, those journalists, publishers or media retailers who displeased the leaders of the ruling party have also suffered under a broad application of Singapore's libel laws. To date, there have been at least 5 different such lawsuits against the media. Clearly, it is impossible for a newspaper or a publisher or a bookseller to vet every word used or every idea expressed in the texts that they handle. Nonetheless, they can be sued when the opinions of one of their authors' works are found to be libelous. Self-censorship emerges as a rational form of protection for the media industry to undertake. The international media who make Singapore their regional printing or distribution center are exposed to the same risks as the domestic media. Additional methods are also available to keep the international media in line. Rather than resort to direct censorship or to block those publications that print critical commentary, the government has launched attacks on the purse strings of its adversaries. As mentioned before, the IHT has had to answer to several lawsuits involving accusations of libel filed in Singapore's courts by Mr. Lee Kuan Yew. It is worrisome that even though these actions affected journalists from some of America's largest papers, there was inadequate coverage on these events in the US and elsewhere. The success of these tactics is evident in that the international media displays an increasing willingness to follow the lead of Singapore's subservient domestic media. Ironically, self-censorship by the international media allows the regime to achieve its goals without having to take more draconian steps that might include detention or arrest of journalists. Restrictive legislation, partial government ownership and the use of libel actions through the compliant court system have led to an exceptionally docile group of newspaper journalists in the face of Singapore's authoritarian-capitalist regime.

A particularly problematic aspect of the failure of some of the Western media to live up to their convictions is that, by backing down before these Asian despots, they offer support to claims that Westerners lack the will to make sacrifices for their beliefs. This is discouraging news to the oppressed who live in hotbeds of repression. If journalists do not seek to protect freedom of speech, then vocal opponents of political oppression have no place to turn to publicize their plight.

Judging from their recent behavior, the international media appear to have no answer to the challenges of Mr. Lee and his PAP comrades. As stated above, the PAP regime has been effective in its cynical policy to impose financial burdens on the owners of those newspapers that condemn Singapore's domestic politics. By giving in to the threats of a despotic government, the international media are abandoning important principles, including freedom of speech and association, which are the underpinning of an autonomous, free press. It is a false tradeoff to jettison such principles in order to protect their short term economic interests. Even if the media are financially sound in the long run, their role as a protector of rights and as agents of change are diluted or totally lost to the general public. By publishing no less than 3 large-print apologies in response to legal complaints about stories that addressed political issues in Singapore during 1994, the *International Herald Tribune* has indicated a willingness to play the game according to rules set by repressive regimes.

It should be clear that Mr. Lee and the PAP regime are determined to take decisive and definitive steps in their pattern of domination over the news media. The years of a hostile and impatient treatment of the PAP's opponents have apparently inspired a self-imposed conspiracy of silence among the news media. Through incremental and persistent harrying of the press, most reports on Singapore have become so uncritical as to appear to be verbatim press releases crafted by Singapore's self-promoting Information Ministry.

Many of the functionaries and leaders of Singapore's government are on record making clear their contempt for the openness of the western media. To preserve their grip on power, they insist that introducing western-style democratic institutions would have a destructive impact upon social cohesion. According to the Singapore Model, Asian democracy does not require individual citizens to have voice in their government or to enjoy more freedom. Restrictions on information flows in general, and the media in particular, are an important element for Singapore's ruling party to impose social control over their fellow citizens.

There are optimists who assume that the "electronic superhighway" provides the vehicle for citizens to be transported towards greater democratic freedoms. While access to the internet does hold considerable promise for the exchange of ideas, there are ways to control this electronic communication. Internet access in Singapore with few exceptions must be through Singapore Telecom, the government telephone monopoly that serves as a local provider of Singnet. This insures that virtually all electronic transmissions can be monitored. With a large stock of national servicemen at their disposal and the active engagement of the youth wing of the PAP on the internet, little is likely to escape the notice of the ruling party.[20]

In order to deflect these insidious influences of the West, the government employs a variety of strategies to restrict media freedom. In light of its credibility as one of the Asian "miracle economies', other Asian countries may seek to emulate Singapore's successes.[21] Countries transitioning from authoritarian socialism are inclined to find the Singapore Model an attractive option. Without doubt, the regimes of Burma, Cambodia, China and Vietnam envy the ability of Singapore's government to govern as a one-party state while delivering economic prosperity. Thus, the affairs of this tiny island-state should interest the rest of the world since they may have an impact far beyond its borders and may affect many more lives than those of its relatively small population.

A decisive element in the campaign of social control is the masterly manipulation of the Rule of Law by Singapore's ruling party. Despite a scrupulous application of laws in the courts, these laws are formulated by an autocratic ruling party. The result is an empty legalism. Following this lead, the regime in China pursues a similar corruption of the law as a means to silence political dissent under the rubric "legal construction." Singapore is an example of a one-party state, without an open and free press, that selectively applies laws against those who challenge the ruling party. Rather than attract headlines by detaining opposition figures, it investigates them for tax offenses or facilitates suits against them for defamation. Mere suggestion of the involvement of members of the ruling party in some impropriety readily invokes a libel suit that government officials are unlikely to lose. This tactic has intimidated and marginalized most opponents of the regime. Smothering the opposition would be difficult without a muzzled domestic press and a relatively tame international press.

Ultimately the aim of social control is to ensure that the dominance of the ruling party is unchallenged. Singapore's neo-Confucian leaders insist that they deserve full respect as well as the automatic loyalty of the citizenry by conducting their duties in a virtuous manner. These political virtues include keeping the peace, providing economic prosperity and not over-burdening the population with taxes. It is notable that there is no reference to advancing or protecting personal freedom.

Whatever the claims of its "virtuous" rule, attacks on freedom of the press by Singapore's regime have earned it a fair amount of external criticism. As mentioned in Chapter 1, several lawsuits have been filed against the *International Herald Tribune* by Mr. Lee Kuan Yew. In August of 1994, Mr. Philip Bowring published a commentary in that newspaper which referred to the existence of dynastic politics in parts of East Asia, including Singapore.[22] The offending passages stated that, "Dynastic politics is evident in 'Communist' China already, as in Singapore, despite official commitments to bureaucratic meritocracy" and also referred to a "battle between the corporatist needs of the state and the interests of the families who operate it." The objective facts are that the younger Lee was elevated to brigadier general at 31 years of age in a peace time army and, as Deputy Prime Minister, he is widely thought to be the heir apparent for leadership. In all events, there are many references to the "Lee dynasty" or to the fact that Lee, the junior, is the prime-minister-in-waiting.[23] The Lees were joined in the lawsuit by Prime Minister Goh Chok Tong, who is apparently seeking to preserve his image as a substantive leader rather than a seat-warmer for the younger Lee. The suit went forward even though the IHT published a groveling apology for printing the reasoned opinion of one of the region's most distinguished journalists.[24] In light of the published expression of contrition, the newspaper had abandoned any means to contest the case, and its counsel appeared in court only to query the size of the eventual awards for damage.

The elder Lee testified in court that he considered the apology to be disingenuous, and he also derided the non-specific nature of its content. This is a remarkable complaint since Mr. Bowring's remarks were not less general and did not mention the Lees by name. Mr. Lee and his son both claim serious injury to their pride and their reputation by what they considered to be unfair attacks upon them. To some, their reaction might appear to be the outcome of a deep sense of political insecurity. However, this would not do justice to the masterful tactics of control applied by Mr. Lee and his followers. Clearly this is all part of a greater scheme to counter-attack their opponents. By choosing those critics whose business affairs place them within the jurisdiction of local courts, Mr. Lee and company engineer the impression that they are treated as undistinguished equals before an impartial system law.

As though to assert a belief that the pen is indeed mightier than the sword, the Prime Minister offered mixed metaphors in an emotional testimony. Mr. Goh intoned that statements associating Singapore with nepotism belittled the many years of effort at creating an image of a corruption-free government. In eloquent terms, the prosecutor likened these few words by Mr. Bowring to a single shot from a gun that wounded 3 of Singapore's top leaders. In spite of these emotional claims about the impact of Mr. Bowring's remarks, everyone familiar with Singapore politics, including most painfully Mr. Goh, knows that he spoke the truth. What transpired was nothing less than a Kafkaesque trial where one can be convicted for repeating the obvious truth. Mr. Goh's attorney insisted that Mr. Bowring's published comments implied that the Prime Minister was "a conspirator, aider, abettor, he is a sycophant, a lapdog… not fit, not competent to run the government."

There is considerable risk in reprinting such statements in the local press in light of the dependency relationship imposed upon Singaporeans and the journalists by the ruling party. Singapore's citizens might be tempted to accept what they were able to read in the *Straits Times* verbatim. Certainly more followed the coverage of the trial than could possibly have read the original article in the IHT that has a circulation of only about 4,000 copies each day.

The outcome of the trial was that the IHT was ordered to pay exemplary damages by the High Court judge, Goh Joon Seng. Prime Minister Goh Chok Tong (no relation to the judge) was awarded the equivalent of about $250,000 while Senior Minister Lee and his son were each awarded the equivalent of about $214,000. Apart from the awards being the highest settlements for libel in Singapore's history, there were several other notable aspects of this trial. First, the plaintiffs used the witness box a soapbox to make political statements. The inconsistent treatment of members of the regime is glaring given that when Dr. Chee Soon Juan attempted to speak in court along similar lines, the judge in his case ruled him out of order. Second, it was most irregular that during the course of the trial, Senior Minister Lee's lawyer mentioned my case as part of his statement. Such observations should have been inadmissible since my article appeared long after Mr. Bowring's and could not be used as a basis for the plaintiff's argument.

These libel actions combined with restrictions on the circulation of the international press are part of a shift in tactics by the regime. The intention behind this campaign is to attack the financial base of media owners rather than to invoke human rights concerns by arresting editors or overtly banning publications. Spokespersons for the regime indicated in court testimony that the high settlement was to serve as an indication that they will impose increasingly heavy costs upon anyone who challenges their authority. Adversaries of the regime were put on notice that they can no longer expect to pay "peanuts" in Singapore when they are forced to appear in their courts before their judges. In setting the exceptional sums awarded in this case, a particularly hypocritical basis for the size of their damage claims was announced. While elsewhere denouncing a decadent trend of litigiousness apparent in other countries, the settlement received by Mr. Jeffrey Archer for about $800,000 in his successful libel case against a London tabloid was cited with great approval by the litigants. Their reference clearly made a favorable impression upon the judge who instructed the IHT to pay about $630,000 in damages to the 3 complainants.

Charges of libel in Singapore have been and are likely to continue to be interpreted liberally and argued by state prosecutors, who, like the judges, have all been appointed by the leaders of the PAP during its uninterrupted administration since 1959. To date, no member of the government has filed a suit against any newspaper or individual for libel outside the confines of their own courts. Unsurprisingly, numerous researchers have raised doubts about the integrity and independence of the judiciary.

Besides libel judgments, newspaper owners' pocketbooks are hit by enforcing limits upon the quantity of issues in circulation ("gazetting") that can be imposed when publications have refused an (unconditional) right of reply to officials in Singapore's government. Insistence by the Singapore government for a right of reply requires that the words of the regime's respondents must appear in print regardless of length or any other editorial considerations. Besides refusal to accept this uncompromising demand, these restrictions might be imposed for any "interference with domestic politics."[25] By running up against the authorities, "gazetting" involves official approval of the number of issues sold and circulating in Singapore.[26] In these cases, there are almost always drastic reductions in the number of the copies that can be placed on sale or are available from subscriptions in Singapore.

There are numerous examples of the bullying of the media. Initially the local press was the target. In 1971, several Singaporean newspaper executives were detained without trial while another local paper was forced to close. Then in 1977, the first of numerous incidents involving the *Far Eastern Economic Review* began with the detention of several of its native Singaporean correspondents. *Time* magazine's circulation numbers were cut from 18,000 to 2,000 for 2 years beginning in October 1986 and have since risen back to about 23,000. Circulation of the *Asian Wall St. Journal* was cut from 5,000 to 400 copies in February 1987 and has recovered to nearly 7,000. Circulation of *Asiaweek* was cut from 11,000 to 500 in October 1987 but has been allowed to grow to 12,000 since then. The *Far Eastern Economic Review* had its circulation cut from 9,000 to 500 issues in December 1987 and currently sells about 4,000 copies. In 1988, *The Economist* chose to close its Singapore offices after its correspondents were denied access to government briefings. Later in 1993, the circulation of *The Economist* was capped at 7,500 copies a week, and it was required to post a security bond of about $125,000 for editing out one sentence of a letter of refutation offered by Singapore's High Commissioner in London. Besides political considerations, a puritanical streak that served as justification for the total banning of *Playboy* and *Hustler* also served as the basis for banning *Cosmopolitan* from Singapore.[27]

A troubling trend of capitulation and latent self-censorship has emerged among the international press operating in East Asia. For example, feeling the sting of these attacks upon it, the IHT has reprinted few of the spate of biting critiques of Singapore's regime by syndicated writers, whereas their columns appear when they address other issues. Several particularly ascerbic articles by William Safire appeared in Singapore's tightly controlled *Straits Times* but *not* in the IHT. One of these condemned the rush to judgment to execute Flor Contemplacion, a Philippine house maid. Another article criticized the decision by Williams College to bestow an honorary doctorate upon Goh Chok Tong. In turn, the treatment of Mr. Safire's columns by the *Straits Times* speaks volumes about its inseparably close connection with the PAP leaders. Apparently, the reprinting of these articles was meant to serve a punchbag for PAP supporters. One has to believe that if William Safire did not exist, the regime would have invented him. He certainly has provided some of the party flacks with ample opportunity to express their loyalty.

Unlike some newspaper editors and publishers, Mr. Safire has refused to shy away from issues that have doubtless raised Mr. Lee's hackles including a reference to the despo-nepotism evident in the PAP government. In a single article, he identified Mr. Lee as a dictator in no uncertain terms, discussed the regime's use of torture, pointed to the corrupt judiciary that takes its orders directly from Mr. Lee, denounced the trampling of the media, and challenged the integrity of Prime Minister Goh.

The atmosphere of fear and dread of the consequences of offending the government is evident in the efforts of a reporter from the *Straits Times* to interview foreign journalists.[28] Of the 30 representatives of the print and electronic media stationed in Singapore, all save two declined to comment on their role as reporters on Singapore and regional affairs. Those who were reluctant to speak did so on orders from their management or did not wish to jeopardize the approval of their press credentials in Singapore. A Japanese press person remarked that "silence is golden in Singapore. But silence is death to journalism."

A new prong in Singapore's attack on the free flow of information has appeared. Visiting journalists now must have special visas since their visits are based upon their work. On the contrary, lawyers or businessmen who visit to hold business meetings or to make business contacts do not face such requirements. Mr. Philip Shenon, a correspondent for the *New York Times*, has been advised that he must meet this requirement. The authorities have refused to renew the employment pass of Mr. Charles Wallace, correspondent for the *Los Angeles Times*. Mr. Ian Stewart, an "uncooperative" freelance journalist for the *South China Morning Post*, who was a resident of Singapore for many years, had to leave when another journalist for the same publication was transferred to Singapore. This hypocritical ruse makes it easy to keep out those journalists whose reporting offends the regime. Journalists who are not circumspect in their judgments of the PAP leaders are almost certain not to receive the required permits.

The combination of intimidating tactics upon individual members of the media, along with costly lawsuits and the direct attacks on media circulation, is having the desired effect. An increasing number of editors advise contributors that articles addressing Singapore must be first be cleared by a battalion of lawyers. Unsurprisingly, few opinion pieces critical of the repressive tactics of the regime are likely to clear such monumental hurdles.

Raising objections to the despotism in this petite country may seem to be a tempest in a teacup. However, Singapore's ruling party has initiated a well-orchestrated campaign to glorify a set of "Asian values" that promote the survival of the ruling party while suppressing the emergence of individual freedoms. Unfortunately, this model is held in great esteem by other repressive leaders in the region. In particular, Singapore's leaders are eagerly sought out for their advice by rulers of the countries transitioning from authoritarian socialism, including those in China. Without protections for freedom of speech in the press, it is certain that abuses of individual rights will go on unabated even as economic growth comes to the rest of East Asia.

Actually Singapore's determined and decisive steps against the media confirm their dread and fear of a free press. If such obliquely negative comments of can prompt such heavy-handed actions, it suggests that this regime fears its days are numbered. Rather than retreat from this Asian tiger, the international media should see that such aggressive posturing conceals a frightened pussycat.

Silencing the political opposition through a clampdown on the media retards the emergence of multi-party politics. Journalists should help widen the political space in such settings and so encourage the development of a civic community in East Asia. Except for the oil-rich states, no other country as rich as Singapore has a government so intolerant of dissent. Surely, after 3 decades of self-rule, the citizens of Singapore deserve better treatment. Perhaps more disturbing is that Singapore's success in silencing the media has provided a model for other emerging Asian economies. In early 1995, Indonesia's ruling party ordered the jailing of several journalists to quiet the nettlesome press corps. In August of 1995, the *Economist* noted that Pakistan's government has begun to apply its libel laws in response to their political critics.[29]

Given the tight legislative control and judicial monitoring of the domestic media, it is unlikely to become a liberalizing force. In his address during the 150th anniversary celebrations for the *Straits Times*, Prime Minister Goh declared that he urged the domestic media "to perpetuate the virtuous cycle of good government, constructive journalism, cohesive society and strong, stable and prosperous Singapore." Nevertheless, it is clear that the expressions of patriotism in the press as measured in terms of support for the current ruling party are the only possible guarantors of continued prosperity.

The historical costs of the absence of the moral force emanating from a free press are striking. Politicians and media moguls reinforced the respectability of Mussolini and Hitler, and their appeasement contributed to the acquisition of the authoritarian grip on power that ravaged Europe. In the case of the Asian Model, it may be true that Asian despots deserve (reserved) praise for overseeing improvements in the material position of its citizenry or for making the trains run on time. Even so, freedom and dignified dissent by the individual are also laudable goals to be promoted.

Western interests in advocating individual rights and democracy in Asia require a concerted effort to unmask the encroaching tyranny supported by the Asian Model. The international media seeking to operate honorably in Asia would do well to remember the words of Benjamin Franklin. If they do not all hang together, they may all hang separately. In reaction to the unreasonable restrictions upon press freedom, perhaps the international media should consider a joint embargo of their publications to Singapore. Businesspersons and others forced to rely upon Singapore's docile local media for their information would be put at a severe disadvantage. Then pressures might be brought to bear in this Jekyll and Hyde land of clean streets and dirty politics.

Political Manifestations of the Singapore Model

Emerging out of the rough and tumble politics of the anti-colonial movement, Lee Kuan Yew and his People's Action Party have developed a unique form of government during its uninterrupted rule. This peculiar mix of strong-arm democracy or *phobocracy* relies upon fear of retribution as the most effective tool of political power and source of social control. Obviously this fear is not only directed toward would-be opponents or actual rivals, but is also directed towards the entire electorate to ensure political support or loyalty. As an illegitimate offspring of democracy, *phobocracy* exhibits many of the ostensible trappings of democracy, including contested elections for parliamentary representatives and a president, as well as an "open" legal system. Behind it all is a subtle and thorough system that politicizes most aspects of Singaporeans' daily life. A report in the *New York Times* stresses the fact that the insecurity afflicts all social classes, including the elite.[30] Ironically, the response of the populace is to become apolitical to avoid the nastiness and "dirty trick" politics of the PAP against its real and imagined opponents.

Phobocracy works so well in Singapore that Mr. Lee and his government wield power from what appears to be an unassailable vantage point. Threats to "punish" voters in constituencies that provide support for opposition candidates have been openly reported in the *Straits Times*.[31] The punishments might take the form of deferred upgrading of government-owned housing or removal of bus routes. Such blandishments would seem trivial were it not for the fact that well over 80% of the population live in public housing.[32] Similarly, in light of the high taxes and duties on automobiles and since nearly all workers live in public housing, they rely almost exclusively upon mass transit facilities.

Another potent element in the success of the regime is the "exit" option taken by many dissidents. Francis Seow and Devan Nair, a former President, and various other defectors from the regime or critics have become exiles. This tactic has also been used to great effect by the Castro regime. A prominent social scientist, A.O. Hirschman, has suggested that there are three basic options available to citizens, i.e., exit, voice or loyalty.[33] Since the regime can effectively muzzle its domestic critics, the only remaining option is loyalty. It is more likely that there is a greatly exaggerated appearance of loyalty.

Criminalizing Political Activity

The government in Singapore has groomed a legal system with the intention of intimidating their critics so as to dissuade involvement in opposition political parties. As described above, the judicial system is rigged to benefit the PAP agenda by limiting the rise of political opposition groups and their ability to rally support around their candidates. These actions have had a disciplining effect upon the populace through the "criminalization of politics."[34] Those foolhardy enough to enter opposition politics face a high probability of finding themselves faced with criminal charges for their actions. It may be true that many other regimes are more brutal in their methods, but few others have been as clinically effective and successful as the ruling party in Singapore. Most of those major opposition figures tried on charges of libel or criminal defamation by members of the ruling party were financially ruined and thus marginalized as credible political figures.

In one extreme case, Mr. Chia Thye Poh, an early ally of the PAP and Lee Kuan Yew in the struggle against the British, spent 23 years in detention under the terms of the Internal Security Act, a relic of the colonial period. To this day, he has never been tried in an open court nor have formal charges ever been filed against him. His imprisonment from 1966 to 1989 was based upon mere suspicion of his communist leanings. It is likely that his release from prison a few weeks before Nelson Mandela's release was timed so that Singapore could avoid the dubious distinction of having the world's longest serving political prisoner. Nonetheless, he was, and continues to be, under house arrest, and is deprived of most of his civil liberties. In more recent years the ISA has seldom been invoked as a means to suppress opposition figures. Instead the government has relied upon more subtle measures and making their opposition behavior seem criminal, the regime is able to deprive from them the status of political martyr.

One such political figure who has been subjected to this criminalization process and relentless persecution is Joshua Jeyaretnam who served for many years as the sole opposition member of parliament.[35] Actions taken against him include libel suits as well as fraud accusations against him both as an individual and as a representative of his political party (the left-of-center Workers' Party). In 1986, he was subjected to an extended commission of inquiry arising from his remarks about the executive branch of government's interference with judicial integrity. In 1987, he was disbarred after being declared unfit by a tribunal headed by Singapore's Chief Justice. Later, his case was heard before the Privy Council in London resulting in a pointed rebuke of the findings in Singapore's courts and advice that he should be re-admitted to the Bar. In response to these findings, the PAP campaigned to portray the Privy Council as an unnecessary legacy of colonialism and moved to abolish access of Singapore's citizens to this court of appeals.

Reflecting again on the case of Mr. Francis Seow, who resigned from his post as Solicitor General, one of the highest ranks in the civil service, he was detained under rough conditions for 72 days when he entered opposition politics and offered his legal services to some political detainees.[36] He was vilified by Mr. Lee and his PAP supporters and badgered by tax officials. Previously, Mr. Devan Nair, despite his credentials as an erstwhile close and loyal colleague of Mr. Lee, was hounded from his position as Singapore's president on rumors of improprieties that were never confirmed by autonomous sources. In light of the actions taken against them, Messrs. Nair and Seow were forced to live as exiles.

Politicizing Criminal Activity

The politicization of crime is part of the wide agenda of the government. Crime enters the political arena to provide the government with a carefully crafted image as protector of the life and property of the citizens. Also, head-lining the real or imagined criminal offenses of foreigners living in Singapore also serves as support for the regime's assertion of superior "Asian values." Widespread reporting on the regime's willingness to impose harsh penalties even for minor crimes was intended to reinforce its tough image both at home and abroad. All these acts should be interpreted as part of a consistent pattern that has region-wide implications.

Perhaps the most celebrated case involved the acts of vandalism by, and subsequent caning of, Michael Fay, an American teenager who lived with his expatriate mother in Singapore. Upon the arrest of Mr. Fay and the others accused in the case, the *Straits Times* published the news in banner headlines that most newspapers reserve for major tragedies or significant affairs of state. Given its image as mouthpiece of the government, the *Straits Times*' collusion with the ruling party is seldom doubted. What became immediately clear was that this case was part of the regime's insistent campaign against the moral defects of the West. While the initial news alleged that those accused were either European or American youths, it was later to be revealed that several Asians were involved. Eventually, the PAP government was able to exploit the case far beyond their apparent intent of damning the corrosive influence of Western culture. Once American politicians became involved, the regime was portrayed as an underdog engaged in a brave struggle against the neo-colonial influences of the world's sole superpower. Ironically, the PAP's apparent willingness to uphold the right of communities to use stiff laws to protect themselves from criminals struck a resonant chord in the US and elsewhere.

Support and approval for the caning of Michael Fay accompanied a debate over the introduction of similar punishments for criminal acts committed in America. However, many observers overlooked some fundamental issues at stake in the case of Michael Fay. Doubts have been raised by Mr. Fay's family as to whether due process was followed. There were powerful suggestions that coercion was applied to extract a "confession," a not uncommon complaint raised by detainees against Singapore's jailers. Furthermore, there seems also to have been some confusion over whether the police purposely allowed for there to be confusion over "plea bargaining." Mr. Fay's parents stated that they were advised that a guilty plea would mean that he would not be caned. According to a report in *The Economist*, one of the accused (another 15 year old American) also confessed after being held for a week *incommunicado*. Upon his release on bail, it was established from passport stamps that he was not even in Singapore at the time of the vandalism. That case was quietly, although begrudgingly, dropped by prosecutors. Few participants in the public debate questioned whether the punishment fit the crime especially when the damage was reparable and the accused were first-time offenders. In all events, the criminal code addressing such actions has been rather subjectively applied. Prior to this well-chronicled case, caning was seldom used as a means of punishment for damage against private property.

Once again, the most fundamental question relates to the rights of the collective community over the individual. Declarations by spokespersons for the government have consistently denounced the individualist-based institutions of the West as a source of moral decay that must be resisted. By asserting that collectivism is a primary "Asian value," the PAP regime provides itself with a convenient argument in support of its autocratic tactics. As public debate and civic discourse are tightly controlled, the final word on the issue is left with spokespersons for the regime alone.

"The courts there would be too incalculable." In a rather obscure manner, Nick Leeson's German attorney, Eberhard Kempf, raised objections to the extradition proceedings initiated by Singapore's authorities. Such an objection confirms the dichotomous image of Singapore's judicial system. On one hand, by following English contract law, its legal system has contributed to Singapore's undeserved reputation as a bastion of capitalism. On the other hand, an equally dismal reputation for twisting the Rule of Law to subvert the civil rights of individuals has earned for Singapore's judges the universal contempt expressed by Herr Kempf.

After a complex manipulation of internal company controls, Mr. Leeson single-handedly did what centuries of wild market swings had been unable to do. After attracting accolades for capturing huge profits, Mr. Leeson's action caused the august Barings Bank to sink under an over-extension of its assets in the arcane market for derivatives. In a move to "save face," and to protect the credibility of its financial markets, Singapore's authorities sought extradition of Mr. Leeson from his haven in Germany. He was summoned to answer charges of fraud said to be committed in the island republic. A substantial body of evidence suggests that he and his lawyers are right to express concern over the fairness of Singapore's court system.

Should the charges of fraud against Mr. Leeson be substantiated, then there is no question that his actions involved a breach of the law in any country. However, his punishment is almost certainly seen by prosecutors and jurists as necessary to preserve Singapore's reputation as a sound financial center. Thus, Mr. Leeson may become a reluctant sacrifice on an altar constructed by Singapore's regime to protect its integrity.

In Mr. Leeson's case, it may be that the rulers of Singapore will try to smother any evidence of the culpability of its own institutions in the tragic events that led to the collapse of Barings. It is widely known that Singaporean exchange authorities were informed of Mr. Leeson's aggressive trading position. Indeed, all the traders in the region dealing with derivatives were aware of what was happening. In turn, Barings executives provided assurance that they held sufficient assets to cover the volume of trading. Now with egg on its face, Singapore's government has been forced to go to great lengths to make Mr. Leeson into a convenient scapegoat for their embarrassment. Once again, the pursuit of a perpetrator of an act, criminal or otherwise, has less to do with justice than with serving the narrow political ends of the ruling party.

In conversations with Mr. Leeson's London-based attorneys, I advised them to mount a vigorous fight against the extradition request to avoid facing Singapore's judges, who are well known for their pro-PAP rulings. Although they did not say as much directly, it was clear that they agreed with my observations. I was told that they were reluctant to "play the human rights card." If the extradition request were granted by the German authorities, it was clear that they feared the regime in Singapore would impose a punitively long sentence in retaliation. In other words, not only was it a foregone conclusion that returning Mr. Leeson to Singapore would result in a conviction, the sentencing would depend upon factors not related to the facts of the case.

Shortly afterwards, the regime acted out its high-handed but spurious sense of justice by executing Flor Contemplacion, a Filipina housemaid. Ms. Contemplacion was accused of murdering another maid by strangulation and drowning the son of the other maid's employer. During her detention, she gave in to her interrogators and finally offered to sign a confession. Prior to the execution, several of her prison mates offered testimony that Flor had been coerced or drugged during her interrogation. One witness testified that she had overheard the father of the dead child revealing that he had killed the maid in a rage over finding his epileptic son to have drowned due to the negligence of his minder. Besides questions concerning the proceedings of Ms. Contemplacion's trial, there were many unanswered questions about her treatment in confinement.

The diplomatic row between Singapore's regime and the Philippine government was intensified after an independent Philippine commission convened. They released a report suggesting that the injuries that led to the other Filipina maid's death could only have been caused by someone stronger than Ms. Contemplacion. After a flurry of recriminations, and several additional post-mortem autopsies, the case was finally put to rest. Both parties agreed to accept the findings of a third party panel of forensic scientists and pathologists, which accepted the original autopsy performed by a team of Singaporean pathologists. Unfortunately, with public attention focused upon these forensic examinations, there were no further discussions or inquiry into the possible coercion of Ms. Contemplacion while she was interrogated, and no inquiry into any mistreatment while she was in prison.

Here again, crime was used for political purposes. The pursuit of her trial by Singapore's regime involved a serious miscalculation on their part, however; it could hardly have gone worse for a partially literate and impoverished domestic servant to be placed in confrontation with Singapore's system of "justice." Upon being assigned a court-appointed lawyer with little criminal trial experience, and facing a pro-prosecution judge, she was found guilty based upon her confession and little more. The father of the dead child was never questioned in court.

Following a request by Philippine authorities to delay Ms. Contemplacion's execution in order to consider newly available evidence, Singapore's officials issued an arrogant refusal. In turn, there was an outpouring of popular outrage among Filipinos against the government of Singapore. The subsequent protests registered by Philippine President Fidel Ramos exposed a serious faultline in the solidarity of ASEAN and reveals the spurious claims for the existence of a set of pan-Asian values. Doubtless, the extradition proceedings for Nick Leeson from Germany will lead to further disclosure of the precarious integrity of Singapore's judicial system.

In all the cases above, the acts of the accused would be considered criminal in most countries. Be that as it may, it is unlikely that any of the five cases involving charges of criminal contempt of court against the media would have been found to have merit in a democracy. These cases all involved the publishing of opinions that found fault with the ruling party. In his summary during my trial, Singapore's Attorney General demanded the imposition of sizable fines to serve as "deterrent charges." Apparently he was expressing frustration by the continual re-emergence of suggestions of the heavy influence of the PAP regime upon Singapore's judges. By insisting that "nothing seems to deter certain people from disparaging the court," he seemed to confirm that the truth will out.

Conclusion

In order to maintain its claim of a "virtuous circle," and to govern without worrying about domestic critics, Singapore's PAP regime has imposed a "vicious cycle" of fear, propaganda and deception. It is noteworthy that they have been especially inventive in their methods and have met with remarkable success. Its idiosyncratic form of democracy (*phobocracy*), replacing rule by consent of the governed with "rule by fear," has relied upon the criminalization of politics and the politicization of crime. The regime has been able to manipulate most of the institutions of a civil society that might have served to limit the intrusion of government into the lives of its citizens. While the local press has been tamed through draconian press laws and indirect control imposed through partial government ownership, a variety of tactics have also been successful in deflecting criticism from the international news media. Costly lawsuits for libel and curtailments of circulation for "unbalanced" reporting have resulted in a cautious approach by editors and contributors of articles that examine Singapore's affairs. Meanwhile, allusions to a mythical set of "Asian values" have been used to justify the wholesale rejection of outside judgments as unwelcome cultural intrusions or inappropriate interference with domestic affairs. The harsh actions taken against the media are a means to a wider and perhaps more ominous end.

Successful pursuit of the PAP's authoritarian-capitalist agenda sends encouraging signals to other regimes that wish to retard further democratic liberalizations in their own countries. Autocrats in the region may seek to follow Singapore's example as a model where economic prosperity and single-party dominance coexist harmoniously. In the absence of outside pressures or the threat of trade sanctions, Indonesian authorities continue a crackdown in East Timor, while closing down periodicals and placing local journalists under arrest. The rulers in Beijing are immune to moral pressure to induce them to discontinue harassment of opposition figures, or to cease the use of forced labor.[37] Meanwhile, conservative nationalists in Japan are able to shape public opinion against national contrition for misdeeds and crimes committed during World War II. There is little reason to expect these groups or governments to act otherwise as long as there is a vacuum in leadership in international affairs.

However, it may turn out that the "Singapore Model" is no model at all.[38] On the one hand, the various factors that combined to generate Singapore's enviable history of economic performance represent a feat that cannot be repeated elsewhere. The initial conditions preceding Singapore's economic takeoff include factors other than its geographic positioning and positive colonial inheritances (dominance of the English language and legal traditions as well as a tradition for honest civil service). Also included were a reasonably equal distribution of income and wealth, relatively high levels of education and training, a high investment rate, and marked increases in labor force participation rates.

On the other hand, increasing fluidity of the international financial market is making it increasingly difficult to attract massive injections of capital for Singapore's export-oriented development policies. Citizens in developing countries in East Asia should hope that their governments look elsewhere when searching for sustainable development strategies. Otherwise, they may find themselves encumbered with the dictates of a political system that retard the development of the sort of political institutions that encourage greater citizen responsibility for their own actions.

Due to the reported successes of Singapore and some of the East Asian countries, as well as the promise of the other emerging economies in the region, the image of an impending "Pacific Century" has become an article of faith. Nonetheless, the observations offered in Chapter 5 suggest that a less optimistic estimation is in order. It is certainly pertinent to examine the implications of the economic and political arrangements of Singapore in this wider, regional context.

Notes

1 An extended study of the experience of East Asian countries with democracy suggests that criticism of Singapore's regime is muted by the strategic importance of access to its ports after the US lost access to Subic Bay in the Philippines. See E. Friedman (ed.), *The Politics of Democratization: Generalizing East Asian Experiences*, Boulder: Westview Press, 1994.

2 In 1991, a "white paper" published by the Ministry of Community Development introduced the notion of "Singapore's Shared Values." The components were (1) nation before community and society above self, (2) family as the basic unit of society, (3) regard and community support for the individual, (4) consensus instead of contention, and (5) racial and religious harmony.

3 A. Jones, "Who Killed Rajan Pillai?" *The Spectator*, July 15, 1995.

4 During 1993, 14 of the 94 complaints of police abuse during investigations were substantiated. The most common form of "soft torture" are sleep deprivation and

aggressive interrogation in super-cooled rooms where the prisoners are either naked or are periodically soaked with water to intensify their discomfort.

5 "Confession of co-accused enough to convict a man," *Straits Times*, February 19, 1994

6 US Department of State, *Country Reports on Human Rights Practices for 1994*. Washington: US Government Printing Office, 1995.

7 *Silencing All Critics*. New York: Asia Watch, 1989.

8 B.S. Frank, J.C. Markowitz, R.B. McKay and K. Roth. "The Decline of the Rule of Law in Singapore and Malaysia," *The Record* (1991, vol. 45, no. 9) New York: Committee on International Human Rights, Association of the Bar of the City of New York.

9 *Political Handbook of the World*, 1993.

10 This election marked the first time that the presidency was more than a ceremonial post. The new duties of the expanded presidency included powers of budgetary review and approval, the responsibility to oversee the countries assets, and the approval of political appointments.

11 *World Competitiveness Report* (1993).

12 Elements of variations on democracy as practiced in Asia are identified by C.D. Neher, "Asian Style Democracy," *Asian Survey* (vol. xxxiv, no. 11) 949-961. These might include a patron-client communitarianism where the individual is subordinate to the group, an emphasis on loyalty to leaders rather than to laws, strict respect for authority and hierarchy, dominant political parties, and a strong state.

13 *Straits Times Weekly*, August 12, 1995, p. 4.

14 Besides the dominant Chinese population, Malays constitute about 15% and Indians about 7% of Singapore's population.

15 "Upgrading: Democracy at Work, Singapore Style," *Straits Times Weekly*, August 5, 1995, p. 2.

16 See D.M. Jones and D. Brown, "Singapore and the Myth of the Liberalizing Middle Class," *Pacific Review* (vol. 7, no. 1) 79-87, and M. Chew, "Human Rights in Singapore: Perceptions and Problems," *Asian Survey* (1994, vol. xxxiv, no. 11) 933-948.

17 M. Hill and L.K. Fee. *The Politics of Nation Building and Citizenship in Singapore*. New York: Routledge, 1995.

18 For a biography of this mercurial personality, see J. Minchin, *No Man Is An Island: A Portrait of Singapore's Lee Kuan Yew*. Sydney: Allen & Unwin, 1990.

19 As it is, Singapore Press Holdings is the only newspaper company.

20 There is a troubling resemblance between the grumbling noises heard in the US Congress about a need for censorship and the announcements of PAP functionaries who offer their rationale for restricting free speech.

21 Responding to claims published in the London *Sunday Times* of impropriety of Malaysian officials in dealings with British firms, Prime Minister Mahathir banned all British firms from bidding on government contracts there.

22 "The Claims About Asian Values Don't Usually Bear Scrutiny," *International Herald Tribune*, 2 August 1994.

23 An entry in the *Political Handbook of the World, 1993* stated, "The 'Lee dynasty' factor continued to dominate Singaporean politics in 1993."

24 The text of the apology is as follows. "The issue of IHT for 2 August contained an article by Philip Bowring on the subject of "Asian Values." The article contained a reference to a "battle between the corporatist needs of the state and the interests of the families who operate it" and "dynastic politics" in Asia and in Singapore. We recognize that this passage meant to readers that Mr. Lee Hsien Loong (currently Deputy Prime Minister and a Cabinet member for 10 years) had been appointed to his present post of Deputy Prime Minister by Mr. Goh Chok Tong (the Prime Minister), and earlier posts of Minister of State and subsequently Minister for Trade and Industry by Mr. Lee Kuan Yew (currently Senior Minister and until November 1990 Prime Minister), *not* (italics in original) on his own merits but purely because he was Mr. Lee Kuan Yew's son; and that there was a battle between the corporatist needs of the state of Singapore and the interests of the Lee family (father and son) who operated it. We admit that these allegations are completely without foundation. We apologize for them without reservation to Prime Minister Goh Chok Tong, Senior Minister Lee Kuan Yew and Deputy Prime Minister Lee Hsien Loong. We undertake not to make further allegations to the same or similar effect." It was accompanied by the signatures of Richard McClean, Publisher; John Vinocur, Executive Editor; and Philip Bowring.

25 In granting the right of an unedited reply to the regime in Singapore, news organizations provide inordinate powers to one of their most strident critics.

26 The following publications continue to be gazetted: *Asian Wall St. Journal*, *Asiaweek*, *The Economist*, *Far Eastern Economic Review* and *Time*.

27 Having a copy of *Playboy* in Singapore is a crime. However, there is virtually no fuss made about prostitution.

28 "Off the Record," *Straits Times*. June 24, 1995.

29 "Anything that Lee Can Do." *The Economist*. August 5, 1995.

30 Kamm, H. "In Prosperous Singapore, Even the Elite are Nervous about Speaking." August 13, 1995.

31 "Vote Will Decide Upgrading Priority," *Straits Times Weekly*. April 18, 1992.

32 Government ownership and control over housing also provided it with the means to dilute ethnic group concentration that might serve as a focal point for organized opposition to its political hegemony.

33 *Exit, Voice, and Loyalty: Response To Decline in Firms, Organizations, and States*. Cambridge, Mass.: Harvard University Press, 1970.

34 These terms are adapted from C. Tremewan, *The Political Economy of Social Control in Singapore*, London: Macmillan, 1994.

35 From 1968 until 1981, the PAP held an absolute parliamentary monopoly. In 1981, Mr. Jeyaretnam became the only non-PAP member of parliament. After the 1992 elections, only 4 of the total of 81 elected representatives were members of opposition parties even though they attracted 40% of the vote.

36 Ironically, Mr. Francis Seow was later to suffer under the system that developed while he served as Solicitor General.

37 From the human rights issue, the use of prison labor by Chinese enterprises provides them with an unfair source of trade advantage.

38 G. Rodan, *The Political Economy of Singapore's Industrialization: National State and International Capital*. Basingstoke: Macmillan, 1989.

Chapter 5

ECONOMIC FRAGILITY AND POLITICAL FAULTLINES ALONG THE PACIFIC RIM

Origins of a Cliché: Images of a "Pacific Century"

During the early 1990's, there was a flood of references to an impending "Pacific Century." On the one hand, a mountain of evidence and anecdotes have been offered to support the projection of the rising fortunes of East Asia. On the other hand, an equally voluminous amount of material has heralded the demise and imminent collapse of the economies and the culture of the West. With little protest and even less introspection about these claims, a new refrain has proclaimed the end of the American Century and its replacement by the Pacific Century.

Journalists, politicians, business leaders, and the general public have been remarkably willing to accept this proclamation despite the paucity of hard documentation. These eager futurologists apparently need reminding that the plural form of anecdote is not "evidence," and a long list of quotations from great figures does not constitute the "truth."[1] Discussion in this chapter will dispute a conventional wisdom on the likely future of economic and political developments in East Asia that has had remarkably few challengers. It should not be surprising that China and Japan will be in the center of the analysis. Japan in particular has pervasive influence upon East Asia since it serves as an economic locomotive for the region, and due to the tendency for its industrial development strategy to be imitated.

Asia's Role in the "Pacific Century"?

At the heart of the discussion of Asian values led by the Singapore School is the presumption that the economic center of gravity is shifting inexorably towards Asia. Even so, predictions of an impending "Pacific Century" remain open to debate.[2] Certain preconditions for the fruition of this rather grand concept should be especially clear. Any claim to a shift of the centrality of global preoccupations from the West to the East depends upon more than convenient references to areas of current economic dynamism. True global leadership must extend well beyond mere economic concerns. This is especially true since economic prowess is made increasingly diffuse due to the growth, and the globalization, of economic activities. Cross-border shifts in capital, technology, information and management skills place enormous pressures upon the leaders of any country seeking to assert their political will, both domestically and internationally.

Whatever its role in the unclear development of the "Pacific Century," there are many factors that limit the prospects of Asia becoming the central focus. This skepticism is driven by a number of ready observations. Dispassionate analysis of the conjuring up of notions of "Asian values" reveals the hollowness of assertions of a homogeneous region that transcends the geographic reference to Asia.[3] It may be true that countries within certain sub-regions may share cultures and underlying values. Be that as it may, regardless of overlapping from religious or ethnic migration, East Asian cultural traditions are considerably different from those in Central Asia and South Asia.

A compelling obstacle to the emergence of Asian-based global leadership is the numerous and diverse sources of instability. Certainly the most critical potential conflicts are found in the apparently irreconcilable tensions between China and Taiwan, and the unresolved rivalries between China and Japan. China's irredentist border disputes with Russia, India and Vietnam mean that most Asian frontiers are in an unsettled and potentially incendiary state. Equally problematic is the issue of Korean reunification, a problem of profoundly different proportions than that of the unification of Germany. Then there are the disputes over the Spratly and Paracel Islands, internal pressures in Indonesia, the continuing instability of Cambodia and Kashmir, political uncertainty in Siberian Russia, and internal disputes over Tibetan independence. It would seem that "pacific" was an unfortunate, and currently inappropriate, aphorism to describe the region that lies along or near the shores of that great ocean.[4]

Prospective leadership among Asian countries is almost certainly limited to that which can be offered by China or Japan, or perhaps through trans-national organizations like ASEAN. Each of these potential sources of leadership exhibits its own set of current problems and unsettled futures. It is obvious that the Japanese have had great difficulty in shaking off the grips of recession in the early 1990's, and the threat of a banking crisis. Similarly, China's uncertain economic and political future in a post-Deng world has preoccupied scholars. However, one limiting aspect of Asian leadership that attracts remarkably little notice is the peculiar combination of xenophobia and racism that exists in many East Asian cultures.[5] Regardless of the calm surface, ethnic and racial animosities are a rampant force throughout most of Asia. In particular, Japan provides a clear example of the maltreatment of minorities based upon institutionalized racially-based judgments that mirror the abhorrent system of apartheid.

Japan's Racial Disharmony

Raising the emotionally charged specter of apartheid outside its original context is almost certain to generate some objections. Surviving victims of that oppressive system of social engineering are right to feel aggrieved by trivialization of their plight and suffering through a tendency to overwork analogies based upon apartheid. In the present case, some Japanese may object that the invocation of such an analogy is an unfair and misinformed assessment of their social arrangements. In all events, apartheid, like fascism, is an odious term often applied to a set of institutions that involve a lesser sense of evil than either of those infamous institutions.

Nonetheless, modern Japan exhibits a variety of legal and social arrangements that bear a disturbing similarity in terms of both cause and consequence relative to apartheid. Given the subtle institutionalization of separatism in Japan, the use of the reference to apartheid as a blunt instrument was purposeful as a means to shock both the Japanese and outsiders into a closer evaluation of Japanese social arrangements. A disinterested consideration of the experiences and life of the minorities living there dispels the cherished myth of Japan as a harmonious community of a homogeneous group of people. On the contrary, even as Japanese-born Koreans have been a particular target of the most pronounced discrimination, members of other ethnic minorities find themselves excluded from the mainstream.

It might be argued that Japan's socio-political system is not as obsessively guided by consciously constructed ethnic and cultural separatist policies as seen in South Africa's. Perhaps Japan's restrictions on minority rights lack the same malice of intent and reflect an evolutionary process that developed over centuries of interactions. However, the Japanese people cannot be absolved of their sins against their resident minorities by asserting that their laws and customs relating to minorities are less invasive or pervasive than South Africa's apartheid system. So the image of Japan's "subtle apartheid" is intended to provide a more complete insight into Japanese culture. Even so, it must be understood that the suggestion of subtlety apparent in Japan's "apartheid" is not meant to imply a lesser impact on its victims. Subtlety as a term of reference here reflects the fact that discrimination against minorities in Japan occurs without the conscious involvement of the perpetrators, or a recognition of its existence by the Japanese or other less involved groups.

An understanding of the arguments offered herein departs from a recognition that apartheid was not merely about racism. For every element of racial superiority underpinning the ideology of South African apartheid, there were equal parts of paternalism that included a concern for order. Japan's "subtle apartheid" has similar constituent elements. On the one hand, many Japanese nationalists are certain of their racial supremacy. On the other hand, the political *status quo* is guided by a Confucian-style of paternalism that places social orderliness at a place of honor in the pantheon of civic virtues. Apparently, Japan's "subtle apartheid" is treated as though it were a necessary feature of ethnic harmony and order.

The establishment of order by any and all means is not a sign of virtuous rule. Perhaps this reveals a flaw in the Asian experiments with democracy. There seems to be a tendency for Asian regimes to avoid the harsh realities of divisive issues in order to create what may be a false impression of harmony. A critical element missing in the public calculus is an acknowledgment of the offsetting costs of the institutionalized methods of discrimination against the Koreans and other ethnic and racial minorities who live in Japan against the presumed benefits of a false sense of ethnic conformity.

Several related points are worth mentioning here. Apartheid, subtle or otherwise, is generated by a sense of hierarchy and driven by a communitarian or collectivist ethic. Were there more appreciation for the rights of individuals, per se, apartheid could never have been enforced. An acceptance of group rights is a necessary, though not sufficient, condition for apartheid to exist. The absence of individualist-based institutions with the support of a Rule of Law is a necessary condition for apartheid-like laws and customs to be able to emerge.

Another point to consider is that the Japanese, and many Asians, seem to consider racism to be the unique domain of a struggle between black and white races, and a problem that does not affect them.[6] There is a tendency to exclude the manifestations of Asian xenophobia and various schemes for cultural protectionism or cultural nepotism as categories distinctly different from what they see as "racism" in the West. The good news is that the forces of modernization may dilute the impulses for institutionalized racial and ethnic separation. Recent developments in post-apartheid South Africa provide considerable support for this optimism. The bad news is that various East Asian regimes have been remarkably successful in implementing policies that delay the impact of modernizing forces.

Apart from the difficulties of coming to terms with their own internal difficulties and treatment of minorities, the official collective amnesia of the Japanese leadership about their actions in World War II remain a bone of contention among their neighbors.[7] While these conditions may undermine or obstruct Japanese hopes of occupying the moral high ground as a leader for the region, there are other circumstances that may weaken their ability to displace the US from its dominant role.

In the unsettled waters of the Sea of Japan and the South China Sea, a strong military leadership is going to continue to be a necessary feature of political dominance in the region. However, efforts by the Japanese to assert their military prowess can be expected to meet with great concern and probably cautionary protest by other regional powers, especially the Chinese. In all events, the necessary amendments to the Japanese constitution to extend or to expand their military commitments would certainly provoke a heated internal dispute. Not even the highly respected commercial prowess of the Japanese economy is solid enough to guarantee a leadership role. Recession in the early 1990's and the fragility of the banking community have been combined with declining yen-based profits for Japanese firms due to rapid appreciation of the currency, a condition which endangers the very foundations of Japan's enviable post-World War II economic record.

China's Fractious Future?

Along the way on its long march toward greater economic prosperity, China faces special problems in terms of a diverse set of fractious political forces. It has often been said that China is a civilization disguised as a state. The inherent weaknesses of Chinese administration are apparent in the inability of the regime to exert centralized control over its far-flung regions. Other indications of centrifugal forces pulling at the central authority in China are evident in the regime's inability to implement a national tax policy as well as overt regional rejection of the various austerity campaigns and the incapacity to control regional corruption. Clearly an inference of a possible breakup of China is based upon several observations of a long-term process.[8]

With the demise of the social contract of the "iron rice bowl" as a basis of support for the central authorities, control from the center is now limited to control over the Peoples' Liberation Army (PLA). While control of the PLA is certainly an important source of power, no government can survive if it depends solely upon the exercise of violence.

Several objections to the suggestion that China might disintegrate can be raised. It would be wrong to dismiss discussion of a possible break-up of China on the grounds that this serves a hidden agenda of "western interests," perhaps as a containment policy. Similarly, a counter-claim could be offered that if a break-up *could* have occurred then it *would* have occurred when morale was at its lowest point after Tiananmen. The Tiananmen Massacre should be seen as just one more step in the loss of legitimacy for the Communist regime. After 1989, many regions have behaved in a successively more independent manner suggesting that China's progression toward break-up is well advanced.

Neither is it adequate to suppose that the numerical dominance of Han Chinese, constituting as they do 90% of the population, serves as an adequate guarantee against a break-up of China. Racial homogeneity simply does not preclude internal strife in China or elsewhere. Civil war is the obvious counter-point, as in Northern Ireland or in nineteenth century America. Assertions of internal racial harmony also ignore historical struggles between the communists and the Chinese Nationalist forces under the Kuomintang (KMT). Just after the collapse of the Empire, China fell apart and developed into separate regions that were united only after successive attempts by the KMT and then the communists. In light of the ongoing general weakening of centralizing authorities, Chinese society appears to be heading back to separate regional development.

There are obvious signs of a weakening of the grip of central control consistent with the break-up scenario considered here. There are reports of piracy in the coastal regions that have implicated the military. At minimum, such behavior implies a collapse in the ability of the Chinese authorities to maintain domestic order. There are similar reports of a widespread increase in warlord activities, one of the most pernicious problems to have plagued inter-war China. Coincidental to the re-emergence of warlords is the abuse of power by municipal and provincial officials. Ready explanations for these turns of events are observable in at least two circumstances. First, regional differences were exacerbated by the uneven development of regions as a result of inefficient economic policies. Second, related to the above, the destabilizing effect of inflation coincidental with current reform is having widely disparate effects, especially upon China's hinterland.

Central planning, with its extensive state intervention in economic and social affairs, is an important cause of uneven regional economic development within China. One considerable element of uneven development arises out of the traditional communist fixation with industrial expansion. While the state generously showered industrializing areas with investment funds, agricultural regions remained underdeveloped. Similarly, regional polarization arose out of the rigidities associated with the monopolistic nature of the communist economy. Unfortunately, resolution of these internal contradictions is not an explicit element of the transition policies.

Peasants were perhaps the most exploited victims of communist-inspired policies. For 30 years, they suffered from low income due to depressed agricultural product prices, and had little access to the social amenities available to urban workers. The broad urban-rural disparity in earnings, incomes, and monetary value of output worsened over time, while peasants' real incomes were either stagnant or fell. Despite reforms in agriculture, collectivist policies have not corrected disparate regional development in China, and have exacerbated regional income differentials. In sum, authoritarian socialist policies not only perpetuated, but also deepened, China's regional divisions. Interest groups are now forming along regional lines in the face of the widening gap in structural underdevelopment. Doubtless, such pressures threaten the continuation of centralized rule in China.

Following the logic offered above, it is inevitable that the transition from a communist, centrally planned economy will lead to further regional redistribution. In reaction to these results, the "losing" regions can be expected to seek the imposition of a heavy tax burden on the regions that are "winners." In spite of significant gains in economic performance, there are still vast numbers of Chinese peasants living in abject poverty who have little hope for respite as the agricultural reform process reaches its limits. Revenues from such a "growth tax" would compensate low growth regions for the disparities in economic success. However, refusal by the high-growth regions to cooperate with all such schemes has already made such tax reform unworkable.

The specter of inflation haunts the Chinese leadership as they seek to reconcile the contradictions arising out of their modernization efforts. Political leaders in China express the same fear and dread of the effects of inflation upon social and political stability as their counterparts in Germany due to shared historical experience. Hyper-inflation is associated with the eventual collapse of the KMT's control over the mainland. More recently, the effects of uncompensated inflation are widely known to have been an important element behind the uprising that lead to the Tiananmen Square massacre. Inflation adds political dynamite to the regional problems, especially in light of the considerable risk of hyper-inflation. The politicization of central banking in China has guaranteed the continuation of substantial subsidies to loss-making state enterprises. In turn, money supply growth continues in an upward spiral that is a central determinant for stimulating inflation. The re-imposition of price controls during July 1994 on various commodities confirmed that political tensions generated by inflation remains a significant source of unresolved conflict. What transpired afterwards was probably the beginning of an inflationary cycle, where early stages of inflation are both a result and later a cause of political instability. Unless the Communist Party officials are willing to privatize or reorganize the heavily subsidized industries, there is little reason to believe that inflation can be brought under control.

In all events, there are ominous signs that power has drifted away from the central communist bureaucracy. Corruption, even among high level party cadres, has reached epidemic proportions. Struggles continue over attempts by the central government to raise its tax base, which is in sharp conflict with provincial authorities who have jealously guarded their own revenues. Imposition of austerity plans has been spasmodic and has impinged upon provincial growth targets, especially in China's coastal region.

To suggest such a cataclysmic event as the breaking up of China (PRC) is undoubtedly a contentious issue. Nevertheless, reflection is the best method to prepare for or to prevent a development of such imponderable consequence. There is substantial evidence that China's long march toward widely shared prosperity might end with a substantially different political geometry than at present. A federal option or a total break-up represent only two possibilities whose probabilities are unknowable.[9]

ASEAN's Place in the Pacific Century

No other nation in East Asia and few multinational organizations are in a position to replace Japan or China in the leadership role that they seem unable to fill. In spite of its long history and projected growth, the Association of South East Asian Nations (ASEAN) provides little assurance in this regard. It is often remarked that the strength of the Association of South East Asian Nations is in summitry. Indeed, summit meetings of ASEAN are normally harmonious affairs rife with public fanfare about their consensus. Beneath all the pomp and circumstance, a steadfast refusal to comment on the internal affairs of their partners is a defining characteristic of ASEAN relations. Apparently, most ASEAN governments consider allowing other regimes to save face to be more important than protecting their own citizens. In all events, given the human rights record of most of these countries, those living in glass houses would be ill-advised not to cast the first stone.

However, as is often the case in interpersonal dealings in Asia, the sense of harmony does not run very deep. A host of problems seethes just beneath the surface. In the case of many East Asian regimes, domestic problems are concealed by an elaborate set of controls implemented by autocratic regimes. The brittle nature of many of these regimes makes it difficult for anyone to pass even the most vague comments upon their activities.

The indifference of some regimes in East Asia to such outrages and crises provides strong support for the perception of the low priority placed upon human life. This observation must be understood in the context of governments ruled by technocrats who impose paternalistic, collectivist ideals which place the interests of the wider community before those of the individual.

Until recently, Singapore and other ASEAN regimes relied upon the image of a communist menace to maintain power. They provided a coherent front that masked repressive means to serve ends that won plaudits from the West. With communism consigned to the dustbin of history, some Asian regimes now justify their rigid authoritarian control by pointing to the threat to their communities from decadent Western influences like democracy and individual rights. Surely, the only certain threat to Asian authoritarian-capitalist regimes from expansion of democratic institutions is the weakening of the iron grip of regimes dominated by one party or a single family.

Meanwhile, West Europeans are vulnerable to criticism for keeping East and Central Europeans at arm's length, especially while Asian economic relations seem to be becoming more inclusive. For example, Vietnam gained membership to ASEAN despite having one of the weakest economies in the region, while Burma is being promoted for membership. Such a comparison is too simplistic. Indeed, establishing free trade among all countries of Europe is desirable. Be that as it may, the European Union (EU) involves a totally different set of commitments among all parties than observed, for example, among ASEAN partners.[10] Joining the EU requires explicit acceptance of a set of shared values and political commitments. Members of the EU accept that others are entitled to apply pressures to ensure that all members live up to these commitments. France and other neighbors would certainly have assisted Germany or insisted upon German actions if vast portions of the Black Forest were aflame, causing regional pollution. ASEAN membership obviously requires no such depth of interaction between or among members. In all events, members of the European Union allow trade with East and Central Europe with few more restrictions than those imposed by ASEAN members on neighboring non-members.

Visible and Invisible Hands in the East Asian Economic Miracle

As pointed out in Chapter 2, a World Bank report published in 1993 applied the term "miracle" in offering an explanation of the sources of the remarkable growth of the high-performing Asian economies (HPAE's). Although this performance is of general interest, it is noteworthy that the Japanese government provided the principal motivation and most of the finances behind the study.[11] For its part, the Japanese government had long been critical of the World Bank's bias in structural adjustment that favored market-based (non-subsidized) lending. Reflecting its own domestic economic policy agenda, the Japanese felt that World Bank credit arrangements should be subordinate to the government interventions dictated by each country's policies for industrial development. In other words, the Japanese felt that their own success with the heavy hand of government intervention provided evidence that government actions are a necessary, though presumably not a sufficient feature of rapid industrial development. Indeed, various agencies of their government have offered their own experiences as a model for other countries to follow. In the eyes of Japanese technocrats, miracles performed in their economy or elsewhere in East Asia were less an act of God and more an act of an enlightened technocracy.

It must have been some disappointment to the Japanese officials involved that the report offered mixed signals on the effectiveness of government intervention. There was a reference to the special role of heavy government intervention in the economy, especially in the cases of Japan, South Korea, and Taiwan. Directing investments towards specific industries that were considered candidates for high growth potential was seen as an important source of job creation in the early development stages of those countries. However, these successes were interpreted as being unique, and there was no suggestion that this constituted a viable option for other countries.

Other equally important policy considerations were also identified as being behind the "miracle." Most important were the ability of these countries to control inflation through a judicious approach to fiscal and monetary policies, as well as by allowing their foreign exchange rates to seek competitive levels. Most of these countries also undertook heavy and sustained investments in education, as well as other aspects of social infrastructure that enhanced the productivity of the work force and the civil service. These expenditures ensured a more equitable distribution of the economic gains referred to as "shared growth." Another feature was the early and continuing emphasis upon manufacturing of export goods to promote growth. Once again, this approach to growth was not offered as a model that should be followed by other developing countries.

Government Intervention Along the Pacific Rim

The World Bank report notwithstanding, no consensus has been formed about the superiority of an "Asian Model" of economic development, whether or not the results are in themselves a miracle. While it is difficult to identify an essential element of this elusive model, perhaps the active role of governments in directing economic policy is the most common element. Arguments that praise government interventions by coordinating investment projects are particularly dubious, however. Among the so-called "miracle economies," there has been a wide range of interventions and promotion policies that have had similarly diverse records of success. While the material successes of rapid development in Southeast Asia cannot be denied, there are strong indicators that this record is soon going to be subjected to daunting challenges. Facing these challenges is especially problematic for the authoritarian-capitalist regimes in the region, which also must confront choices that endanger their continued dominance. Refusal to adapt to the constantly changing realities associated with the new global economy may lead to decreased rates of economic growth and in turn weaken their principal source of political legitimacy. Continued relaxation of government controls over their respective economies shall also undermine their political dominance. The choice is double-edged in that authoritarian-capitalist regimes must either adapt or die. Yet even if they do adapt, they will limit their chances for survival.

An underlying thesis in the above discussion points to the long run interdependency of economic and political freedoms. This interdependency is most evident in the pressing challenge that political leaders face in seeking a balance between policies that aim to support an orderly society while promoting individual freedoms. In the interim, individualist capitalism can be expected to continue in its confrontation with the authoritarian-capitalist regimes of East Asia and its imitators. Those government officials who would seek to imitate the "Asian model" should understand both the nature of its rise and the prospective decline in its credibility. In the end, comparative advantages as the basis for continued growth can be expected to shift towards those countries with responsive institutions and economic arrangements that are attractive to globalized capital. Despite its potent political implications, the most important issue to address is increased flexibility in information as the basis for future production.

Public Policy and the New World Economic Order

Efforts by some US politicians to block ratification of the Uruguay Round of GATT provided evidence that gridlock politics continues to thrive in Washington, DC. Yet there would be reasons for optimism even if the opponents had succeeded to obstruct its passage.

It may be that approval of the measure, and the subsequent formation of the World Trade Organization (WTO), is a clear and welcome signal of an increasingly broad commitment to global free trade. Nonetheless, changing circumstances in the world have rendered attempts by governments to impose protectionist rules upon world trade to be increasingly ineffective, at least in the long run. Meanwhile, the span of time for long-run economic adjustments is shortening. There is also a new and broad consensus forming, whereby political obstructions to trade are seen to be as counter-productive, in that they serve only special interests while imposing costs on the general public.

It is increasingly apparent that a new set of realities defines economic relationships along global lines in a manner that has no historical precedence. Consequently, policies designed to protect local or domestic markets are becoming virtually meaningless as concepts. The internationalization of markets requires an understanding of a new set of political realities. In drafting public policies that affect business decisions, politicians must understand that input and output prices are being set on the world stage in an unprecedented manner.

The start of the latest phase in the globalization of markets began with the European integration process, accompanied by the world-wide response to the liberalization of London's financial market in 1986. International capital flows exploded during the 1980's, whereupon both international portfolio investments (bonds or stocks) and foreign direct investments continue to experience annual growth rates of 25-30%. The economic and political repercussions of the internationalization of capital markets, as well as the increased interdependence of the world's economies brought about by the ready access to technological change, can be interpreted as a "new world economic order" (NWEO).[12]

An important aspect of this new international trading regime is that it reduces the impact of interventionist and protectionist policies. Capital now readily seeps around protectionist barriers. "Foreign" producers can readily endogenize their capital and become "domestic" producers. For example, leading Japanese automobile manufacturers responded to American, and then European Community protectionism by establishing themselves first in the USA and then in the UK. More recently, NEC, a Japanese electronics giant, has relocated a major segment of its computer production to Scotland.

The relocation of productive activities arises out of both push and pull factors. Public policies that reduce operating costs and lessen risks will attract capital. In general, the expanding presence of such arrangements encourages companies to develop into multinational enterprises. As production capacity for these firms becomes planned globally, a large capacity in one region balances production requirements in another.

Although the NWEO limits the impact of economically irrational decisions, efficiency losses will continue to emerge from interventionist policies. The majority of these losses fall upon the most vulnerable and relatively immobile input, labor. The wider information flows that normally follow market expansion will make citizens more aware of the real costs of protectionism. As consumers, they will pay higher prices for a more limited range of goods in protected markets. As workers outside of the protected sector, there will be fewer job opportunities due to the lower purchasing power of consumers. As producers, they face higher input costs when they compete with protected industries for resources.

Most economists acknowledge that protectionism destroys domestic jobs by being inhospitable to capital. Nonetheless, there is widespread confusion, fear and anger among citizens in low-growth, high-unemployment Western economies. With competition in all goods and services markets going global, some politicians in countries in a weak competitive position will promise to create jobs at home by promoting domestic industries. However, the higher visibility of the costs of protectionism to their citizens, and the immediate reactions of investors ensures that any effects of such policy are temporary. In this sense, the NWEO is likely to change the functioning of representatives in very real ways. One beneficial effect is a reduced acceptability of interventionist legislation prompted by demands from special interest groups.

By generally reducing the sphere of interventionist policies, a step is taken towards a form of international "market democracy," wherein consumers express their preferences in an increasingly global marketplace. Wider markets tend to provide every consumer with more choices. They also weaken the impact of interventionist policies, since internationally formed prices cannot be permanently altered by the actions of national governments.

The NWEO also reduces the relevance of formalized agreements for either regional economic integration (free trade areas like ASEAN and NAFTA or common markets like the European Union) or those which broaden global trade (GATT-WTO). It also means that the considerable stress in the negotiations over the Uruguay Round of GATT on international relations can now be avoided. Similarly, it is no longer necessary to waste domestic political capital within the USA, Mexico and Canada during the implementation of NAFTA. Once politicians and diplomats comprehend the ramifications of the NWEO, they can direct their attention to more central issues in such negotiations. The relevant political choices to be made are between self-inflicted stagnation under protectionism and a sustained economic growth from ever-widening trade and capital flows.

Politicians or producers who ignore global economic forces are likely to find their policies doomed to failure. Protectionist policies may raise economic growth in the short or medium terms before gains in one sector are offset by losses in others. The adage that "all politics are local" may still be true. However, the NWEO dictates that, in order to ensure continued economic growth and prosperity, in the future, politicians must understand that "all business is global."

Shifting Capital Flows in the 1990's

Volatility in Asian emerging markets in the beginning of 1994 provides a strong signal of a wider trend. The simple fact is that much of the glamor and high returns are rapidly disappearing in East Asia, inducing international investors to look elsewhere for higher returns. This turn of events has crucial implications for Singapore, as it is more dependent on foreign capital investment than most other economies in the region. Market fundamentals have shifted in favor of other regions, such that the economies of East and Central Europe (ECE) and Latin America are poised to become the focus of new attention. The following remarks point to a variety of elements which point to specific elements of the shift of comparative advantage from East and Southeast Asia toward East and Central Europe, perhaps most especially for Western-based investors.

Pull Factors for Future Flows of Capital to Other Regions

1. *"Clean slate" of institutions during their transformation process.* The political leaders can be expected to avoid failures by imitating development models with proven track records.
2. *Highly skilled (surplus) labor.* ECE has a particularly promising combination of high productivity and relatively low real wages.
3. *More ready geographic access to mature (import-oriented) markets.* The markets of North America and Western Europe have institutional arrangements to slot in the developing economies of Latin America and ECE respectively.
4. *Fewer cultural differences for Western investors to reconcile than exist in other areas.* Both ECE and Latin America possess a distinct advantage by sharing European traditions and historical links.
5. *Essential qualities of "true" entrepreneurs are more consistent with Western political and cultural institutions.* Entrepreneurs tend to be iconoclastic in nature and exhibit a willingness to challenge the *status quo*, including government authority. Most Western institutions are premised upon and often offer rewards for individualistic behavior that lead to a readiness to be risk takers.
6. *Benefits from reverse brain drain.* The ECE countries are presently recipients of net inflows of émigrés with well-developed management/financial skills and with established business contacts outside the region. As a consequence, they have a readily available quantity of skilled managers with similar cultural and ethnic backgrounds to guide highly skilled workforces.
7. *Disposition to openness and ready access to economic data.* It can be expected that there will be a continued distrust of control over economic data and other aspects of civil society reminiscent of the communist era.
8. *Success depends upon market responses.* Merit and the capacity to meet requirements of consumers in a competitive market are principal avenues

for success. Positive-sum outcomes are possible where consumers are better off in that anguished competitors can seek alternative openings in other markets.

9. *Investment opportunities from privatization.* Many state-owned enterprises in Latin American and Europe continue to be available for sale.

Problems with Future Capital Investment in East Asia

1. *Commitment to present political order.* Political hubris and authoritarian tendencies are likely to lead to a static set of political arrangements along with an inflexibility and lack of eagerness to adapt to new institutions. The certainties arising from prevalence of one-party dominance of the polity are offset by rigidity and reluctance to change.
2. *Labor market shortages.* Many Asian economies tend to suffer from a lack of both skilled labor and managers. As a consequence, real wages can be expected to rise, causing a shift in comparative advantage.
3. *High likelihood of trade frictions and disputes.* Absence of reciprocal trade practices due to an instinctive tendency to exercise control over economic and political matters can be expected to lead to disagreements over commercial practices.
4. *Cultural differences.* Confucian values, hierarchical governance, traditional institutions and authoritarian tendencies complicate discussion of commercial and human rights issues.
5. *Tendency for governments to set conditions for commercial success.* In many instances, commercial activity tends to be determined by access to special arrangements (*guanxi*) and crony capitalism. Where this exists, there is likely to be endemic corruption.
6. *Problems arising from continued brain drain.* The absence of individual freedom induces free thinkers to seek free environments.
7. *Tendency to restrict access to economic data.* Official control over access to economic statistics impedes meaningful debate over the future of economic development.
8. *Success may depend upon collusive arrangements with government officials.* Monopoly privileges and exclusive, special treatment close off opportunities to other producers. These zero-sum games tend to drive up costs and prices.
9. *Little effort to privatize in East Asia.* Fewer investment opportunities since privatization schemes are not well advanced in the region.

In considering the above, there was no intention to compose an exhaustive list of the sources of comparative advantage. Given the proper circumstances, rapid shifts in global dynamics can eliminate or accentuate any of those indicated to favor or disfavor countries in a particular region. Singapore's heavy dependency on foreign investment (75% of total investment) makes it particularly vulnerable to the shifting whims of international capital. If foreign investment undergoes a significant decline, Singapore will face higher costs in terms of domestic resources in order to move into higher value-added production. It will also push the time horizon for the technological upgrading further into the future.

Economic Limits upon Political Stability

In general, East Asian economies are confronted with a number of structural weaknesses. This list need not be taken as a prognostication of dramatic reversal in the fortunes of the region. Nonetheless, these issues can be expected to impose constraints on their ability to continue such high rates of economic growth. Since governments in the region must deliver continued economic prosperity as the basis for their political survival, these issues are of considerable interest.

Continuation of economic growth will be hampered until the infrastructural weaknesses that exist in many of the countries are remedied. Regardless of their great potential, China and Vietnam have poor internal communication and transportation facilities. These facilities are crucial both for the development of their own domestic markets and for foreigners to have access to their consumers.

East Asian exports are in narrow product lines that are not included among the necessities of life (e.g., food and energy). Therefore, there will be enormous pressure to operate with greater flexibility in response to uncertain demand. For example, Japanese exports are heavily concentrated in consumer electronics and automobiles. The economies of other countries in the region export similar or even less sophisticated products. As markets become saturated with durable consumer items, much of the export production will then rely upon the replacement market. In order to broaden their economic base, East Asian economies must develop a capacity to export their services. Political arrangements in many of these countries place hindrances upon information flows.

Similarly, export markets for the region are very thin, as evident in their heavy dependence upon access to sales in advanced industrialized economies, especially North America. While Japan has provided impetus for growth in production, the demand for the output depends heavily upon the fortunes of North America and Europe. Even though there is an increasingly lesser likelihood for the imposition of trade-impeding protectionist policies, there are risks of mis-managing trade relations. This is apparent in the disregard exhibited by many of the regimes in the region for human rights, a problem that is becoming increasingly intractable.

Most East Asian economies are heavily dependent upon imported raw materials, including energy, and will remain so for the medium term. There are considerable regional resources, especially oil in the South China Sea and in Siberian Russia. Development of these reserves will continue to be restrained by internal political instability and international disputes. Even though there is an abundance of cheap labor in many of the countries, there is a shortage of skilled labor. As these shortages drive up wages in the more advanced economies of the region, they will lose a principal source of comparative advantage. Up to now, Japan's economy, and those of most of the mini-dragons, has handled difficult situations reasonably well with a dearth in their endowment of natural resources. Nevertheless, as new emerging markets come on line, the competition for critical resources will become increasingly acute.

As mentioned previously, institutional deficiencies are generating inhibitions upon original research produced in the region. Consequently, there is dependency for access to technological innovations in many fields. Japan may lead the world in the filing of new patents, but most of these are in a few fields and are the outcome of industrial research. Much of Western technology arises out of independent research institutes or universities and covers a wider range of fields. This dilemma may be resolved by noting that even though most Asians hold education in high regard, most schooling there is based upon rote learning. An imposed set of hierarchical structures also inhibits free thinking and the challenging of received wisdom that might generate new ideas or approaches. Those contributions that have emerged from East Asia are in narrowly focused areas.

Another area of potential difficulty for East Asian economies is found in the effect of hierarchical tendencies upon the operation of firms. A contrast with the recent successes in the West, America in particular, might be in order. Most of the growth in US productive capacity and employment has been derived from the formation of independent, small and medium sized enterprises (SME's). An opposite set of forces is at work in Japan, where the prevalence of large industrial groups (*keiretsu*) drives the formation of SME's and binds them in long term contracts. About four out of every five workers in Japan are employed by SME's that, in turn, produce about two-thirds of total output. Consequently, due to the nature of their relationships with the *keiretsu*, Japanese SME's have considerably less flexibility, are less able to source cheaper inputs, and are not free to develop their own new markets. This approach to production will spread as Japan's large firms move to offshore locations in the region, and so will the associated inflexibility.

The arguments in the above section indicate how social conventions can affect economic activity. We have already discussed the use of illusion and the adherence to face saving in challenging some of the images created by the regime in Singapore, and observed that many other Asian countries exhibit similar patterns of social behavior. A provocative analysis of Japanese production techniques has challenged the impression of high quality Japanese products by offering substantial evidence and argumentation that indicates the contrary.[13] After living in Japan while working at a research institute, the authors found that Japanese culture reinforces the importance of images over reality, impressions over substance. As an expert in industrial engineering and quality control, one author of the study points to numerous contradictions in the obvious lack of quality in products, especially those consumed in Japan. Perhaps the most noteworthy observation is that in 1993, Hondas were nearly 13 times more likely to be recalled than were General Motors cars. In summary, the myths of quality in Japanese products are promoted by the exaggerations of Japanese politicians, the media, and business executives while consumers played into the charade. This problem is compounded by public reinforcements. For example, American automobile makers are 6 times more likely to make a public announcement of their recalls than their Japanese counterparts. It appears that the hopes of Japan's producers to remain viable competitors depend upon maintaining these illusions of the superior quality of Japanese products. Should this illusion disappear, the economic vitality of the whole region will be shaken.

There is no intention here to assert that any of these faults on their own, or in combination, will halt the steady march towards modernization of this dynamic region. The level of expectations of Asians has been raised by the early successes of their neighbors, and they can be expected to strive towards moving up the economic ladder. In the end, the inability of governments to meet the expectations of their eager citizens may be expected to lead to a transformation of East Asia's political landscape that would equal its rapid pace of economic transformation.

Political Limits to Economic Developments: A Skeptical Note on the "Pacific Century"

Commentators in both the East and the West offer projections of an approaching "Pacific Century" with a mix of enthusiasm and gloom. Their perceptions converge in an assumption of the inexorable rise of Pacific Basin economies, such that they become the new economic center of gravity. However, this observation may be based upon a set of dubious premises. While the material advance of developing economies in this broad region is welcome news, there are various weaknesses in the underlying assumptions of the anticipated dominance of the Asian dragons and tigers into the next century. It is of no small consequence that the manipulation of this idealized view of the future for narrow political purposes may unnecessarily spark inter-regional tensions.

On the one hand, more than a few of the "optimists" who offer images of an impending "Pacific Century" are apologists for despotic regimes in Asia. Posing as promoters of certain "Asian" values that they deem to be superior, they rail against decadent western values of individualism and liberalism. Material advancement is offered as an indisputable justification for the literal or figurative imprisonment of their citizenry. Ironically, this optimistic chorus often hails the arrival of an Asian Renaissance. In so doing, they overlook the implications that this metaphor suggests an advancement from a dark age of despotism and misery similar to that experienced in pre-Renaissance Europe. It remains unclear whether the appropriate interpretation of this "renaissance" is a projection into a future without the current repressive regimes, or is a commentary on their own slow progress from a now-distant escape from colonialism. Neither case is an especially flattering interpretation.

On the other hand, protectionist-minded "pessimists" in the West evoke a dreaded image of the calcification of the industrialized world, forecasting it as being unable to compete with the labor-surplus conditions and market-friendly policies of developing countries in East Asia. This viewpoint incites an adversarial atmosphere and, by so doing, encourages the costly imposition of restrictions on international trade flows. Interventions in international trade continue to have political currency, even though there is a wide understanding that protectionism imposes costs on the wider population of consumers and taxpayers in order to confer benefits upon specific groups of producers and workers.

Among the optimists and the pessimists are those who regard the future as simply an extrapolation of current trends. In such a viewpoint, the enviable economic growth rates in parts of Asia are taken to be a reliable harbinger of the future. However, rigid thinking along these lines implies an image of the future that is built upon shaky foundations. To be prepared for the next century, regardless of geographic focus, static models of unchanging conditions must be rejected. The globalization of commerce along with the high degree of fluidity in capital markets requires that policy makers must address the need for responsiveness and flexibility to an unknowable future. Only those models that incorporate an element of the dynamics of long run adjustments offer useful insights. There can be no living on one's laurels in the new global market place.

Some of the regimes in the Pacific Basin might be tempted to assume that their recent material progress is the consequence of some immutable set of circumstances, including the political *status quo*. Nonetheless, this self-serving myopia overlooks the impact of a frozen set of political institutions where, for example, one-party or one-family regimes control political arrangements in many Southeast Asian countries. More generally, many Asian regimes are combining their own peculiar combination of economic decentralization with political centralization under the authoritarian-capitalist model.

Authoritarianism too often provides a misleading impression of political stability. In the long run, economic growth and progress are served by the mediating influences of non-governmental institutions and the conversation emerging from civil society. Such arrangements are necessary features which counterbalance the governing elite, preventing it from dominating and atomizing the rest of the community. Contrary to more open societies, authoritarian-capitalist regimes impose a paranoiac control over interpersonal communication and the flow of information. These controls obviate independent corroboration of data and discourage the formulation of new ideas that might challenge the enforced orthodoxy of the regime.

Such restrictive arrangements are almost certain to curtail the potential for economic growth. Survival of authoritarian-capitalist regimes depends upon strict social controls to ensure that any political opposition remains diffuse and marginalized. Similarly, interventions into domestic commerce demand that only trusted party sycophants have access to economic power. As private property rights and contractual arrangements are weakened by the prevalence of "rule by rulers," instead of the rule of law, "lawless order" masquerades as law and order. In the end, a system built upon party patronage must face the looming specter of political corruption, along with accompanying contradictory impulses and uncertain incentive structures. These arrangements can only yield a bitter harvest. Keeping citizens in line through a "rule by fear" is an unstable political equilibrium. Autocratic regimes cannot hope to inspire deep loyalty even if public support appears to be vocal and spirited.

In order to maintain power, and faced with the absence of loyal support derived from open democratic rule, these regimes find it increasingly costly to buy out or to co-opt the middle class. Overly-generous compensation to encourage the loyalty of civil servants also has its limits, especially if it distracts the educated elite from entering into more productive activities. Following this strategy is likely to result in the homegrown entrepreneur becoming an endangered species. True entrepreneurs are able to make their own market niches without entering into a symbiotic dependency with governments. These individuals are the promoters of progress and growth.

Governments can only approximate or pretend to fill this role, since the necessary attributes of entrepreneurship go beyond the mere instinct to buy low and sell high. Entrepreneurs spark economic growth through a characteristic contrarian nature. Their market positions are made through a drive to upset the *status quo*, whether this means challenging market leaders or government officials. By choking off the atmosphere for free thinkers, authoritarian regimes will encourage a brain-drain and discourage the emergence of homegrown entrepreneurs.

Aside from "frozen politics," several other institutional arrangements also impose limits on the bright prospects of continued Asian development. For example, *guanxi* is a widely acclaimed set of informal social networks and contacts that is practiced, and its importance is underlined in most business settings where Chinese traders dominate. These complex inter-relationships often have a basis in an intertwined set of political and family connections. By most accounts, these are an all-important element in carrying out successful business transactions in Asia and elsewhere. Whatever its presumed value to individuals, as was discussed in a previous chapter, this ancient system is little more that a zero-sum redistributive game. As elsewhere, individuals and, more likely in the Asian context, families may extract large benefits through privileged access to or contacts with bureaucracies or suppliers.

Eventually the limit to the advantages of *guanxi* is reached since a multiplicity of contracts cannot all be supported by carefully nurtured arrangements. In simple terms, the costs of nurturing begin to outweigh the benefits derived from the relationship. Such networks become less important when there is greater transparency of contracts and contacts.

Ironically, *guanxi* involves several sources of internal contradiction. If access is too exclusive, then there is little incentive for outsiders to endeavor to penetrate a market. However, an extension of the existing *guanxi* arrangements to accommodate newcomers, deflates its value to each and all. Perhaps worse, if government officials try to enlarge the sphere of activities that require *guanxi*, this will lead to an increasing loss of efficiency that makes outside investment less attractive. Similarly, as these arrangements are informal, or at least outside of the law, they cannot be expected to be stable since no legal protections are available to aggrieved parties.

A significant problem here is that the modern global economy seems to be destined to rely heavily upon judicial enforcement of contract law and the protection of property rights. Transparency of contracts within a judicial system that offers protection to individual contract parties is certain to become an increasingly important determinant of comparative advantage. Western contract law is grounded in a determination to protect individual interests in economic, as well as political, arrangements. In general, moves by Asian authoritarian-capitalist regimes to de-emphasize the importance of individuals have the strong potential to hinder economic opportunities. In the absence of individualist-based economic institutions, outsiders are more likely to be obliged to consort with commercial elites whose economic influence contributes to an inefficient oligopolistic market structure. Crony capitalism, with its reliance upon ersatz entrepreneurs who cut shady deals with a corruptible government, is a poor substitute for the innovative undertakings of "true" entrepreneurs.

Reliance upon "Asian values" does not seem to be have been enough to stem rampant corruption in most countries in the region.[14] Endemic corruption is worst among emerging economies in Asia, but even South Korea and Japan face enormous problems. In a recent survey of the perceptions of persons involved in international commerce, Singapore rated highest among other Asian states in terms of ratings by foreign managers in terms of perceived corruption, only ranking below New Zealand and Denmark. Yet one has to wonder if the perceptions and definitions of corruption as they pertain to Singapore are too narrow. Surely corruption should include other abuses of power beyond the problem of simple bribery or fraud by politicians or bureaucrats. Doubtless many respondents have overlooked the often repeated evidence of the dependency relationships of various organs of government to the ruling party that would be an important indicator of corruption. For example, testimony from independent sources provides some evidence of the compliance of their judicial systems. Some of these sources have been cited above and include the English Privy Council, the US Department of State, the New York City Bar Association, AsiaWatch, and, most recently, Mr. Alan Jones, member of the Queen's Council. Some might also find it corrupt that the ruling party can pass astronomical pay increases to high ranking elected officials with virtually no public debate. Similarly, decisions made over the disbursement of the mandatory pension contributions to the CPF and the use of these funds are closed to public scrutiny. Eventually, the political costs of corruption can include the collapse of ruling coalitions, as experienced several times in Japan, which is ranked at about the same level as Singapore.

Obviously, it is important for these governments to control perceptions about the extent of corruption. It is in this area that the tradition of "saving face" becomes important in deceiving voters as well as prospective investors. By promoting consensus and limiting dissent, it is easier for leaders and entire governments to hide their failures. It is especially ironic that the World Bank report on the "miracle economies" of East Asia pointed to the "relative lack of corruptibility of the public administrations in Japan and Korea" given the numerous and widely reported scandals involving corruption. Differences in perception and reality involve the imposition of high economic costs for high corruption countries in putting a brake on their growth prospects by reducing the profitability of engaging in clean business activities.

On the one hand, economic growth is encouraged through a selective but extensive scope of market interventions at the micro level, while at the macro level the economy is prodded to follow export-oriented policies that are supported by massive infusions of inputs of capital and labor that cannot be repeated. On the other hand, authoritarian restrictions on political discourse stand in sharp relief against the impression of wide-ranging economic freedoms. Political stability becomes a codeword for thwarting challenges to the primacy of the ruling party. Where support is prompted by the promise of continued prosperity or stability, critics of the government are marginalized or eliminated. Most of these regimes offer a thin veneer of "democracy" in order to appear to be credible to outside parties. In the absence of a civil society, political conversation is reduced to a monologue of petty despots guided and supported by technocrats whose loyalty is as important as their skills.

It is far from clear that the social and political control imposed by authoritarian-capitalist regimes constitutes an equilibrium arrangement. Perhaps the end result of democratic reforms is that archaic institutions will be swept aside through the choices of individuals whether their origins are Asian or European. It is possible the eventual set of institutions will be distinctly different to any of those that currently exist. On the one hand, despots and autocrats are mortal. On the other hand, the effects of modernizing influences associated with economic prosperity provide a potential means to weaken their grip on power. It may be possible that Singapore's leaders can avoid some of the increasingly complicated political issues associated with the processes of modernization. The problem is that it may be just as likely that Singapore's rapid spurt of economic growth is little different from that experienced by postwar Germany and Japan or even Soviet development in its earlier stages.

Several Asian institutions share the dubious distinction of exhibiting an inherent tendency to stifle the driving forces of economic development. This may seem to be a preposterous claim in light of the recent record of the "miracle economies" of East Asia, but there are good reasons to believe that long-run adjustments may reverse the fortunes of those Asian tigers and dragons that are ruled by authoritarian-capitalist regimes. These institutional arrangements are associated with, but not limited to, corruption, the prevalence of crony capitalism and the institutional bias in Asian authoritarian-capitalist regimes against individualism. Historically, certain aspects of Asian cultures have engendered institutional arrangements that stifle the enterprising spirit underpinning the innovative process necessary to spark and to sustain economic growth. For example, the Schumputerian process of "creative destruction" depends upon several layers of commercial and managerial activity. At the highest level are entrepreneurs who through their contrarian behavior stir economic and social progress. They undertake actions that others fail to see as profit-generating opportunities and by so doing make their way in life by upsetting the *status quo*. A lower level of activity is undertaken by management administrators who merely implement or follow rules in the operation of a business enterprise. Such management administrators seek their rewards through their knowledge of rules rather than their expertise or success as an innovator.

Under crony capitalism, those who rise to the top of an organization and are careful not to offend the ruling party can expect to have secure positions. Their incentive structure is related to maintaining the *status quo*. Even in Japan, lacking the pressure of outside directors, presidents of corporations exercise autocratic powers, allowing them to survive even in the face of plunging profits. What emerges is a hierarchical, top-down decision-making managerial authoritarianism whereby top managers are increasingly remote from their workers. While the detachment of top level managers from production lines and lower level managers might be expected to result in increased internal frictions, the insularity of authoritarian managers is not confined to internal dynamics. There is also a likelihood for the development of insensitivity to the market that prefaces a decline in the status of the firm as business opportunities are missed.

True entrepreneurs, by contrast, concern themselves with front-line operations and are poised to take risks. As a necessary feature of their actions, entrepreneurs open opportunities for themselves by upsetting the existing market arrangements and exploiting the situation to their advantage. Many Asian institutions weaken the payoff for entrepreneurial activities while rewarding a more conservative managerial style. There is no doubt that a "parasite economy" can generate economic growth through encouraging technology transfers and by attracting multinational investments. The real question boils down to whether such high rates of economic growth can be sustained. There are several restrictive factors in these cases, one of which presupposes a continuing technological gap emerging from a dependence upon technology transfers. As suggested above, another question arises as to whether economic growth can continue without homegrown entrepreneurs whose presence is a necessary basis for continued economic dynamism.

While promoters of the "New Asian Model" seem to have grasped some understanding of economic mechanics, they fail to understand the competitive dynamics behind cultural and political evolution. As a consequence, despite eschewing economic protectionism, many East Asian regimes have instead been tempted to impose "cultural protectionism" as a means to maintain the political *status quo*. Efficiency can be seen to impact upon cultural developments in much the same way as it impacts upon economic developments in markets. In turn, institutional efficiency is observable as in those social arrangements that allow for the pursuit of individual life purposes within a collective setting such that others seek to imitate them. Although political leaders may wish to impose a set of institutional arrangements upon their citizens, these arrangements will ultimately be compared with results that appear outside their own borders or regions. In this sense, competitive forces test the capacity of institutions to facilitate human interaction and to allow individuals to fulfill their goals. An important element of the process of modernization are the evolutionary, and sometimes revolutionary, changes in institutions. Just as global economic progress depends upon the free trade of goods and services, cultural progress arises out of an open competition between political and cultural institutions regardless of their cultural or geographic origin. On the one hand, the reactionary interferences by Asian authoritarian-capitalist regimes are apt to fail in the long run. On the other hand, these same interferences can be expected to contribute to a premature end of the promises of a "Pacific Century."

In all events, the "miracle" economies in East and Southeast Asia may be no different and no more sustainable than was the exceptional performance of the Soviet economy or the post-W.W.II economy of Germany. It is possible that despots can initially meet with considerable success in directing the development of immature economies. Meanwhile, the East Asian dragons have been behaving like the rest of the developing economies by relying upon access to technology and markets in the West. Without producing their own domestic entrepreneurial talent and self-generated technological advances, these countries shall follow the developed economies in a continuing dependency relationship. Some economists have recognized that it is relatively easy to implement a set of efficient policy initiatives in the early stages of development.[15] Given the opportunities of a global economy, it would require a substantial number of stupid policies and unstable institutions to hold back economic development. Like Germany and America prior to World War I, the "miracle economies" of East Asia have probably benefited as much from widening product and resource markets as they have from their own choice of development strategies. Furthermore, the complicated political relationships that evolve along with a modern economy are certain to impose a limit upon whatever gains might be generated from authoritarian leadership. There is no reason to expect that Asian despots shall have any greater long term survival than elsewhere. As the rate of economic growth begins to slow, their basis of political legitimacy shall be challenged and the ensuing political instability will lead to change.

Conclusion

Unfortunately, the same institutional arrangements that have been credited with the exceptionally high growth rates in East Asia are also capable of undermining their long run economic possibilities. In more recent years, the "miraculous" performance of many Southeast Asian economies has been dependent upon the success of the Northeast Asian economies, notably Japan and South Korea. As new emerging markets come on line, the convergence of economic structures, combined with the continuing duplication of productive capacities, poses serious challenges to the Asian dragon economies. Aggressive global competition will challenge the growth potential of "parasite" economies since they will face difficulties in expanding export markets in the face of competitive pricing. Similarly, the rapid introduction of new technology will benefit those countries that are the original innovators.

In all events, there is little likelihood that the large trade imbalances that existed between Asia and the West in the 1980's and early 1990's are sustainable. Besides the political tensions that may limit these imbalances, Western governments are committed to reducing their budget deficits. In turn, there will no longer be a need to tap the savings of Asians that provide offsetting payments for trade deficits. These observations should not be perceived as negative posturing against the honest efforts of the people of an impoverished region to improve their lot. Rather, the intent here is to expose the narrow interest groups and representatives of ruthless regimes who benefit from the rhetoric surrounding the proclamation of a "Pacific Century." A much better, and more inclusive, concept is that of a "Global Century," where a rising tide of global free trade lifts all ships.

Notes

1 See B. Cummings, "What is a Pacific Century—and How Will We Know When it Begins?" *Current History* (1994, vol. 93, no. 587) pp. 401-406.

2 A wide-ranging discussion of this issue can be found in, A. Dirlik (ed.), *What is in a Rim? Critical Perspectives on the Pacific Region Idea.* Boulder: Westview Press, 1993.

3 The internal difficulties of attempting to define the area geographically should be evident in the fact that both "Pacific" and "Asia" are terms and concepts that were introduced by Europeans.

4 See B. Buzan and G. Segal, "Rethinking East Asian Security," *Survival* (Summer 1994) 3-21. For a less pessimistic view, see J. L. Richardson, "Asia-Pacific:

The Case for Geopolitical Optimism," *National Interest* (Winter 1994/95, no. 38) 28-39.

5 Chu, Chin-Ning. *The Asian Mind Game: Unlocking the Hidden Agenda of the Asian Business Culture—A Westerner's Survival Guide*. New York: Macmillan for Rawson Associates, 1991. pp. 8-9.

6 Before going to China I had lived in South Africa where individual Africans were most often treated with respect although national policies deprived them of certain rights. By contrast, the government of China offered a helping hand to African countries. Meanwhile, Chinese citizens treated individual Africans very badly. I was struck by the abusive treatment of Africans by ordinary Chinese who spat at them or abused them verbally on the streets.

7 One indelible blight on the Japanese war record has been thoroughly chronicled by G. Hicks, *The Comfort Women: Sex Slaves of the Japanese Imperial Forces*. St. Leonards, Aus.: Allen & Unwin, 1995.

8 For differing views on China's economic and political cohesion, see J. A. Goldstone, "The Coming Collapse of China," and Yasheng Huang, "Why China Will Not Collapse," in *Foreign Policy* (Summer 1995, no. 99), pp. 35-68.

9 Additional discussion and references on this issue can be found in G. Segal. *China Changes Shape: Regionalism and Foreign Policy*. London: Institute for International Strategic Studies, 1994.

10 With the admission of Vietnam and the impending offer of membership to Burma-Myanmar, ASEAN increasingly assumes the look of a club for incumbent despots.

11 See A. Fishlow, C. Gwin, S. Haggard, D. Rodrik, and R. Wade. *Miracle or Design: Lessons from the East Asian Experience*. Washington, DC: Overseas Development Council, 1994.

12 Discussion of these general issues, albeit from a different starting point, is found in P. Krugman, "Competitiveness: A Dangerous Obsession," *Foreign Affairs* (March/April 1994), pp. 28-44.

13 R. Eberts and C. Eberts. *The Myths of Japanese Quality*. Upper Saddle River, N.J.: Prentice Hall PTR, 1995.

14 *Asian Risks, 1995*. Hong Kong: Political and Economic Risk Consultancy, 1995.

15 See M. Olson, *The Rise and Decline of Nations: Economic Growth, Stagflation, and Social Rigidities*. New Haven: Yale University Press, 1982.

Chapter 6

THE DIN OF DEMOCRACY AT THE DAWN OF THE "ASIAN CENTURY"

Family values, political correctness, freedom of speech, life-style choice, academic freedom. This list of pressing issues is the subject of debate throughout America in a political setting that has been variously described as nasty or brutish, and anything but solitary or short. Pundits and politicians there and abroad proclaim that conflicts over these issues provide clear signs that both America and Western civilization may be heading for disintegration. In turn, authoritarian leaders in Singapore and elsewhere point to these and other problems in the West to justify their strict repression of civic conversation.

An alternative interpretation of the apparent disharmony is in order. What Americans in particular are experiencing is a healthy demonstration of the free-wheeling democratic traditions that gave birth to that country in the first instance. It is easy for those less familiar with American history to mistake unfettered debate for disruption, or to see bruising political campaigns as a sign of systemic breakdown. The battles, real or imagined, over political correctness, and the pull and tussle of the political arena, are important ingredients of multi-party democracy. Were the leaders of the Asian authoritarian-capitalist regimes truly secure and confident of their leadership they would welcome such cut and thrust politics without hiding behind submissive judges and draconian laws.

There is particular irony both in the existence and the expression of such strong doubts about Western democratic ideals that seek to guarantee freedom of expression. Although there is uncertainty over future prosperity, and appropriate questions have arisen about the viability of the Western economic and political systems, they continue to be widely imitated throughout the world. Meanwhile, internal struggles over moral issues seldom divide communities or polarize politics for long periods of time. The exceptional cases like the former Yugoslavia offer proof of this rule. For example, American universities may be embroiled in charges and counter-charges of "political correctness," but these debates represent the unavoidable and healthy growing pangs of free discussion. In all events, it would be inappropriate to lose sight of the benefits of extensive freedoms for individuals and the community. Most clashes of ideas within the framework of Western institutions should be interpreted as part of a process rather than as an end result.

By contrast, despite all the controversy over the role of Singapore's leaders in the debate over "Asian values," the debate has not included ordinary citizens or the normal range of civic associations. Ideas from the Singapore side have come almost exclusively from government officials, and have been exchanged in a transoceanic dialogue. As such, there has been virtually no spontaneous input from scholars in Singapore's institutions of higher learning, nor have dissenting views found a voice in the domestic media. Therefore, it is not surprising that expressions of the superiority of "Asian" values have often reflected a mono-dimensional argument. Singapore, and some other Asian regimes, have warned their citizens of the costs of Western individualism by offering images of an unbroken landscape of crack-infested neighborhoods inhabited by unmarried mothers on welfare. Most of these failings have been placed at the feet of Western institutions which promote individualism. Then, it is conveniently forgotten that the creativity arising from Western institutions provides the innovations and creates the wealth allowing others to purchase Asian products.

Meanwhile, the merits of the presumed pan-Asian values are promoted without examining the associated costs to their communities within this value system. Filial piety, a strong sense of collectivism and a grab-bag of other values, including some recognizable in the West as "Puritan ethics," are portrayed as the unique source of economic success in Asia. It is also contended that the absence of these values explains the decline and moral decay of the West. Scant attention is paid to the social costs to Asians arising from "face saving," or to the economic costs of *guanxi*. Neither is there an accounting for the impact of the intimidating tactics of one-party regimes that inhibit the questioning process and discourage challenges to the status quo, or to the limits that retarded political arrangements might put upon economic growth. Similarly the Asian concepts of filial piety and unquestioned respect for authority have been shamelessly manipulated by cynical and thin-skinned leaders who are allergic to criticism. In turn, outsider's expressions of concern for the lack of individual freedoms for Asians tend to be dismissed as neo-colonial meddling. Western concerns over human rights tend to be ridiculed or derided as schemes obstructing the economic policies of Asian authoritarian-capitalist regimes.

In sum, authoritarian-capitalist regimes in Singapore and elsewhere justify the imposition of the visibly repressive hand of government intervention by pointing to short-run gains while conveniently overlooking unintended long-run costs. As the costs of stunted economic growth become apparent, they can be expected to generate additional social and political costs. Eventually, an economically secure and politically mature population will demand that their governments acknowledge a measure of the national quality of life that must include abstractions such as individual freedoms and rights.

Survival and success in the open and highly competitive international economic order that is emerging require flexible institutions and innovative, risk-taking entrepreneurs. Whatever the economic successes recorded to date under authoritarian capitalism, there is a lack of a nourishing environment for the development of these requirements. In reality, the cruelty of the choice to trade off political freedom for rapid economic growth is that opting for short-run gains comes with the expense of long-run losses. Of particular concern is the illusion of stability emerging from the state of "lawless order," when legal systems are molded to match the whims of the ruling parties.

Transplanting Democracy?

Spokespersons for the "Singapore School," and other proponents of the Asian model, argue that the form of democracy that has blossomed in the West will find Asia offers fallow ground. Instead, they allude to a geographically-specific form of "Asian democracy" that they hope to make credible by using the vocabulary of democracy. Judging by their actions as governors rather than by their words, it is clear that their political system is a poor replica of democracy since they exclude one of the defining elements of democracy, i.e., protection of citizens from tyranny. There should be little debate that this essential element of democracy relates to the provision and promotion of individual rights and liberties. Claims of cultural relativity and regional specificity for democracy to enter this debate are appropriate only if they address contingent or variable conditions rather than the necessary conditions of democracy. For example, Asians or Singaporeans might have different ideas from Europeans or Americans as to what issues are to be decided through application of the tools of political democracy. It would appear that assertions about a form of democracy peculiar to Asia represent false advertising for a political system seeking to disguise oppressive regimes.

The strongest claim of apologists for Asian authoritarian-capitalist regimes is found in the observation that there is little in their cultural traditions to support the emergence of individual freedom. There is historical evidence that differing cultural habits in the East and West have resulted in distinctive contributions to political institutions. Whereas democracy is undeniably the great contribution to political arrangements from the West, bureaucracy remains the great contribution of the East. While liberalism and individual freedoms prospered in the West, many Asian institutions developed within an instinctive conservatism among ruling elites that implemented institutions based upon paternalistic collectivism. However, this logic would suggest that medical patients in earlier centuries would prefer being bled or having leeches attached to them to be cured, due to their lack of exposure to modern healing practices, over modern medical procedures. Asian citizens may not have first hand knowledge of a given political system, but it is impossible to know whether they would reject it until it is known to them. Only political Luddites, or true dictators, would suggest that their citizens have no interest in, or are disinterested in, changing their preferences when presented with advances in either modern medicine, new technology, or alternative schemes that govern social interactions.

Ultimately, the economic and social institutions associated with the so-called Asian model and its strange relationship with democracy will be forced to stand the test of time. This is of particular concern since present or past economic successes are not reliable indicators of future performance. Despite the political concern attached to trade deficits between East Asian economies and some of the advanced industrialized economies of the West, most economists accept that different saving and consumption patterns allow such imbalances to be sustained over long periods of time. In and of themselves, trade surpluses are not desirable nor are trade deficits an indication of economic disorder. Those countries that experience deficits are no more harmed than are those that run surpluses necessarily blessed. It is of more significant concern to the long term growth patterns if there is a continued "intellectual deficit," where ideas and innovations continue to flow from West to East or as free-thinkers immigrate from East to West. In the post-industrial international economic order, those communities with the most flexible political institutions and economies will be most able to innovate and will have the best chance of enjoying continued prosperity. It will become increasingly difficult to rely upon the short time horizons of trade-based economies with their heavy dependence upon technology transfers from other countries. Success can be expected to come to those countries whose entrepreneurs can effectively challenge both the economic and the political *status quo*. These latter actions are especially important when governments try to impose economically irrational policies. It is arguable that the pre-conditions for future economic prosperity reside in a setting that guarantees individual freedom and rejects collectivist repression.

In carrying out its "virtuous" rule, Singapore's PAP regime has been especially inventive and remarkably successful in suppressing the development of demands for individual rights and multi-party democracy. Its distinctive form of democracy (*phobocracy*) operates by substituting the rule by consent of the governed with "rule by fear." With the local media as subservient to the PAP regime as *Pravda* was to the Soviets, a variety of tactics have been successful in deflecting criticism from the international media. As discussed earlier, costly lawsuits for libel and curtailments of circulation for "unbalanced" reporting have induced editors and publishers of foreign publications sold in Singapore to be very cautious in offering articles that examine Singapore.

Virtual Democracy and "Lawless Order"

So it is within the carefully constructed context of Singapore's "virtual" democracy that an increasingly insecure group of rulers seeks to continue single-party rule. Survival of the ruling party of this Leninist state can be enforced with a thin base of political support due to its *phobocratic* rule by fear and an Orwellian control over information flows. Singapore's arguably enlightened dictators have imposed a quarantine on the rulers, distancing them from citizens and their ideas or preferences while sustaining their well-documented disregard for the rights of individuals through the intellectual construction of a list of shared, pan-Asian values.

The debate over "Asian values" has arisen at the time when a watershed has been reached in the confrontation between Western democratic countries and authoritarian-capitalist regimes. This pivotal moment occurred when the Clinton administration provided continuing MFN status to China in spite of its wanton disregard for human rights. This signaled that diplomatic pressures on human rights would be removed from the trade agenda. If other regimes are as successful as Singapore in silencing the international media, a huge gap in moral and political resolution will open up in the struggle to resist dictatorial aspirations. With the loss of these two sources of external pressure to temper authoritarian regimes, the moral force of human rights groups and other non-governmental organizations (NGO's) is considerably diluted. By imposing greater internal repression with the harassment of American and other citizens in combination with attacks on the international media, one of the world's smallest countries has been able to exploit the lack of political and moral will in the world's sole superpower. While appeasement of despots is a poor basis for foreign policy, neither can it serve the long run commercial interests of media owners.

It is perhaps more difficult to transplant the "Singapore model" elsewhere than it is to transplant democracy in Asia. Given its small population, those factors behind Singapore's performance would appear to be difficult to apply in countries with much larger populations. More importantly, increased mobility of international financial capital can be expected to increase the difficulty in attracting the foreign financial resources that were combined with other elements of Singapore's development strategies. Given this evidence, citizens of countries that hope to benefit from the take-off stage of development can only hope that their governments look elsewhere in selecting economic and political models.

Some futurologists and enthusiastic promoters of the electronic superhighway optimistically assert that the wider global access to the internet is an effective and sure means to undermine authoritarian rule. Presumably, this simplistic view is based upon the expectation that governments will find that censorship of the vast numbers of interlinked conversations to be difficult, if not impossible. Nonetheless, most repressive regimes have not ignored this possibility and have begun to devise ways either to control the electronic revolution or to manipulate it to serve their own ends.

As indicated in previous chapters, Singapore's government is well known for its obsessive desire to exercise control over the thoughts and lives of their citizens. Brigadier General George Yeo, Minister for Health and Information and the Arts, has announced the regime's intention to build defenses against outside influence so that Singaporeans do not make choices that stray from the PAP agenda. In his words, "immune systems" must be constructed to encourage citizens to discriminate between good and bad influences. If the past history of the government is any indication, its highly visible hand will be offered to assure that citizens understand what it believes is right and wrong for them. Apparently, the PAP's intention is to exploit the information revolution by using the electronic media to expand their authoritarian control.

Singapore's National Computer Board (NCB) announced its program "IT2000," which involves ambitious plans to create a computer-linked, high tech economy by 2015. The plan is for Singapore to become a global media hub. Evidence of their progress is seen in that most government agencies computerized over the past 10 years, and many private sector firms have followed suit. In what might appear on the surface to be a benign move, the government has encouraged the establishment of a grassroots network to report feedback on what is considered acceptable in the media. By defining an explicit role for the Young PAP (the youth arm of the ruling party) to police the internet, this may be the first time a political party has attempted to manipulate the electronic media for its own specific political purposes.

In January 1995 the regime undertook a more explicit attack on privacy. The authorities applied a complex computer program that sifted through

80,000 private electronic mailboxes in search of pornography. Obviously, the same program would allow them to copy e-mail messages and could be used to detect politically sensitive key words in such correspondence. Except for large corporate users, private internet users must enter through Singnet, which is served by the government telephone monopoly. Therefore, there are no restrictions upon the access by government to files sent over electronic mail. With the government's track record, it is predictable that they intend to implement very efficient internet censorship and install an effective "surf police."

The regime must resolve what appears to be an insoluble paradox in its hope of promoting Singapore's reputation as a world class media center amidst extensive controls. It is difficult to understand how it can be expected to develop into a regional or global information center with internet controls and the banning of private satellite dishes. In a move that involved the "privatization" of Singapore Broadcasting Corporation (SBC), it created 5 new, distinct operating companies that are completely owned by the government through Singapore International Media, Pte. Ltd. As the successor to the SBC, operations of all the subsidiaries of SIM are financed by license fees paid by television and radio owners as well as government subsidies.[1] With strict government monopoly on domestic TV broadcasting, and a near-monopoly on radio transmissions, Singapore's role as an Asian information hub can be expected to be weighted down by the PAP's conservative agenda.

In light of recent developments, an open or spontaneous dialogue about the regime's approach to governing is not to be expected. The government's official position on the nature of public discussion and consultation on political issues was laid out by Prime Minister Goh Chok Tong and Mr. Chan Heng Wing, his Press Secretary, in a series of letters published by the *Straits Times* (7, 13, and 28 December 1994). In this forum, it was clear that the regime would not allow its authority to be challenged by "writers on the fringes." Those who wished to comment regularly on politics were instructed that they should enter the political arena openly, or keep quiet. In turn, critics were advised to avoid making remarks that might undermine the respect for the PM by "denigration and contempt." Further, while there "will always be some limits to openness and consultation," they promised that the limits of discussion would widen over some unspecified period of time. In the meantime, the government intends to "stay in charge of the agenda... not by suppressing discussion, but by defending its policies, rebutting and debunking criticisms which are wrong, and accepting constructive suggestions." Clearly the government will unilaterally decide for the rest of the population whether suggestions are constructive or not. Additional signs of the prickliness of the regime were found in the steps taken in late 1994 to censure advertisements for Sustagen (a milk-based nutritional supplement for children), Qantas Airlines, and Citibank due to content that the regime's cultural arbiters felt might undermine filial obedience or impair domestic instincts towards thrift.

Pursuit of its repressive media policy reveals the hypocrisy of Singapore's regime in terms of its double-standards relating to press freedom. Whereas the apologists for its regime denounce the traditions of "excessive" openness of the Western media, they demand and receive a generous hearing from the international media to allow them to air their views. Meanwhile Singapore's domestic media avoids confrontation with the government as a distinct editorial policy. In turn, the general public faces similarly severe restrictions on their access to the editorial pages for any critical remarks of the government that they might offer.

Singapore's determined and decisive steps against the media seem to confirm their dread and fear of a free press. If the critical comments of a university professor or the remarks of a journalist can prompt such heavy-handed actions, it confirms that this regime must fear that its days are numbered. Rather than retreat from this Asian tiger, the international media should interpret the aggressive posturing as the whining of a frightened pussycat. In the end, silencing the political opposition through a clampdown on the media retards the emergence of multi-party politics. Journalists have a duty to step forward to help widen the political space in such regimes and so encourage the development of a civic community in East Asia.

Swimming Against the Democratic Tide

While there are some encouraging signs of liberalization in some countries in East Asia, Singapore is providing a model of continued authoritarian repression that some of the emerging economies may be tempted to follow. As indicated in Chapter 4, the PAP follows a clear pattern of controlling the local media and intimidating the international media by restricting the circulation of print as well as broadcast media, or by applying a broad interpretation of libel actions and possibly the expulsion of journalists. These disruptions of the free flow of information have allowed the People's Action Party to consolidate its power and to hold office without any serious threat of interruption. Erstwhile communist governments in the region would doubtless like to maintain power while undergoing market reforms. They are certain to look approvingly at the success of Singapore's regime in marginalizing the media and weakening its political rivals while achieving strong economic growth. Perhaps equally troubling is that promoters of these policies are being placed in areas that had a long standing reputation for supporting a free press. For example, in early 1994, Mr. Lee Kuan Yew's former press secretary was offered a prominent media position in Hong Kong.

Final Thoughts

Considerable evidence has been presented that indicates that many of the public impressions about Singapore are the outcome of a relentless propaganda campaign. The success of the regime in presenting an acceptable image to the rest of the world is based upon its deft duplicity in stage-managing the image of its primary institutions. A bifurcation of the judicial system occurs whereby the rule of law is applied to protect commercial interests, especially of foreign investors, but it is often abandoned in cases that involve politically sensitive issues. Government economic policies are equally schizophrenic, in that crony capitalism and extensive government intervention guide domestic economic matters while there are many fewer barriers to international trade and investment. Notwithstanding its deep commitment to authoritarian rule, the regime has been very effective in creating an illusory affinity with democracy. However, if democracy is understood to be a set of experientially fair rules that allow citizens to elect officials that operate as an accountable government, then Singapore should not be considered a truly democratic country. To discourage their citizens from demanding the liberating aspects of institutions that promote individualism and multi-party democracy, Singapore's regime has shifted its rhetoric towards identifying with Asian institutions that are more amenable to its centralized, authoritarian rule. As suggested above, liberation of the individual should not be allowed to lead to the imprisonment of the community. It is no more desirable for governments to try to improve the aggregate position of the community by imprisoning the human spirit. It is impossible to imagine a healthy forest when individual trees have been cut off from sources of sustenance. There is little evidence that Asians, or any other groups, accept that the suppression of the human spirit is a social arrangement superior to one that allows for and encourages the elevation of the human spirit. There is an obvious flaw in political arrangements that obstruct spiritual nourishment and impose a heavy dependency relationship between citizens and their governments for their political rights and tastes and beliefs; in short, for their own sense of self.

People who have not lived in Singapore, or those who have entered into a symbiotic relationship with the PAP, may feel that allusions to the regime's capacity to rule by fear are exaggerations. Indeed, this objection is reinforced by the fact that the government has no record of political assassinations or of brutal, physical torture. However, the imposition of fear is a pervasive and deeply instilled psychological dread that affects the citizens of Singapore in many subtle ways. There is a belief that the visible and invisible hand of a big-brother government can reach into every nook and cranny of their lives. As provider of most of the housing, disloyalty to the government can affect the quality of one's living arrangements. As provider of most school services, educational opportunities can be limited to outspoken critics of the regime. As one of the most important employers, those who show their disaffection with the PAP would put at risk their job security. Given the regime's insistence that the interests of the community always be placed above those of any individual, there is an understanding that private space will not be respected. As indicated earlier, most citizens and expatriate residents expect that their telephone conversations are monitored by the authorities. Similarly, there is a pervasive suspicion that the content of any other modes of conversation might be compromised by informers or other methods of eavesdropping. This is confirmed by the knowledge that access to the internet is closely controlled by the government. Many of my former colleagues who remain at the National University of Singapore have either chosen to ignore my e-mail messages to them or requested that I cease further transmissions due to their fear of losing their positions. As mentioned before, the extent of interference and fear is so pervasive that Singapore's regime can be defined in terms of near totalitarian control.

The material performances of Singapore and some of the other so-called "miracle economies" have been guided by similar development strategies. In more general terms, their ruling parties instituted a set of arrangements that involved the centralization of politics combined with decentralization of the economy that has been referred to here as authoritarian capitalism. While some governments have moved toward democracy, other regimes in East Asia are beginning to cast an approving eye toward this capitalist model that allows for continued one-party rule.

There are reasons to believe that the potential for economic performance in these countries is limited by the contradictions inherent to authoritarian-capitalist institutions. One source of inefficiency is found in the tendency for the "politicization of commerce" whereby rent seeking inspires market interventions or where special market access is offered to supporters of the regime. Such crony capitalism should not be expected to be a sustainable source of economic growth. Similarly, the tendency exists for there to be a "commercialization of politics" whereby political parties become involved in business in order to maintain their domestic political hegemony by gaining access to revenue sources independent from their citizenry. The "politicization of commerce" in authoritarian-capitalist regimes, in combination with other Asian institutions, works against the development of home-grown entrepreneurs. A dearth of a domestic stock of "true" entrepreneurs can only lead to a continued dependency upon research and development from outside the region. In light of these contradictions, and given the changing nature of the global economy, policies of the past cannot be expected to deliver the same "miracles" in the future.

Singapore's autocratic leaders might be said to have a charmed existence. They pay themselves significantly more than any of their counterparts in the world. Having deprived their domestic critics of a voice, they have imposed a cleverly manipulated propaganda campaign that allows them to exploit the general lack of outside information about this tiny island state. Meanwhile, leaders of other authoritarian governments, certain expatriate businessmen and other self-serving opportunists sing loud praise of Singapore's regime while remaining totally mute when it comes to criticism of any sort. In addition, the regime can rely upon a cowed general public to provide it with substantial, but declining majorities, thereby providing an illusion of democracy. To round off the delusion that Singapore operates under democratic institutions, there is widespread agreement that the regime is able to rely upon a cooperative set of judges whose appointments and promotions have been in the hands of the PAP leaders for the past 3 decades.

Interest in the unfolding events in Singapore should be motivated by a concern for the same basic issue that divided the antagonists in the Cold War. At stake is whether social, political, and economic institutions should be based upon collective arrangements driven by the heavy-hand of government, or whether individuals should be allowed to express their choices in a free environment and be protected by a true rule of law. The new struggle promises to be between liberal democracy and authoritarian governments that hide behind the vocabulary of democracy, and that construct a set of legal and political institutions to serve their hegemonic agenda. Singapore's paternalistic authoritarianism seems to be premised upon an assertion that people cannot be trusted to disregard their own interests when faced with difficult problems. This observation is almost certainly correct. Nonetheless, it does not necessarily support the presumption that the toughest decisions of a given community ought to be to be left to a few, powerful leaders, especially if they are not fully accountable to the community. It is the indisputable fallibility of individuals that should convince citizens of the need for limiting the role of government and restricting the concentration of power in the hand's of an elitist party or a dynastic family.

As is made clear by the above personal account, I have offered the analysis here after being a firsthand observer of the economy and political structure in Singapore. Admittedly, it is difficult to avoid the seductive propaganda and the co-opting influences associated with living there. Nonetheless, it appears that the rapid economic growth recorded in Singapore and other countries in the region is based upon a peculiar set of circumstances. A non-sustainable momentum of growth has been based upon massive increases in the quantity of inputs and a dependency relationship upon Western markets and technology. As these Asian economies approach the levels of Western economic development, their growth will have to slow, because their institutional arrangements do not generate the sort of entrepreneurs that introduce growth for other economies. As economic growth slows, the increasing dissatisfaction with the political regimes will create the seeds of political instability leading to change. It is indeed unfortunate that Asian citizens may have to wait for economic disaster before they are able to escape the trap of "lawless order" imposed upon them by their autocratic leaders.

Singaporean citizens have good reason to be proud of their individual and collective accomplishments. After all, it was their contributions within an environment of capital-friendly policies that allowed their country to join the exclusive club of high performing East Asian economies. Even though they played such a key role in their joint material advances, they remain impoverished in terms of the sort of political freedoms that serve both as a means and as an end to sustained economic growth.

Authoritarian-capitalist regimes in Singapore and elsewhere that wish to maintain power can expect to confront an unhappy choice. On one hand, they face the risks of having a more free and open democratic dialogue within a competitive setting without controls on the press. On the other hand, restricting information flows as a means to eventually maintain political control shall lead to decline in economic performance. This predicted decline in living standard improvements should cause an upset in the existing social contract whereby citizens tolerate authoritarian repression in exchange for material payoffs. With their shrinking means for co-opting the emerging middle classes, the regimes must then decide either to step up repression or to introduce reforms. These issues will inevitably generate tensions among their neighbors in the region. Meanwhile, emerging economies in other regions of the globe will be likely to develop a comparative advantage that attracts investment capital away from East Asia.

Happily, there is no doubt that the next century will witness a continuation in the rising fortunes and growing political importance of East Asia. Even so, it may be premature to anticipate that a simplistic extrapolation of the recent economic performance in the region will be an accurate harbinger of its post-millennial achievements. It may be just as likely that the authoritarian-capitalist regimes will set another record. Perhaps they will match their rapid pace of economic development by consigning themselves to the dustbin of history more quickly than their predecessor, authoritarian socialism.

Note

1 These subsidiaries are: Television Corporation of Singapore; Radio Corporation of Singapore; Caldecott Productions International, Pte. Ltd. which is a commercial production house; SIM Communications, Pte. Ltd. which handles transmission and distribution services for other SIM companies as well as for outsiders; and Singapore Cablevision Pte.`Ltd. which provides devices to descramble 3 channels for a monthly fee as substitute for cable network that is to expand to 30 channels by 1998.

Appendix

YOU MAY NOT LIKE IT, EUROPE, BUT THIS ASIAN MEDICINE COULD HELP

Kishore Mahbubani

SINGAPORE — While the guns are almost silent in East Asia, Europe is surrounded by conflict. This "ring of fire" stretches from Algeria across North Africa, then reaches its climax in the vicious fighting in Bosnia. From the violence in Georgia to the explosions waiting to happen in Kosovo, Macedonia and Albania, more lives are lost daily on the periphery of Europe than in the entire Asia-Pacific region, with its much larger population.

This is not an accident. It is a result of the strategic incoherence in Europe's approach to its immediate environment. East Asian, meanwhile, is making relatively sound decisions.

There are several flawed elements in Europe's policies. The first is the belief that Europe can secure peace for itself by concentrating on internal unification and detaching itself from its periphery. To an observer from East Asia, these efforts — whether on deepening unification through the Maastricht treaty or widening unification by including "similar" European countries — seem akin to rearranging living room furniture while flood water is coming in under the door.

It is puzzling that Europe is trying to draw up its ramparts, cutting off its neighbors from its growth and prosperity. By contrast, the strategic impulse in East Asia is to draw all societies into the region's dynamism, starting with Burma and Vietnam and eventually including North Korea.

Europe has no choice but to deal with three big forces on its doorstep which will not go away: Russia, Africa and Islam. The EU has had a marginally successful strategy toward Russia, although questions remain. But Europe's strategy toward Africa and Islam is fundamentally flawed.

In the long view, it might have been a strategic error to admit socially and culturally similar states into the EU ahead of Turkey. This sent a signal that no state in the Islamic world, no matter how secular or modernized, would be admitted into the house of Europe. An opportunity was lost to demonstrate that an Islamic society could cross cultural boundaries and become like any other modern European state.

The EU's snub of the Islamic world has been magnified enormously by European passivity in the face of the genocide in Bosnia. Few in the Islamic world (or elsewhere) can believe that Europe would have remained as passive if Muslim artillery shells had been raining down on Christian populations. It does not help that European governments condemn the reversal of democracy in Burma while endorsing a similar reversal in Algeria.

Such double standards are easily shrugged off by cynical, sophisticated Europeans. But they underestimate the enormous price Europe is paying for alienating a force, Islam, that it will have to live with for the next 1,000 years.

A second flaw in European strategy is the assumption that other countries will remake themselves into social models of Europe, that the natural progression of history will lead to all societies becoming liberal democratic and capitalist. For most Europeans this assumption was vindicated by the Soviet Union's collapse.

This profound belief in the superiority of the Western idea creates a unique weakness or blindness for Europe — an inability to accept that other cultures or social forms may have equal validity.

A third flawed element is Europe's effort to lock in its high living standards by raising clever new barriers to free trade and by sustaining high subsidies.

Here the contrast between U.S. and European policy is striking. The United States has taken a relatively bold leap by entering into a free trade agreement with Mexico, thereby crossing a cultural as well as a socioeconomic divide. In fact, it had little choice. If America did not export some low-paying jobs to Mexico and gain high-paying jobs in return, Mexico could not and would not stop exporting Mexicans northward.

The only permanent solution to illegal immigration into Europe is to export some low-paying jobs (in return for high-paying jobs) and enter into free-trade agreements with North Africa.

This strategy is more likely to work if the EU promotes, rather than hinders, global free-trade regimes that will integrate Europe and its neighbors into the rising tide of prosperity in the Asia-Pacific. But to allow Europe's neighbors to compete in their areas of natural advantage, European agricultural subsidies will have to go.

Within a few decades, as its neighbors (particularly Africa) soar, Western Europe will be confronted with impoverished masses on its borders. Increasing numbers will slip in, to join the millions already there, exacerbating serious social and political tensions. Unless these masses feel they are part of European prosperity in their home countries, they will feel that they have no choice but to move into the EU itself.

There is a danger that these flawed elements in European strategy will be exported to the rest of the world. In the long run, if Europe persists with an "Atlantic impulse" — moving toward continental rather than global integration, exporting political development ahead of economic development while ignoring social and cultural differences and creating new protectionist barriers to lock in untenable welfare state policies — it will lead to grief.

Were the EU to become totally preoccupied with its immediate problems, this would be a loss not only for Europe but for the rest of the world. Mankind could benefit immensely if a new synergy were created between the newly revitalized Asian civilizations and the rich creative heritage of Europe. To achieve this, Europe must learn to approach the world differently.

❖❖❖❖❖❖❖❖❖❖❖❖

The writer, permanent secretary in Singapore's Foreign Ministry, is expressing a personal view. This comment was adapted by the International Herald Tribune from a paper he presented at the recent annual conference in Vancouver of the IISS.

International Herald Tribune, October 1, 1994.

INDEX

BIOGRAPHICAL NOTE

Dr. Christopher LINGLE is a native of Atlanta, Georgia, USA (born: 2 October 1948). He is an economist and has served as a university lecturer since earning his doctorate from the University of Georgia in 1977. Most of his academic career has been spent outside of the USA as a university lecturer living in Africa, Asia and Europe. He is an ardent and active supporter of individual rights.

In January 1995, he joined Georgia State University in Atlanta as an Adjunct Professor of Economics. From September 1993 until November 1994, he held the position of Senior Fellow in the European Studies Programme of the National University of Singapore. Previously, he served as Associate Professor of Economics at Loyola University (New Orleans, Louisiana). From 1981 to 1984 and then again from 1989 to 1991, he taught at the European Center of Miami University in Luxembourg and subsequently at the stateside campus. During this time he was also Adjunct Professor, Departement de Droit et des Sciences economiques, Centre Universitaire de Luxembourg. He was also tenured as a Senior Lecturer at the University of Natal in South Africa. In the first half of 1987, he served as a Visiting Foreign Expert in Economics at the Shanghai University of Finance and Economics in China.

Dr. LINGLE's research interests and publications are in Political Economy and International Economics with a focus upon public policy issues in Europe, East Asia and Southern Africa. His work has appeared widely as chapters in books, in the international press and in numerous academic journals. Most recently, his research has focused upon the marketization and democratization processes of authoritarian regimes as well as the relationship between democracy and economic development.

He was recently tried and found guilty, *in absentia*, in Singapore following his published commentary in the *International Herald Tribune*. He described tactics of repressive regimes in East Asia, yet named no country nor any government officials. Nonetheless, Singaporean police officers interrogated him in his office as well as his home on 2 separate occasions and also confiscated research materials. Fearing arrest and trial, he left Singapore and resigned his position at the National University before charges were filed against him. Upon being found to be guilty of contempt of court, the High Court in Singapore assessed heavy fines against him, and he was charged to pay court costs. At the time of preparation of this manuscript, a civil lawsuit filed by former Prime Minister, Mr. Lee Kuan Yew, was pending.